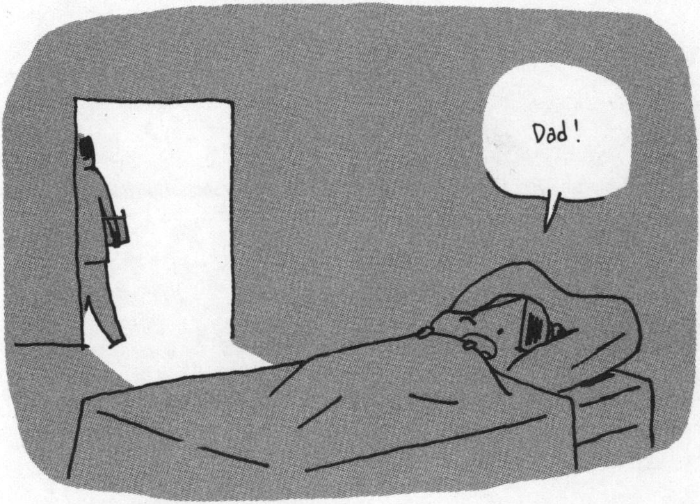
Dad!

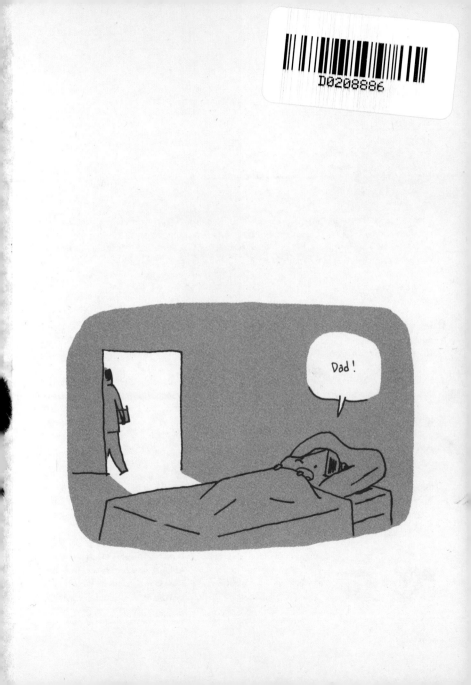

Also by Guy Delisle:
Even More Bad Parenting Advice
A User's Guide to Neglectful Parenting
Jerusalem: Chronicles from the Holy City
Burma Chronicles
Pyongyang: A Journey in North Korea
Shenzhen: A Travelogue from China
Albert & the Others
Aline & the Others

guydelisle.com
drawnandquarterly.com

First paperback edition: October 2015
Printed in Canada
10 9 8 7 6 5 4 3 2 1

Library and Archives Canada Cataloguing in Publication. Delisle, Guy. [Guide du mauvais père 3. English] *The Owner's Manual to Terrible Parenting*/Guy Delisle; translation by Helge Dascher. Translation of: *Le guide du mauvais père* 3. ISBN 978-1-77046-214-4 (pbk.) 1. Fatherhood–Comic books, strips, etc. 2. Parenting–Comic books, strips, etc. 3. Graphic novels. I. Dascher, Helge, 1965–, translator II. Title. III. Title: *Guide du mauvais père* 3. English. PN6733.D44G8613 2015   741.5 971   C2015-902367-X

Drawn & Quarterly acknowledges the financial support of the Government of Canada through the Canada Book Fund, the Canada Council for the Arts, and the National Translation Program for Book Publishing, an initiative of "Roadmap for Canada's Official Languages 2013–2018: Education, Immigration, Communities," for our translation activities.

This work, published as part of grant programs for publication (Acquisition of Rights and Translation), received support from the French Ministry of Foreign and European Affairs and from the Institut Français. Cet ouvrage, publié dans le cadre du Programme d'Aide à la Publication (Cession de droits et Traduction), a bénéficié du soutien du Ministère des Affaires étrangères et européennes et de l'Institut Français.

Liberté • Égalité • Fraternité
RÉPUBLIQUE FRANÇAISE

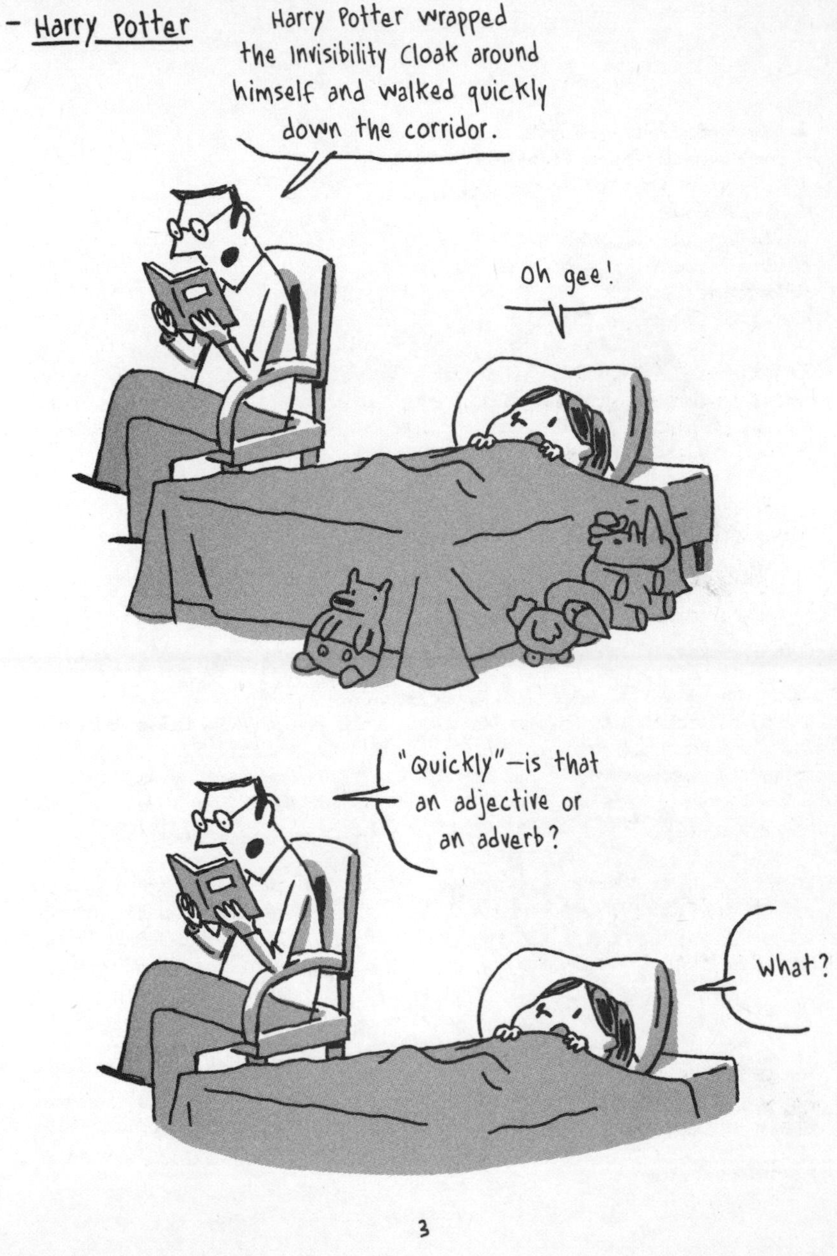
- Harry Potter
Harry Potter wrapped the Invisibility Cloak around himself and walked quickly down the corridor.
Oh gee!
"Quickly"—is that an adjective or an adverb?
What?

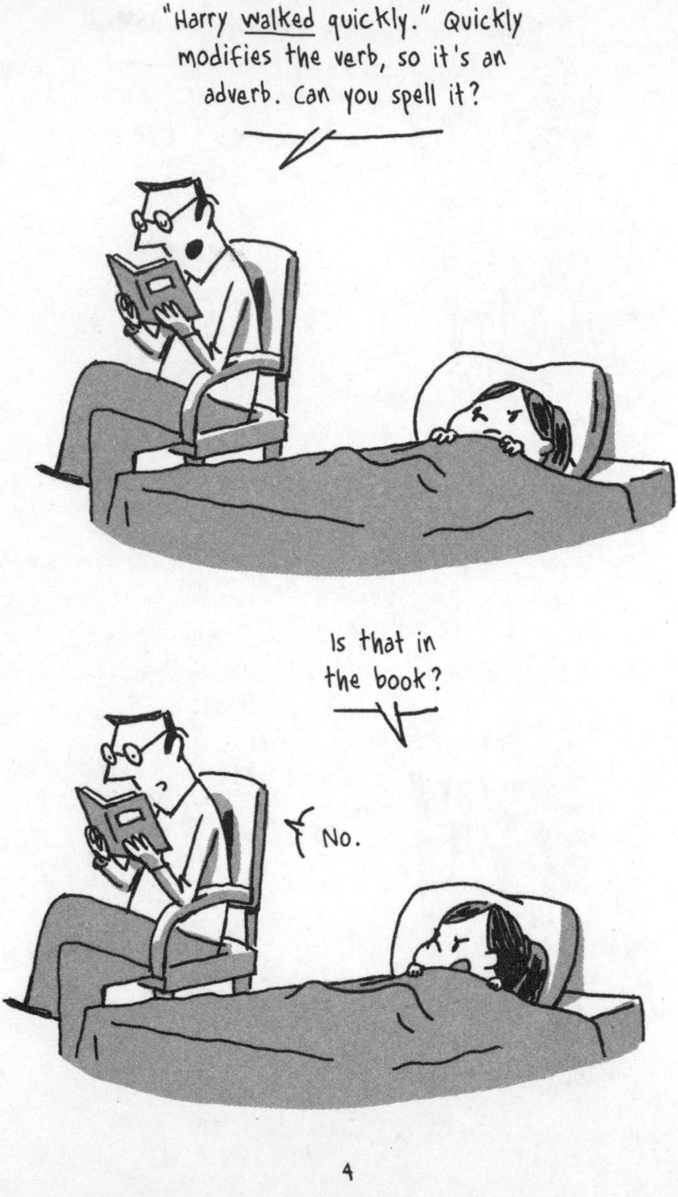
"Harry walked quickly." Quickly modifies the verb, so it's an adverb. Can you spell it?
Is that in the book?
No.

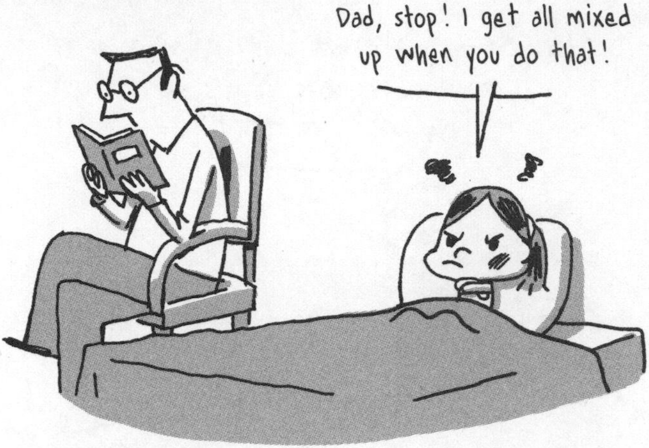
Dad, stop! I get all mixed up when you do that!
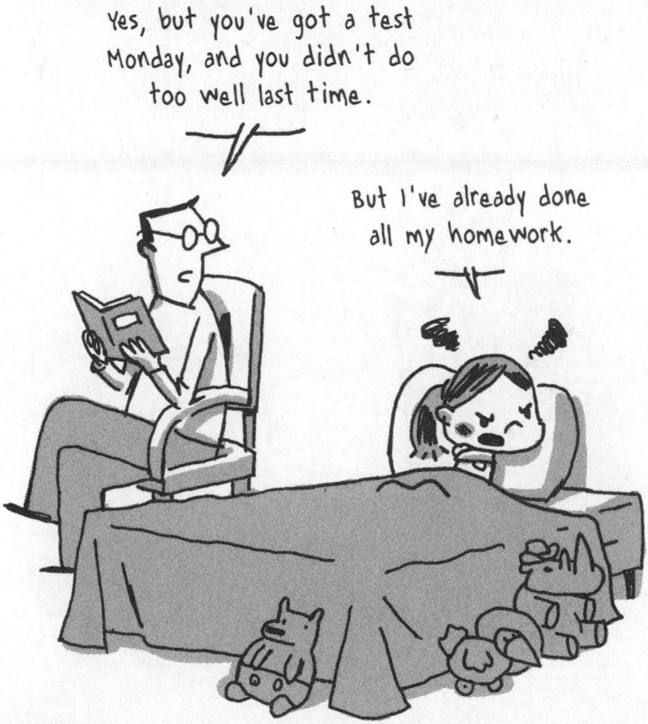
Yes, but you've got a test Monday, and you didn't do too well last time.
But I've already done all my homework.

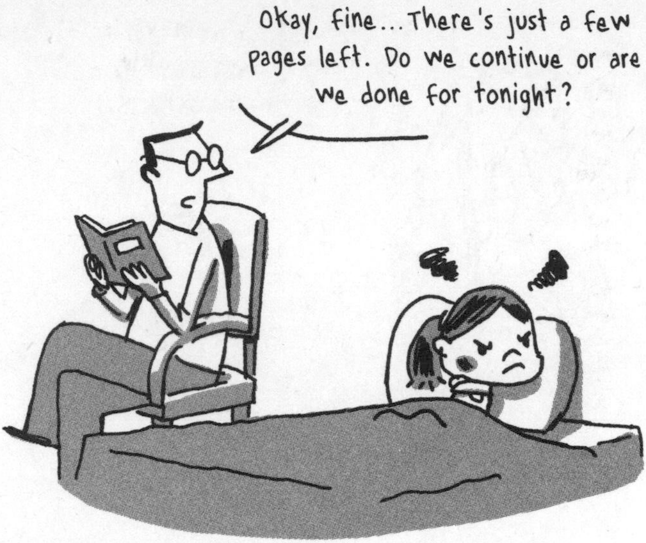
Okay, fine... There's just a few pages left. Do we continue or are we done for tonight?

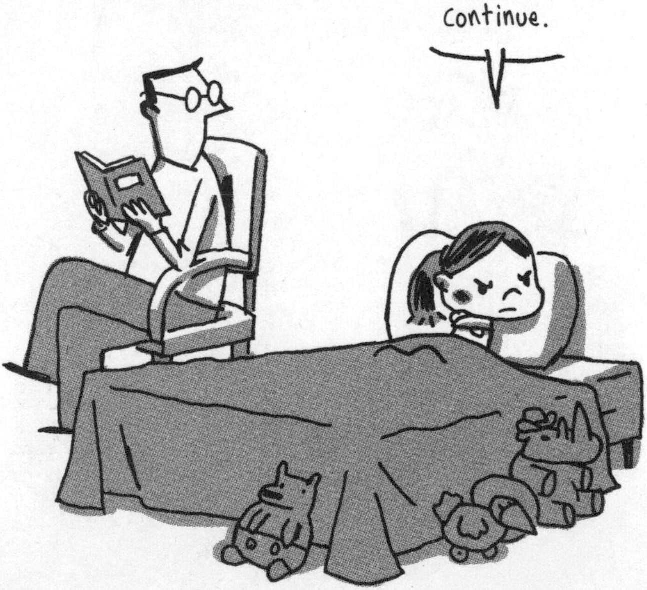
Continue.

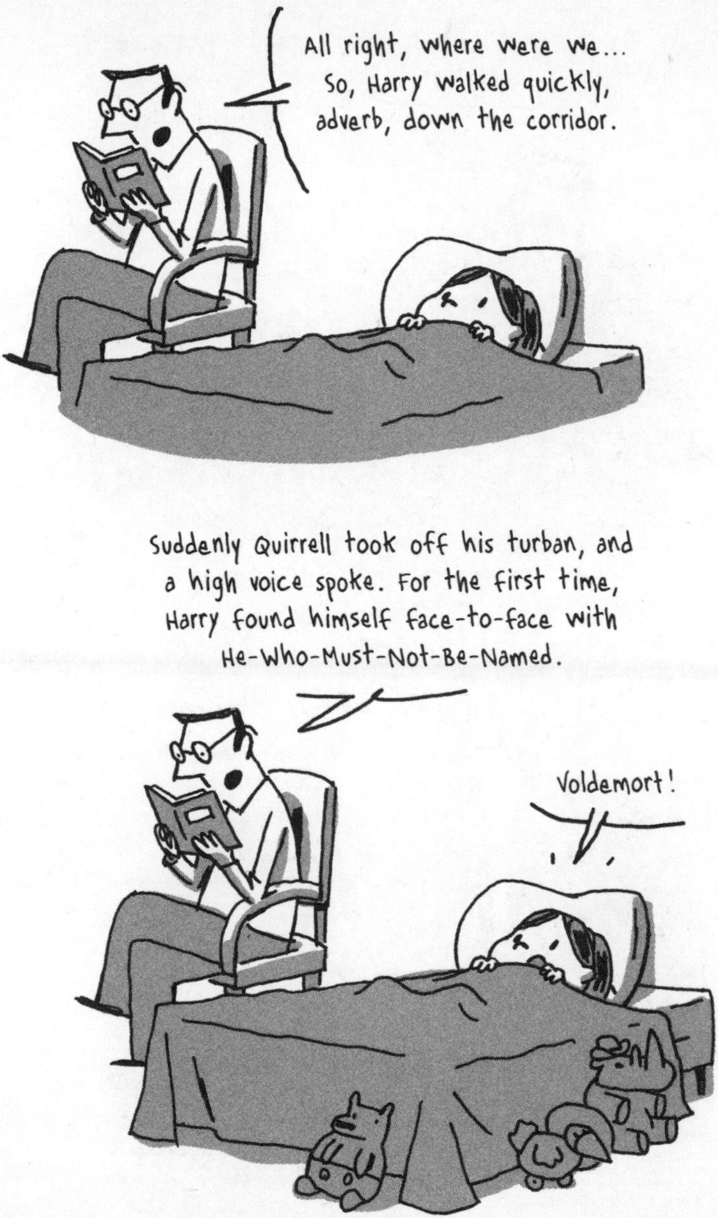
All right, where were we... So, Harry walked quickly, adverb, down the corridor.
Suddenly Quirrell took off his turban, and a high voice spoke. For the first time, Harry found himself face-to-face with He-Who-Must-Not-Be-Named.
Voldemort!

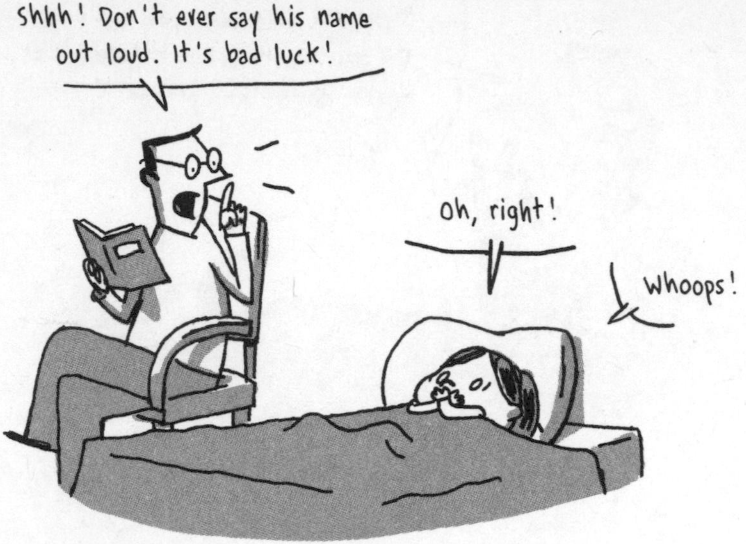
Shhh! Don't ever say his name out loud. It's bad luck!
Oh, right!
Whoops!

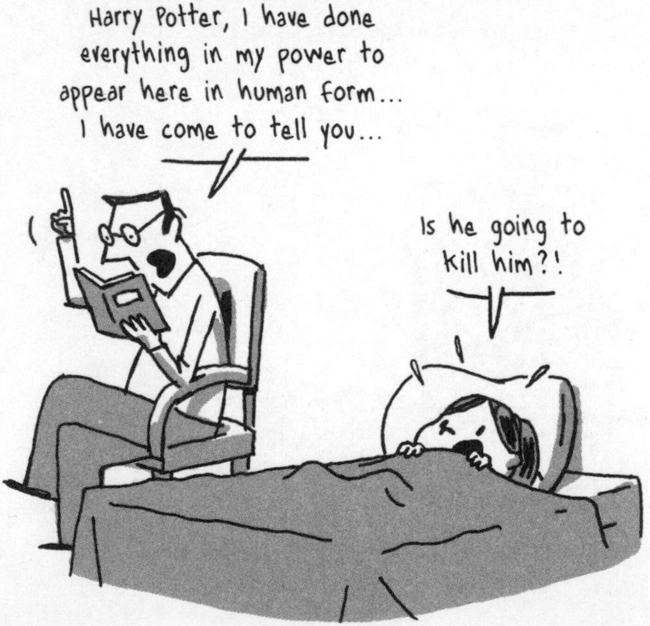
Harry Potter, I have done everything in my power to appear here in human form... I have come to tell you...
Is he going to kill him?!

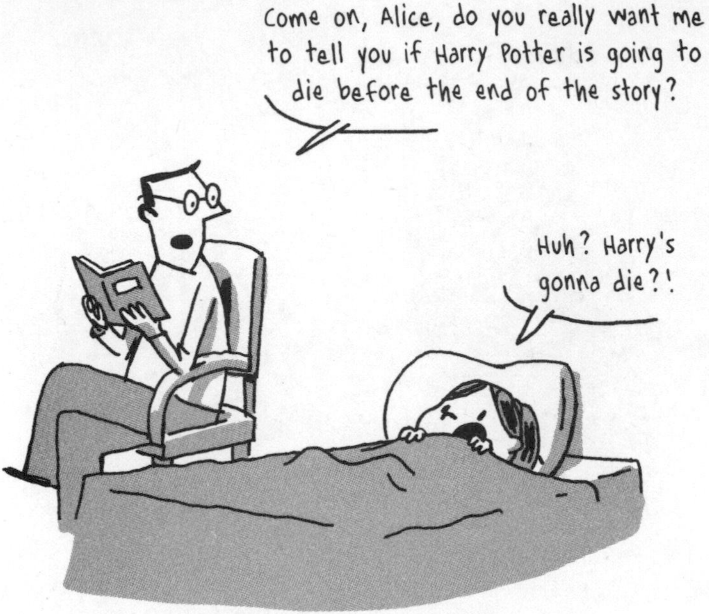
Come on, Alice, do you really want me to tell you if Harry Potter is going to die before the end of the story?
Huh? Harry's gonna die?!

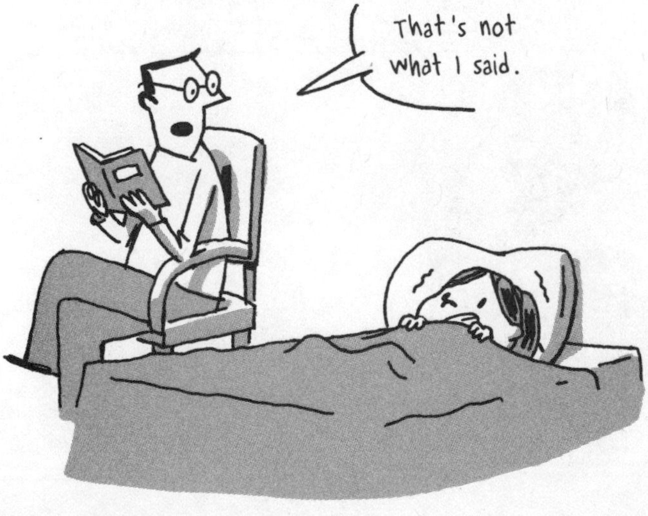
That's not what I said.

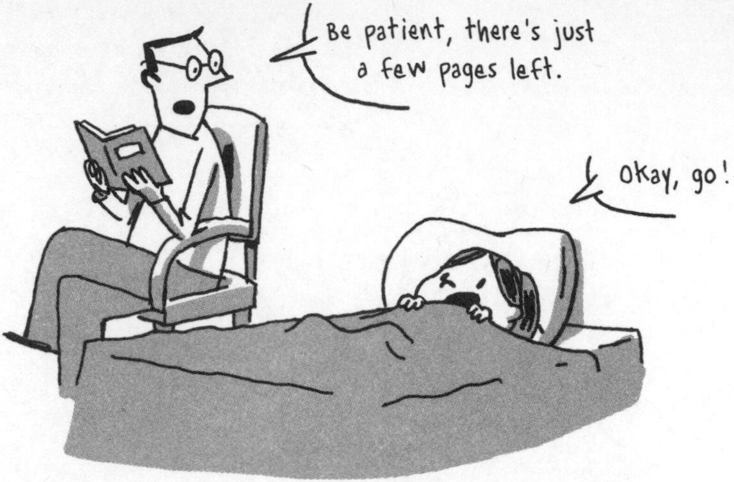
Be patient, there's just a few pages left.
Okay, go!

Harry stood frozen with fear. Voldemort drew closer. His eyes gleamed blood-red and his face was twisted with hatred. He said...

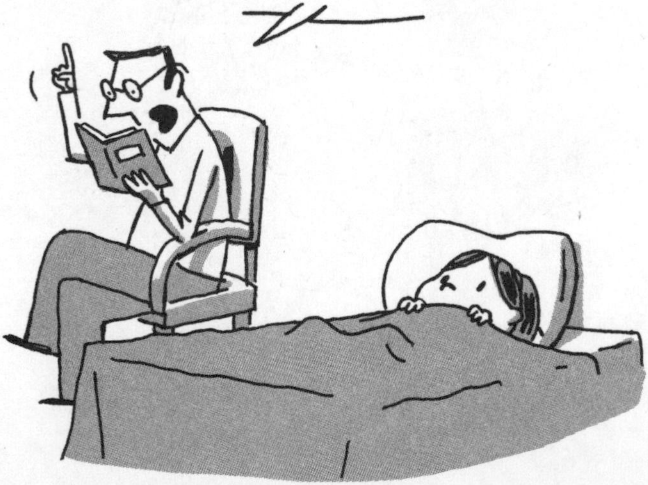

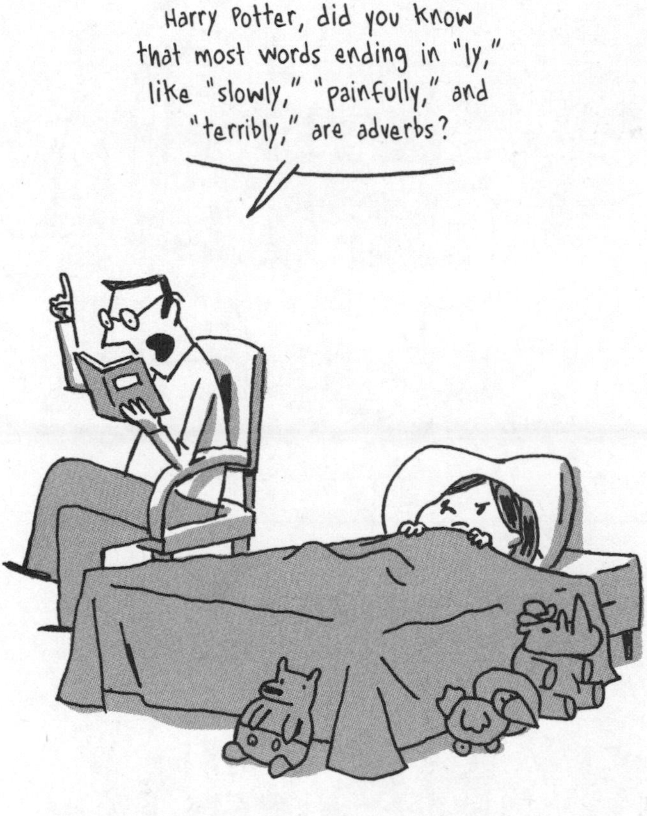
Harry Potter, did you know that most words ending in "ly," like "slowly," "painfully," and "terribly," are adverbs?
Delisle

– In the garden

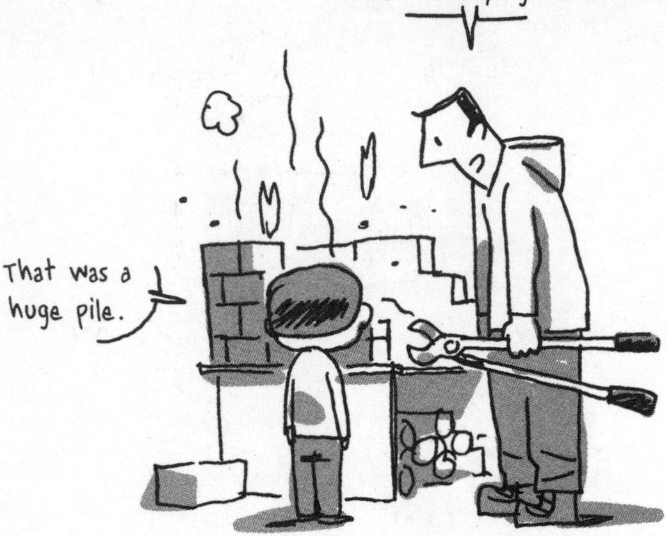
Okay, I think we've burned all the leaves and little branches that were lying around.
That was a huge pile.

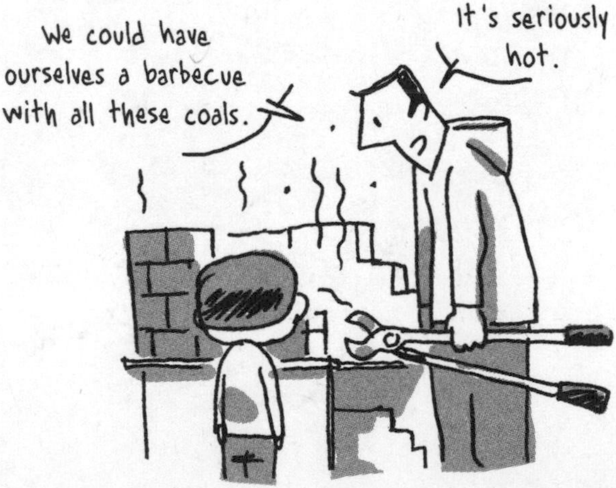
We could have ourselves a barbecue with all these coals.
It's seriously hot.

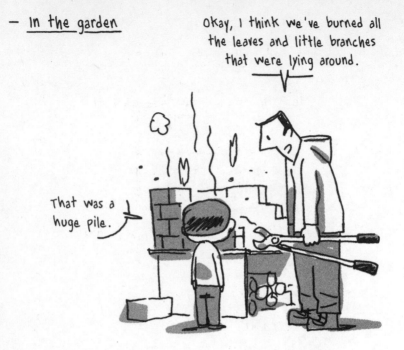

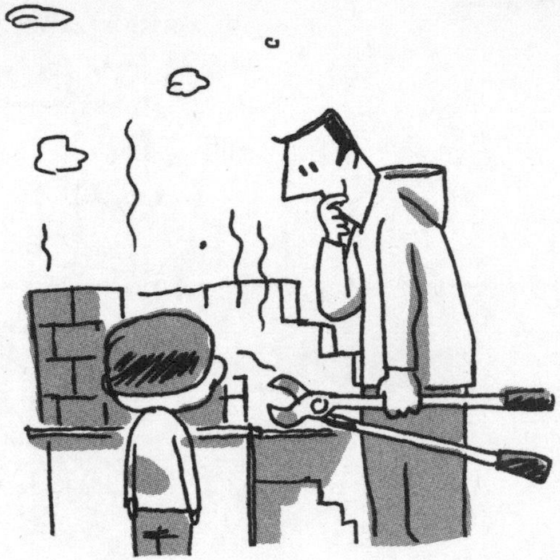

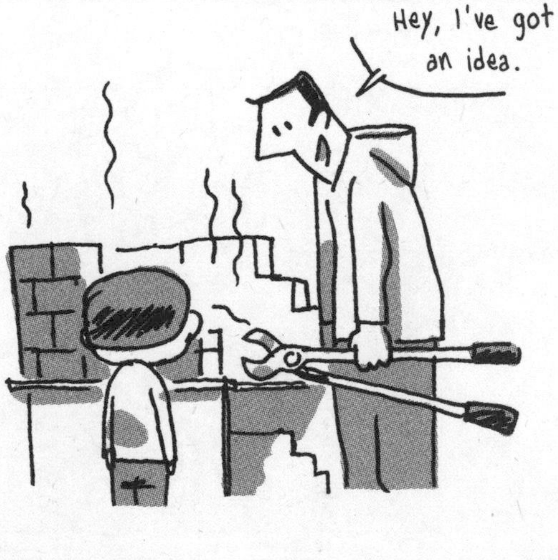
Hey, I've got an idea.

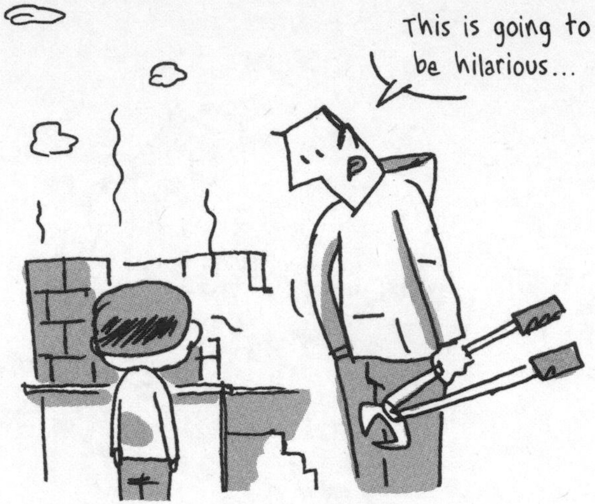
This is going to be hilarious...

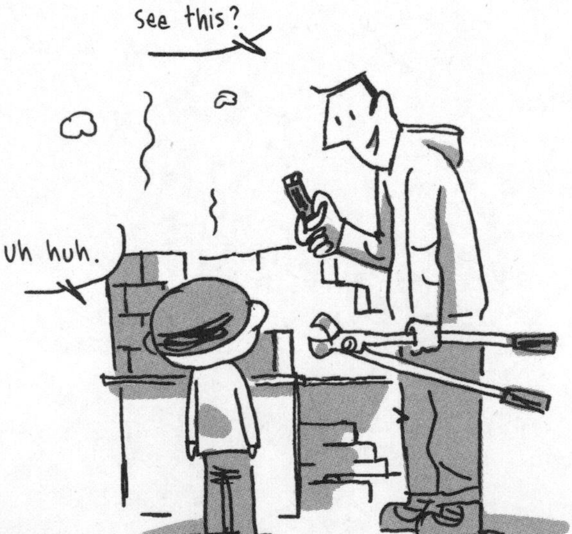
See this?
Uh huh.

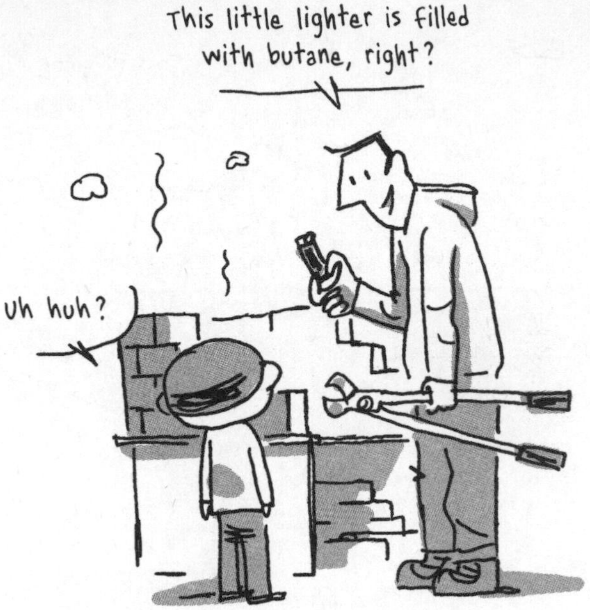
This little lighter is filled with butane, right?
uh huh?

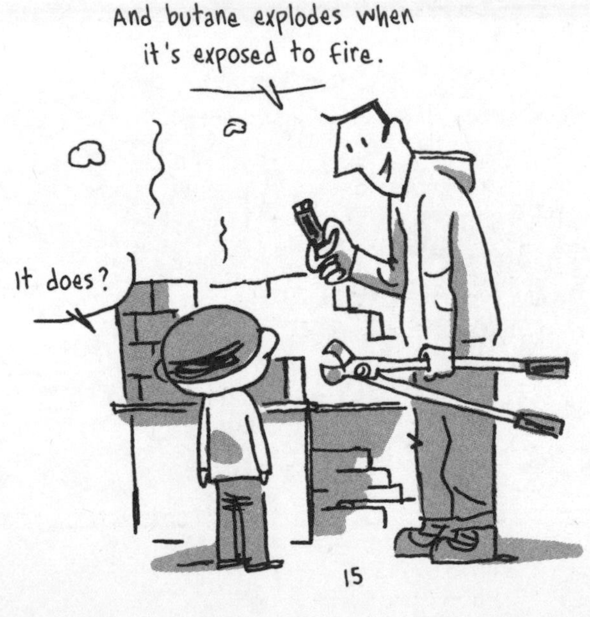
And butane explodes when it's exposed to fire.
It does?

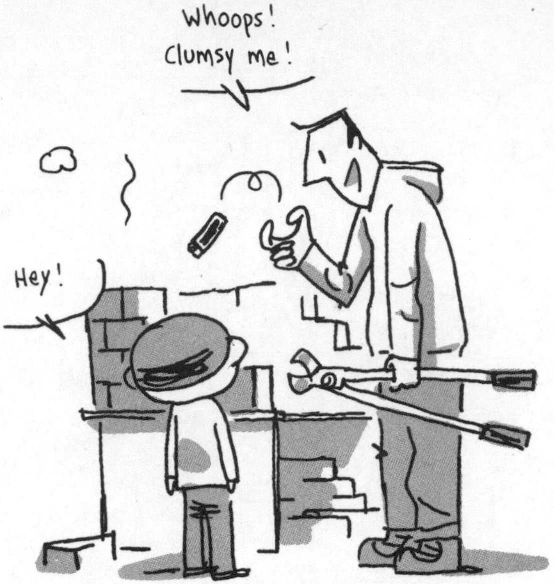
Whoops! Clumsy me!
Hey!

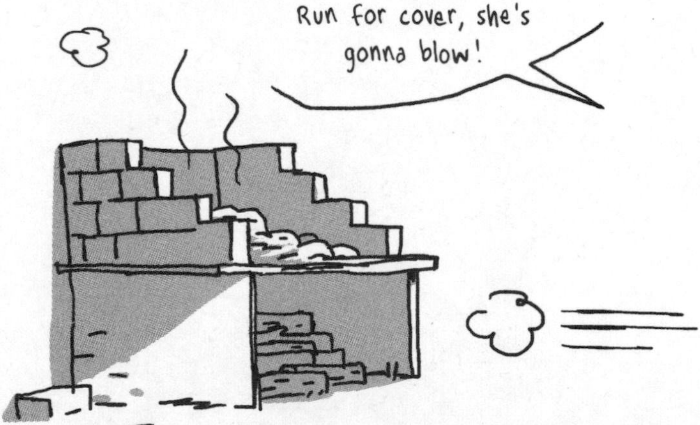
Run for cover, she's gonna blow!

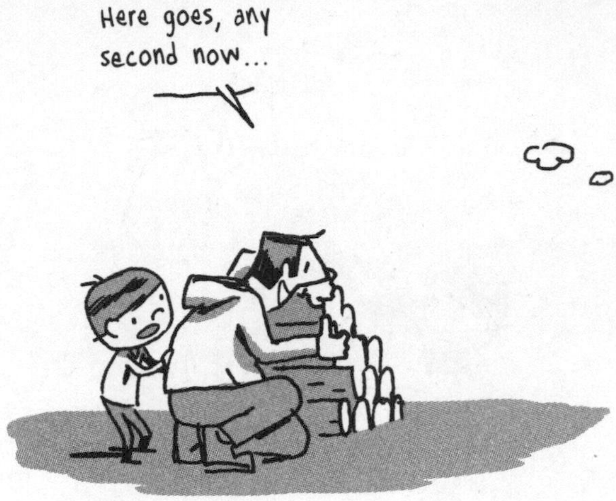
Here goes, any second now...

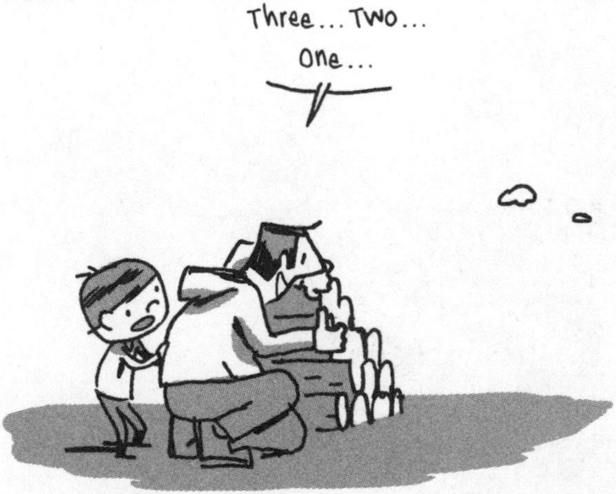
Three... Two... One...

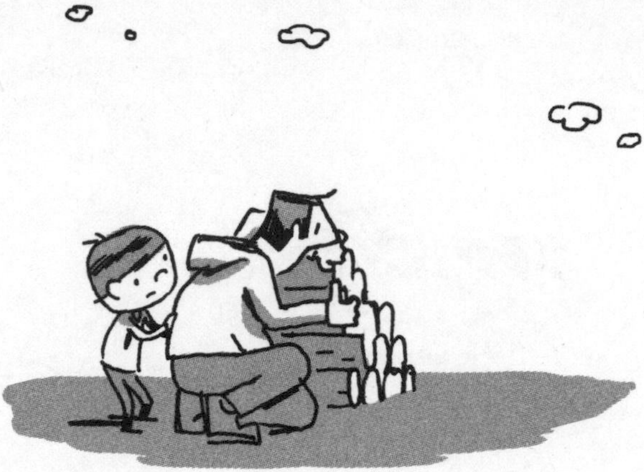

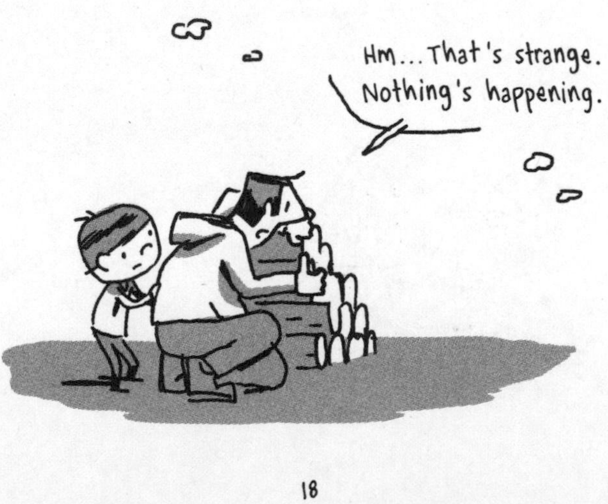
Hm... That's strange.
Nothing's happening.

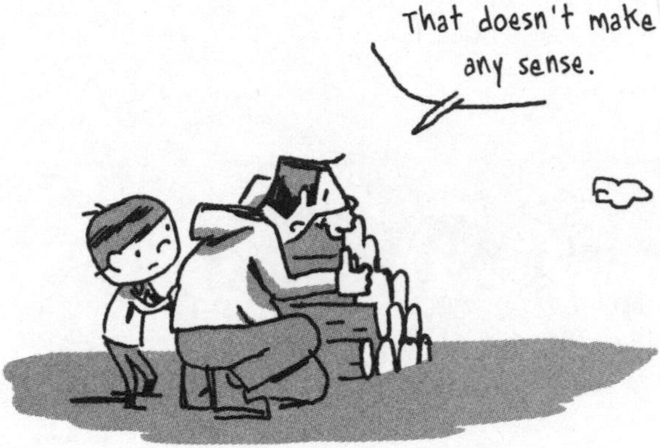
That doesn't make any sense.

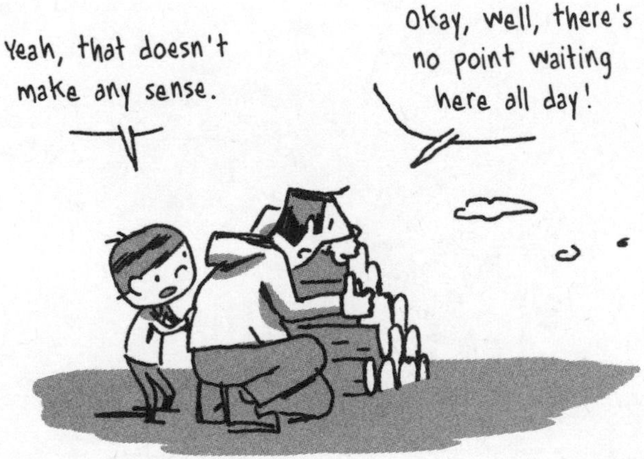
Yeah, that doesn't make any sense.
Okay, well, there's no point waiting here all day!

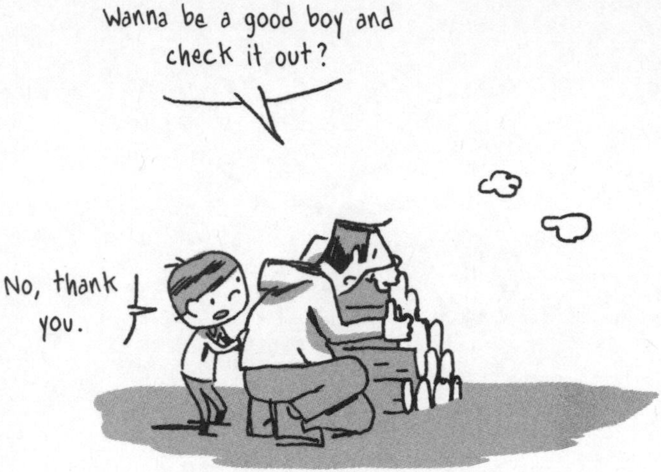
Wanna be a good boy and check it out?
No, thank you.

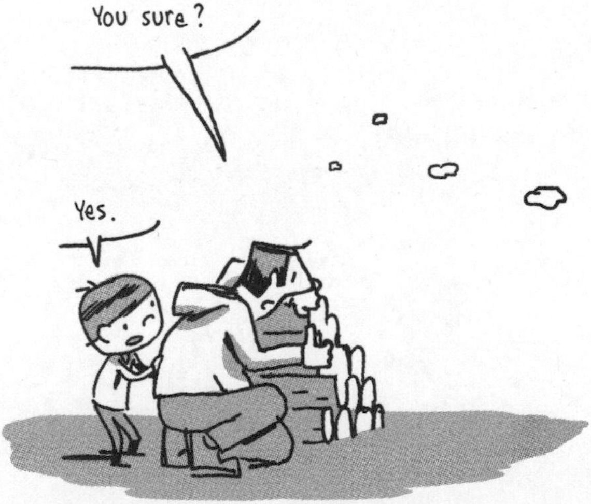
You sure?
Yes.

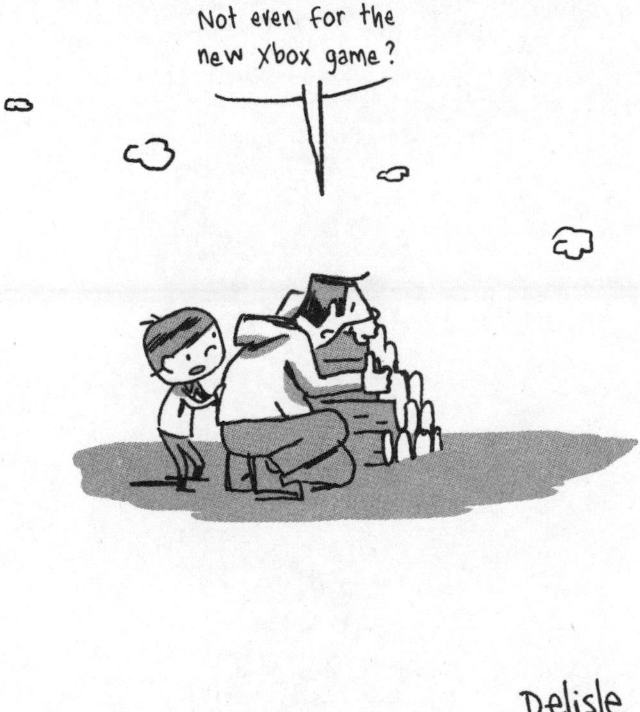
Not even for the new Xbox game?
Delisle

- After school

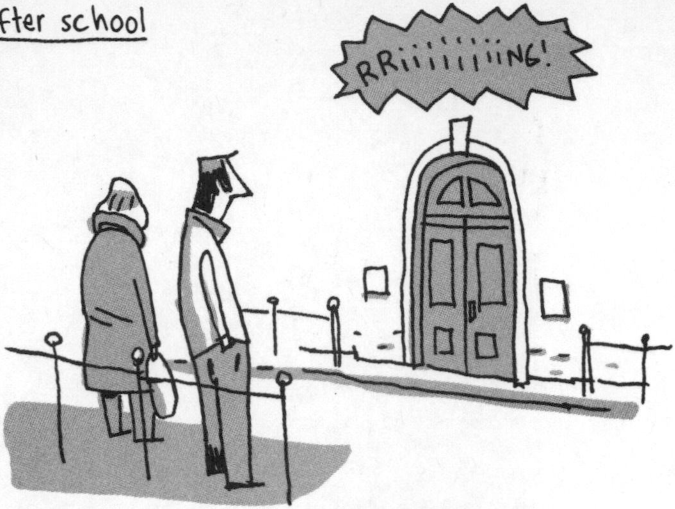
RRiiiiiiiiNG!

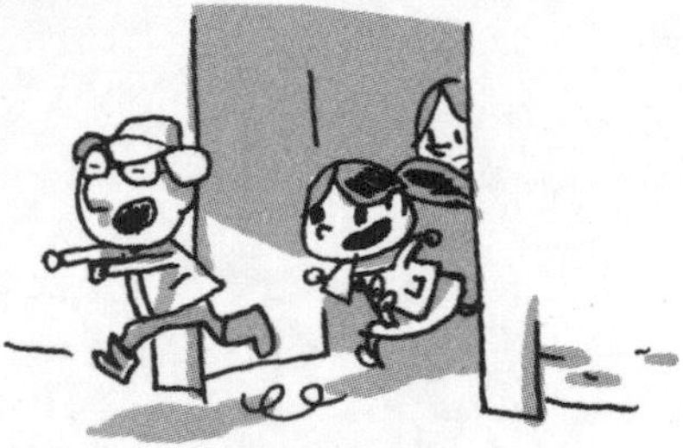

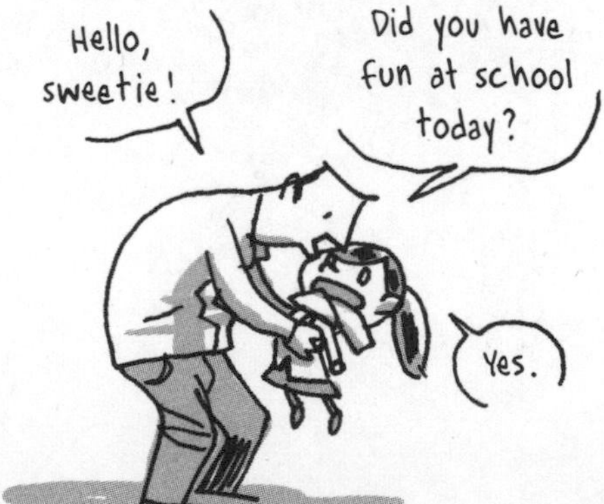
Hello, sweetie!
Did you have fun at school today?
Yes.

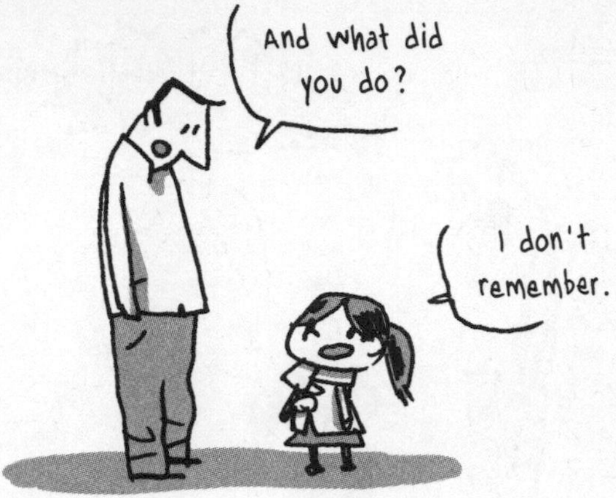
And what did you do?
I don't remember.

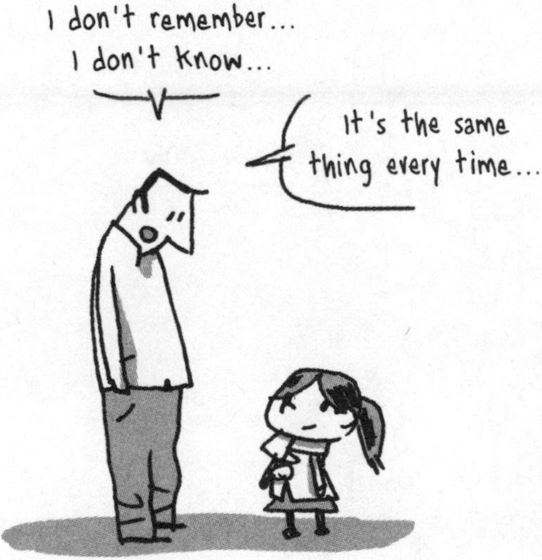
I don't remember... I don't know...
It's the same thing every time...

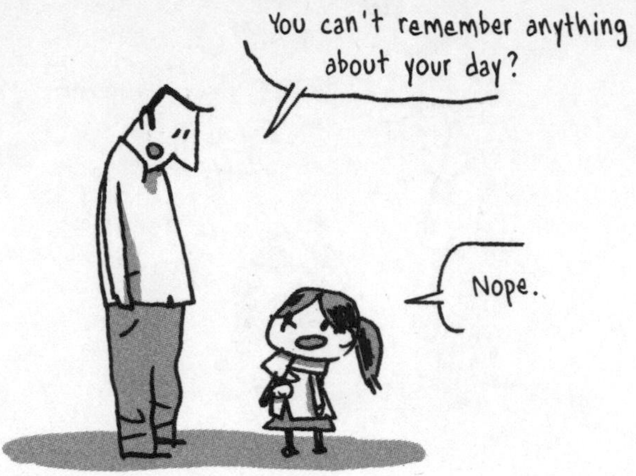
You can't remember anything about your day?
Nope.

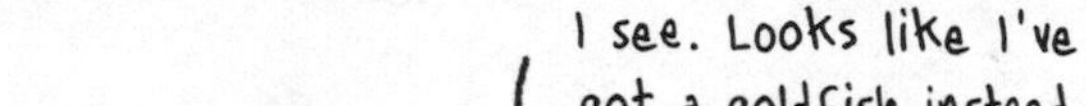
I see. Looks like I've got a goldfish instead of a daughter.
Ha ha!

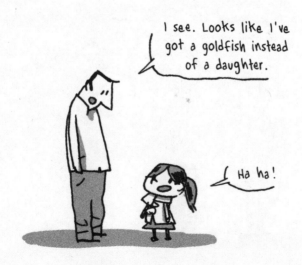

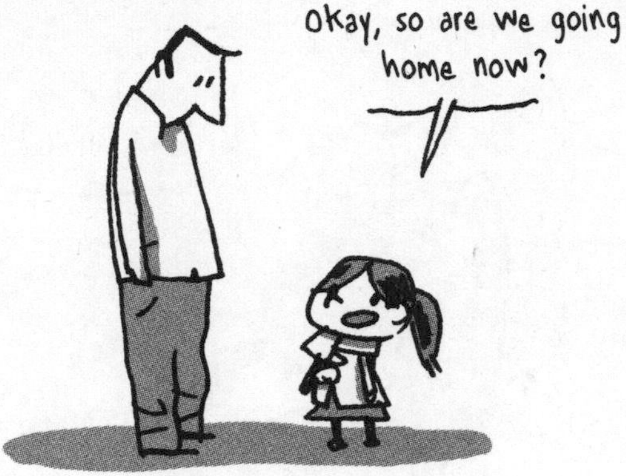
Okay, so are we going home now?

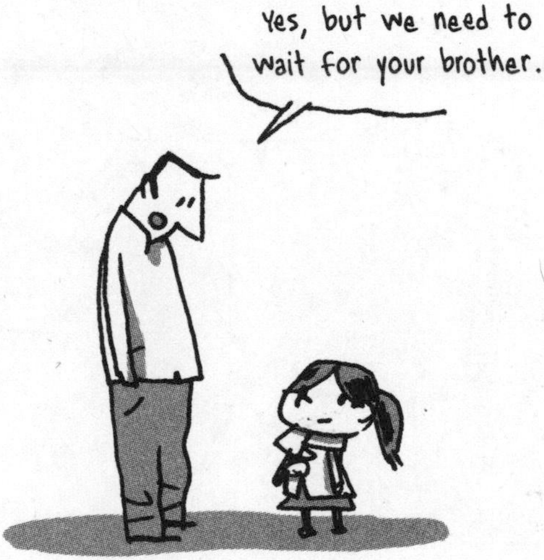
Yes, but we need to wait for your brother.

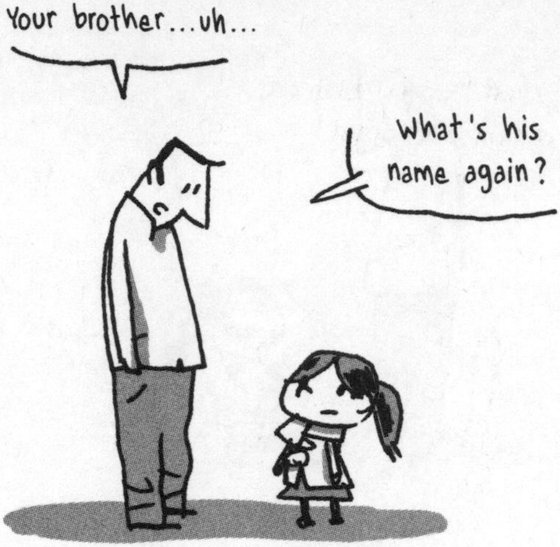
Your brother...uh...
What's his name again?

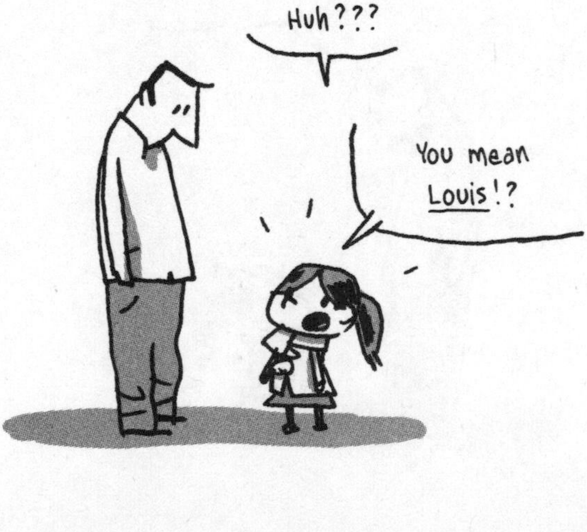
Huh???
You mean Louis!?

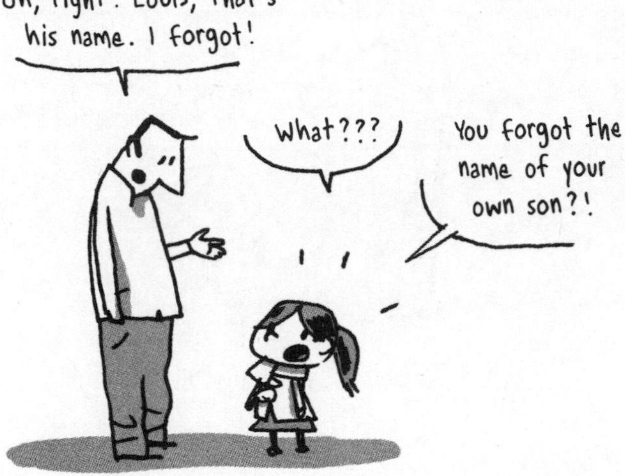
Oh, right! Louis, that's his name. I forgot!
What???
You forgot the name of your own son?!

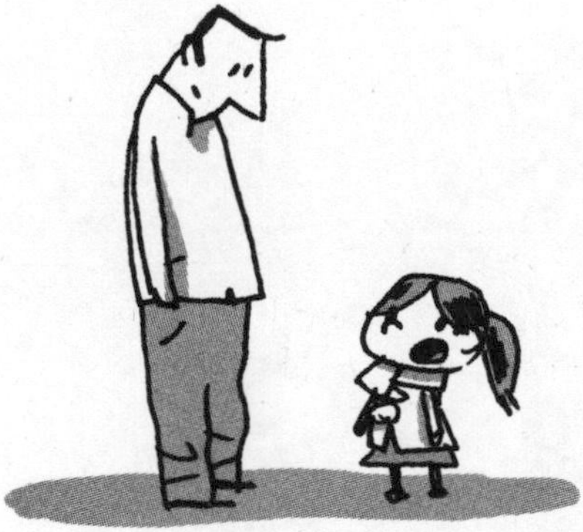

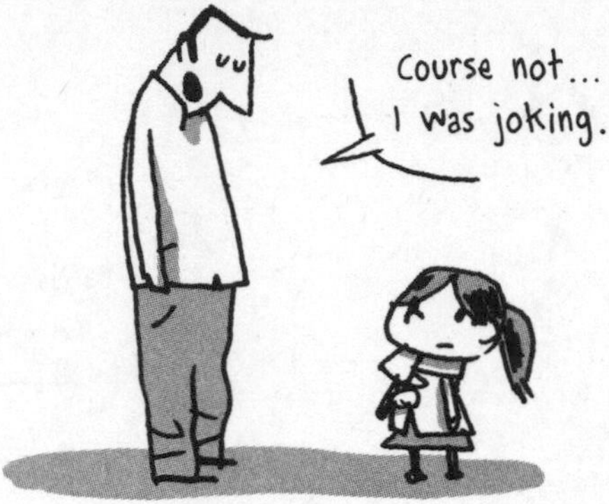
Course not...
I was joking.

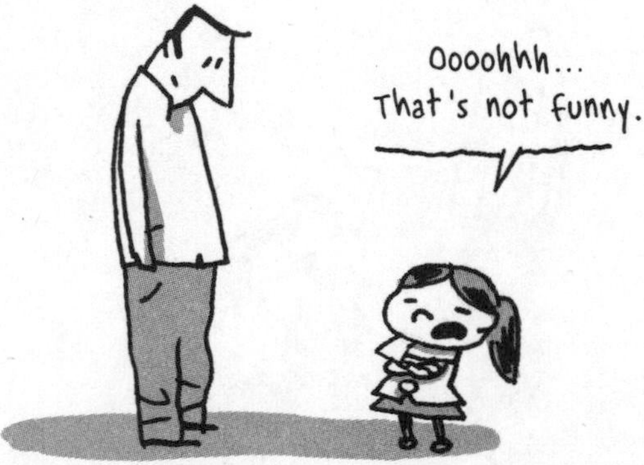
Oooohhh...
That's not funny.

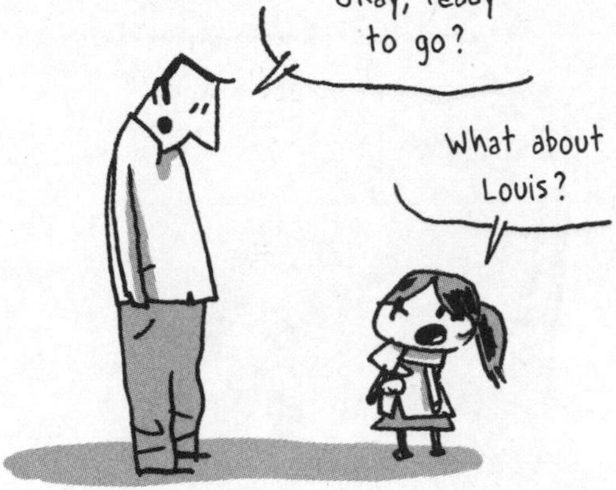
Okay, ready to go?
What about Louis?

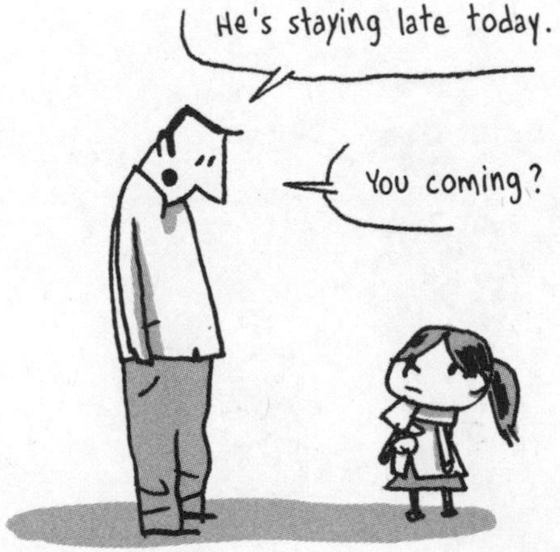
He's staying late today.
You coming?

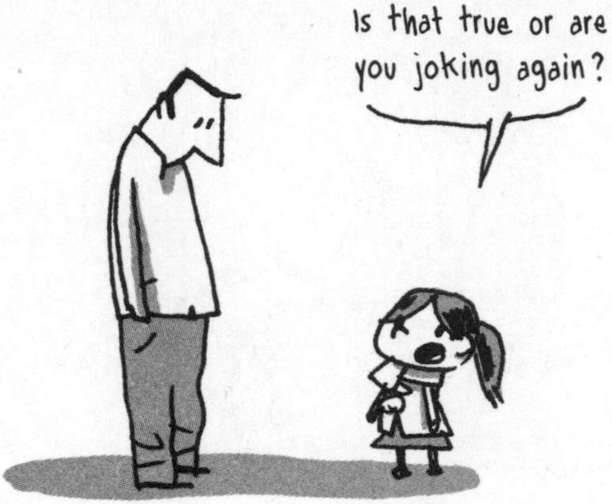
Is that true or are you joking again?

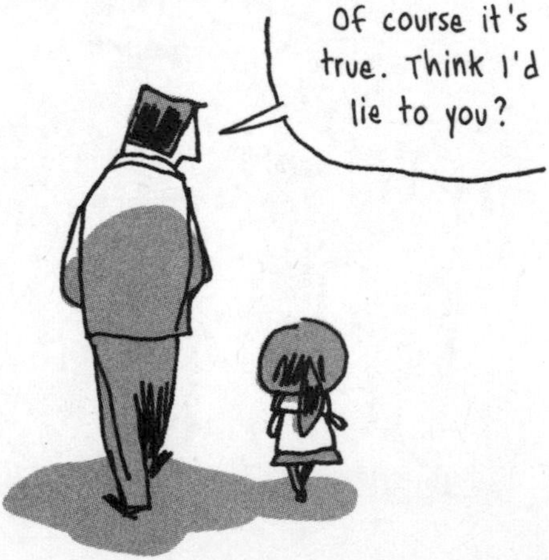
Of course it's true. Think I'd lie to you?

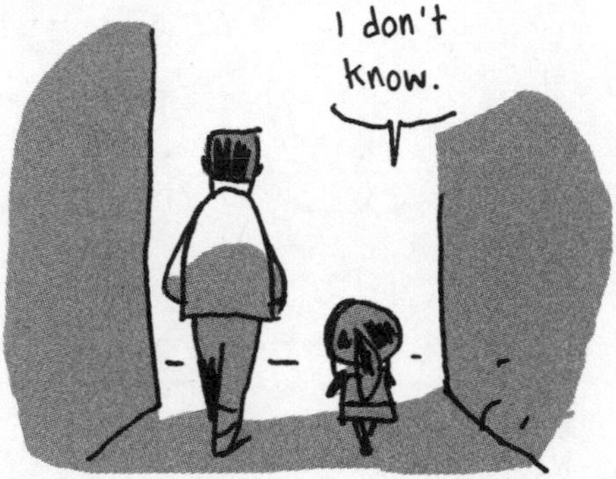
I don't know.

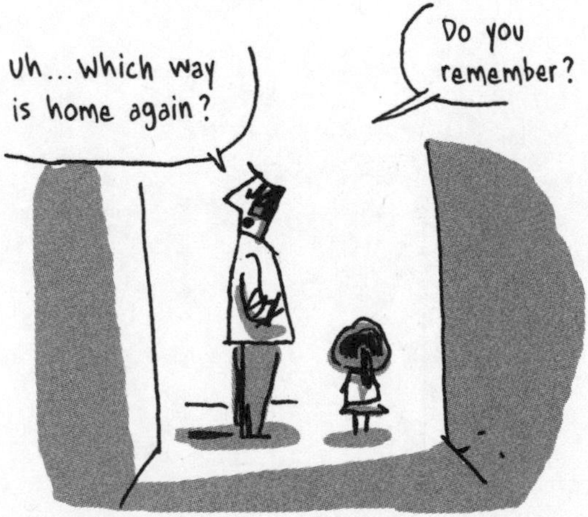
Uh... which way is home again?
Do you remember?

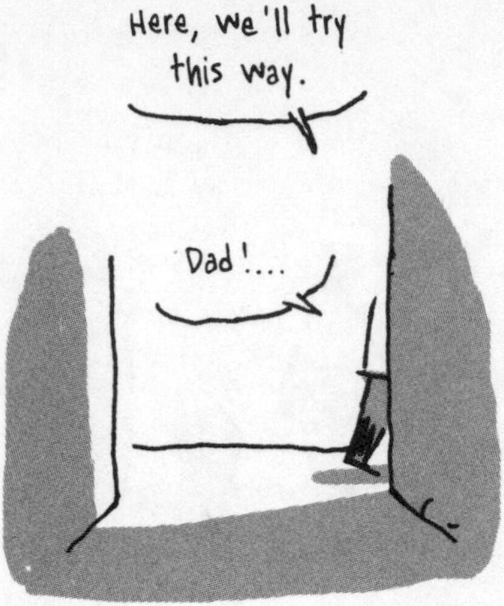
Here, we'll try this way.
Dad!...

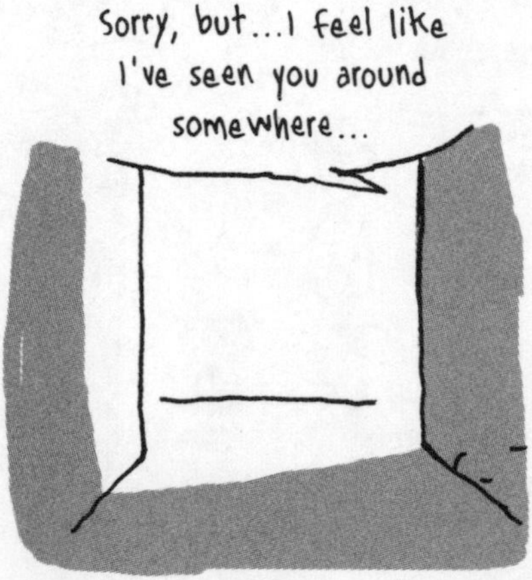
Sorry, but...I feel like I've seen you around somewhere...

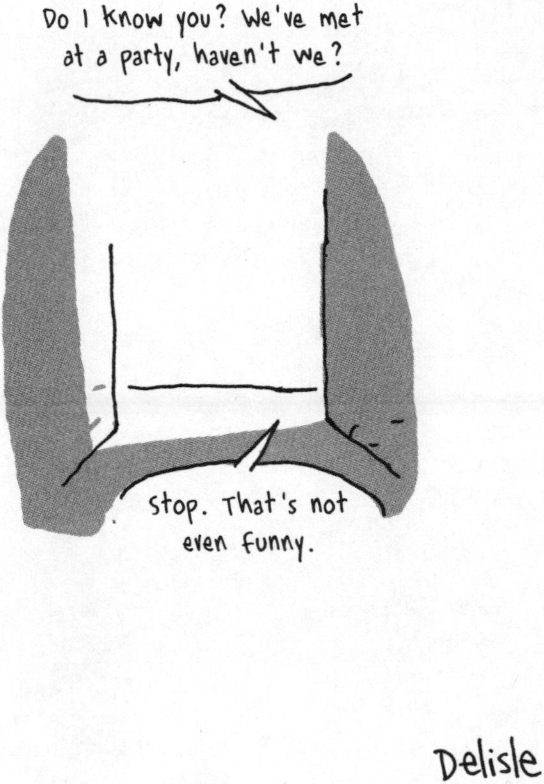
Do I know you? We've met at a party, haven't we?
Stop. That's not even funny.
Delisle

- Sunshine

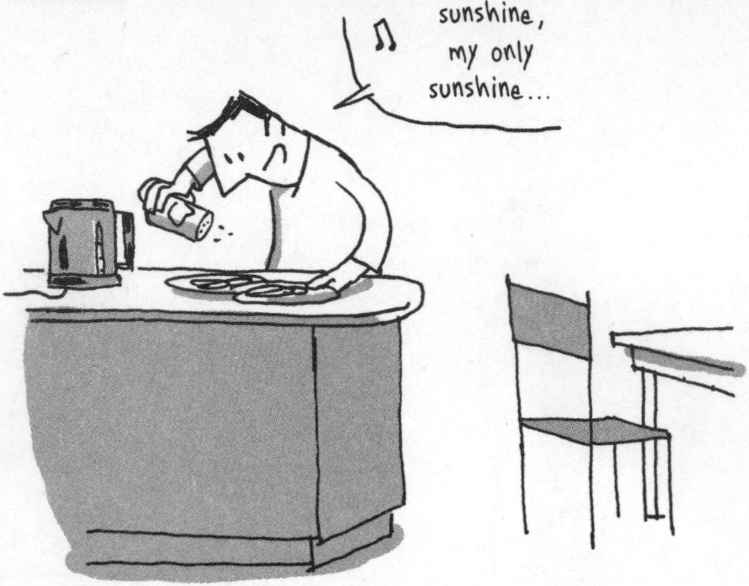

You are my sunshine, my only sunshine...

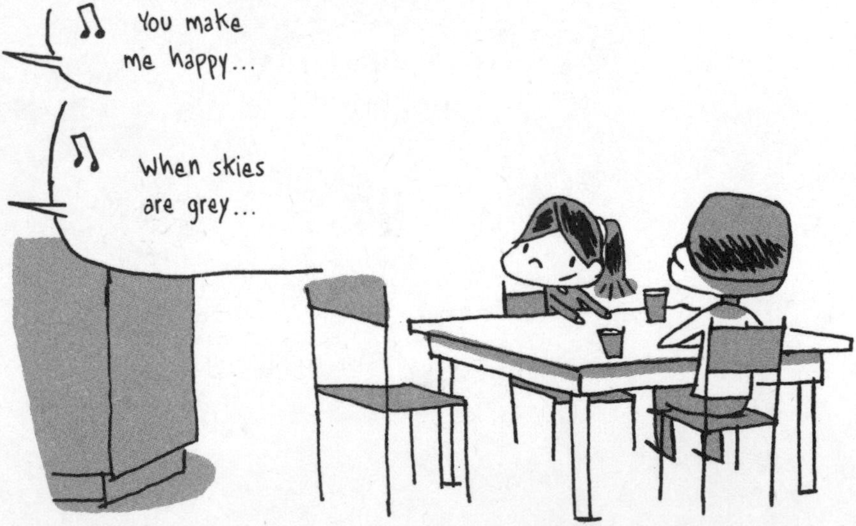

You make me happy...
When skies are grey...

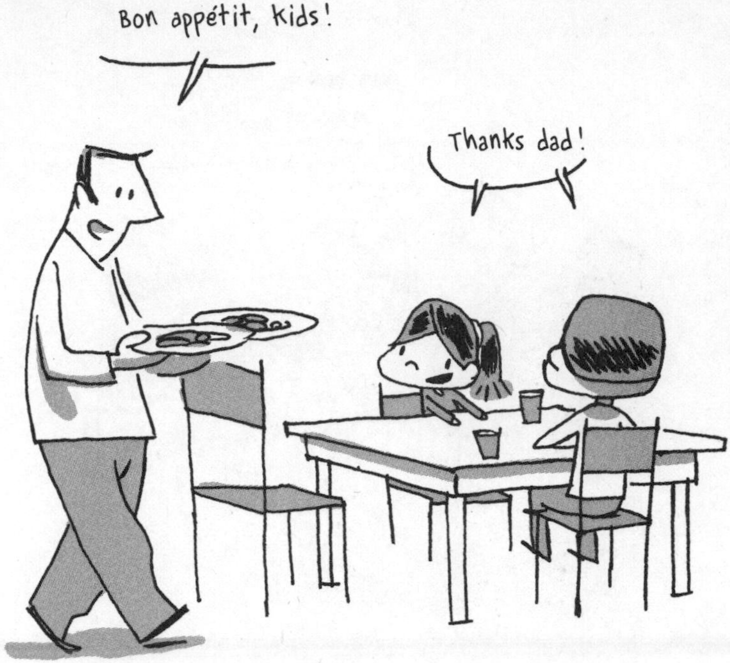
Bon appétit, kids!
Thanks dad!

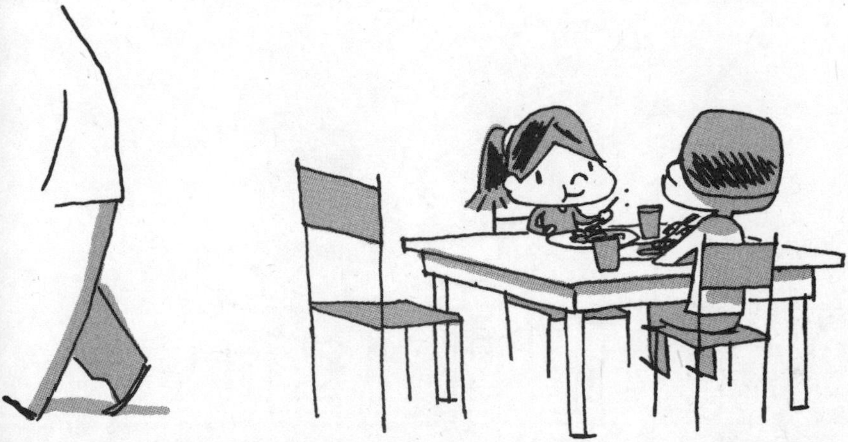

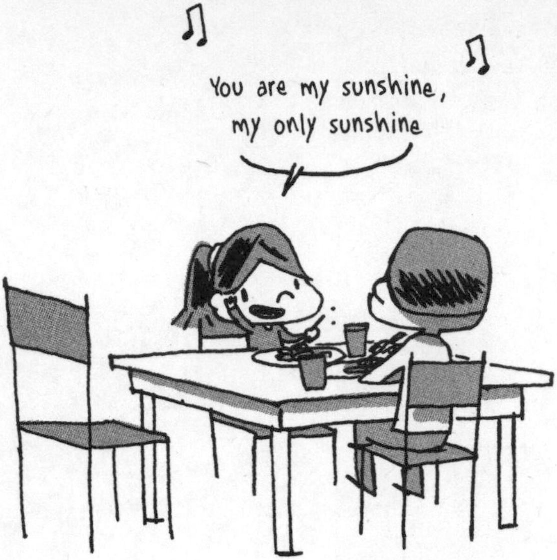
You are my sunshine, my only sunshine

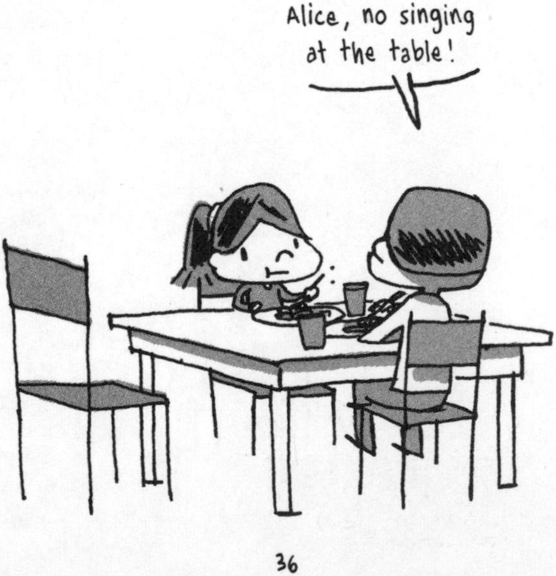
Alice, no singing at the table!

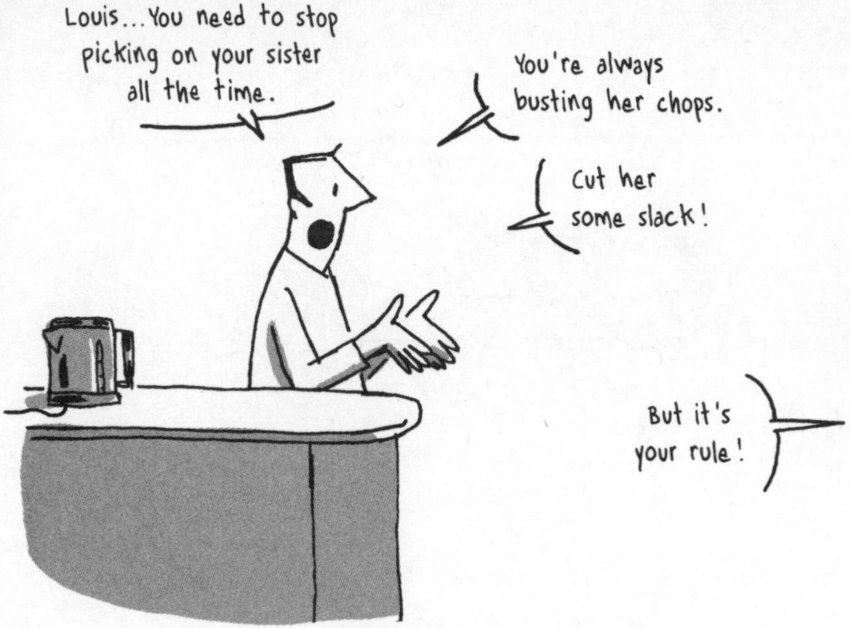
Louis... You need to stop picking on your sister all the time.
You're always busting her chops.
Cut her some slack!
But it's your rule!

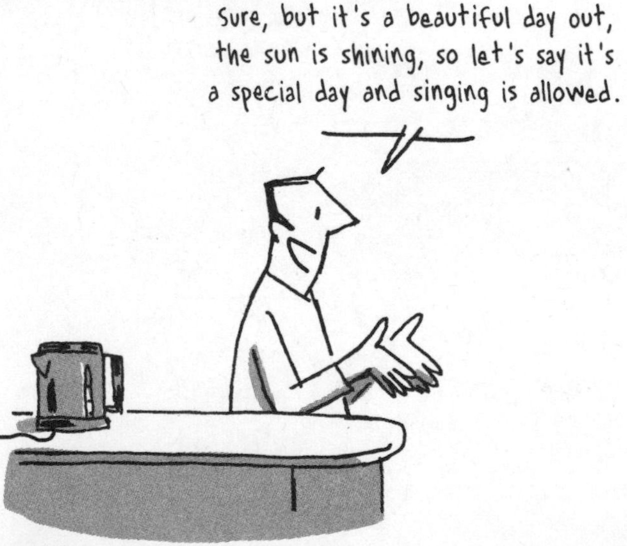
Sure, but it's a beautiful day out, the sun is shining, so let's say it's a special day and singing is allowed.

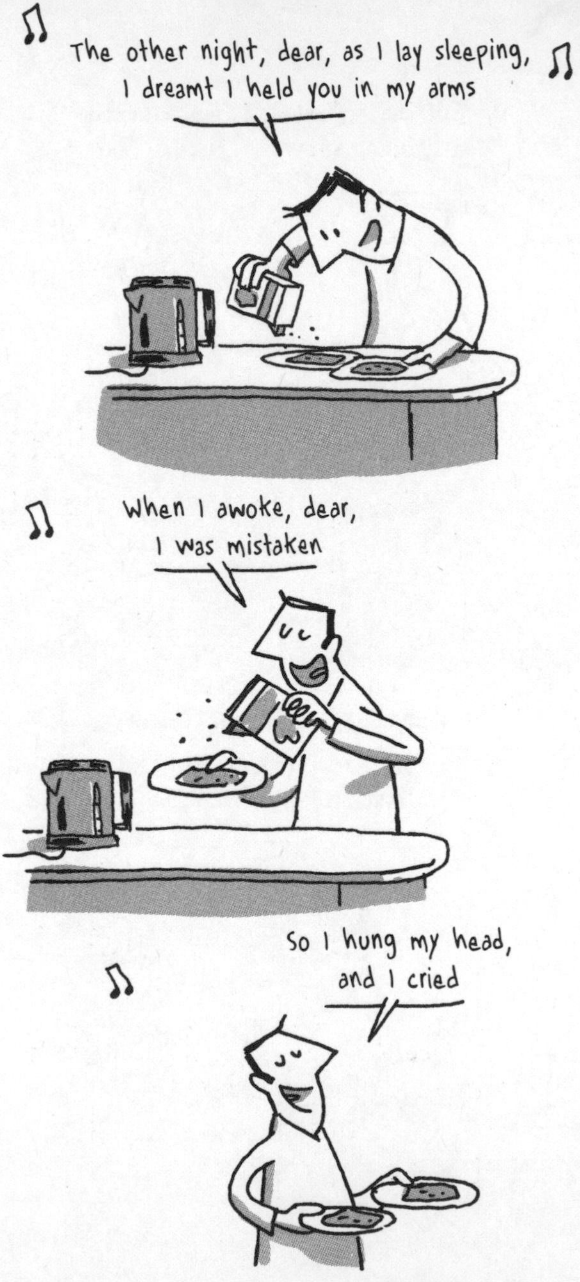
The other night, dear, as I lay sleeping,
I dreamt I held you in my arms
When I awoke, dear,
I was mistaken
So I hung my head,
and I cried

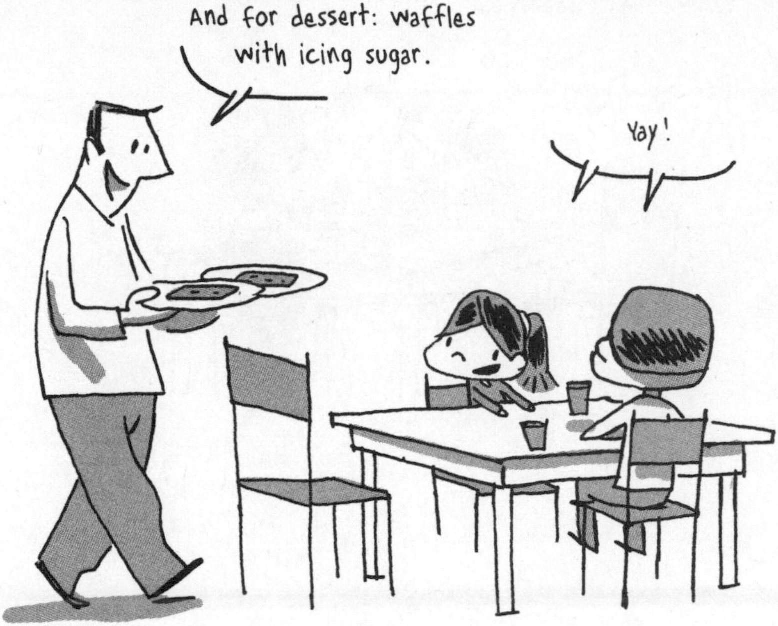
And for dessert: waffles with icing sugar.
Yay!

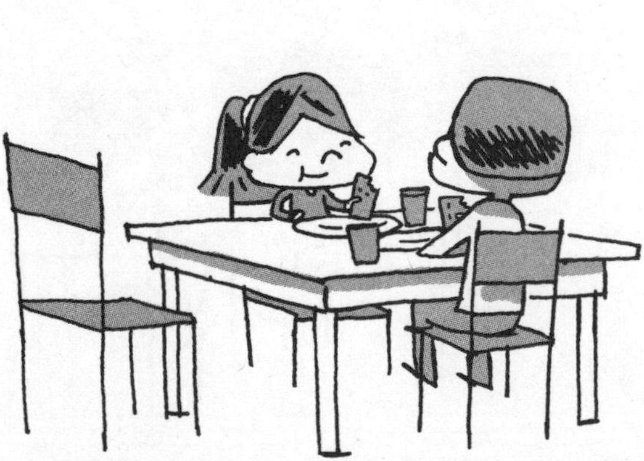

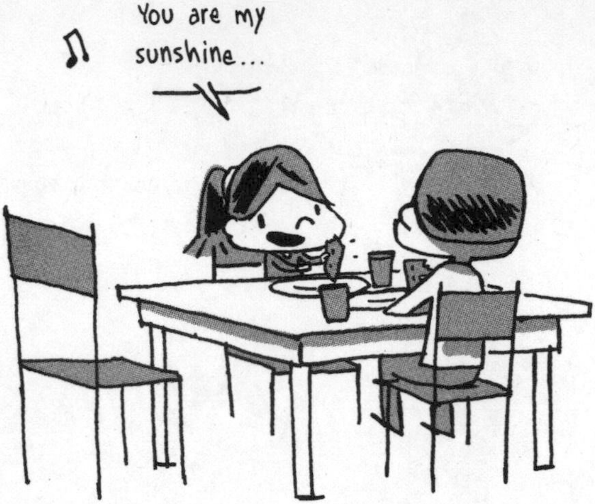
♫ You are my sunshine...

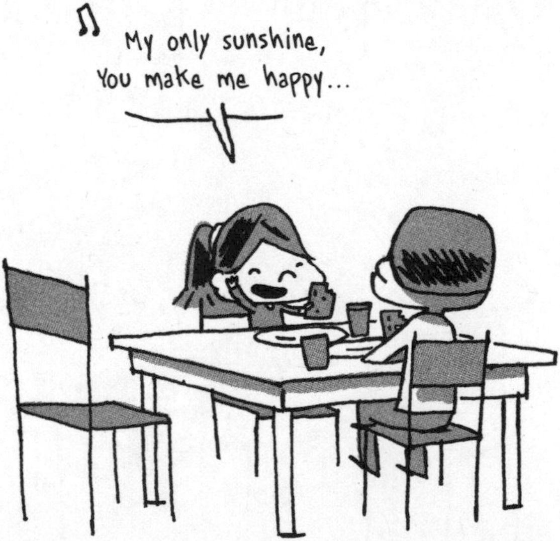
♫ My only sunshine, You make me happy...

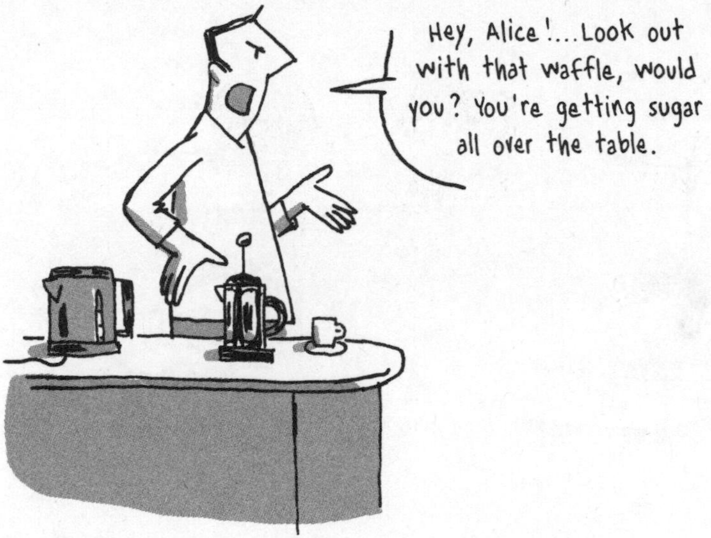
Hey, Alice!... Look out with that waffle, would you? You're getting sugar all over the table.

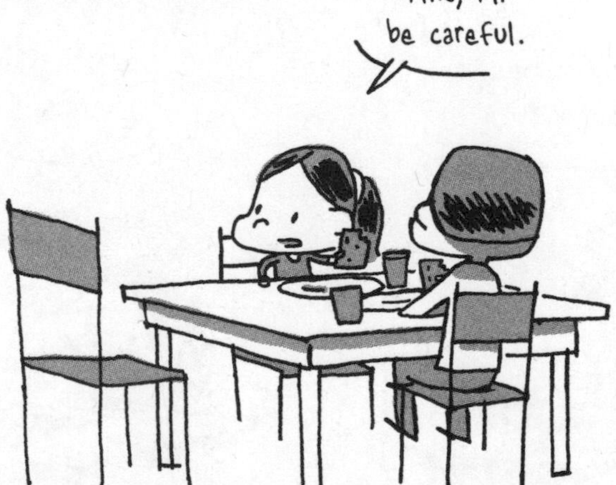
Fine, I'll be careful.

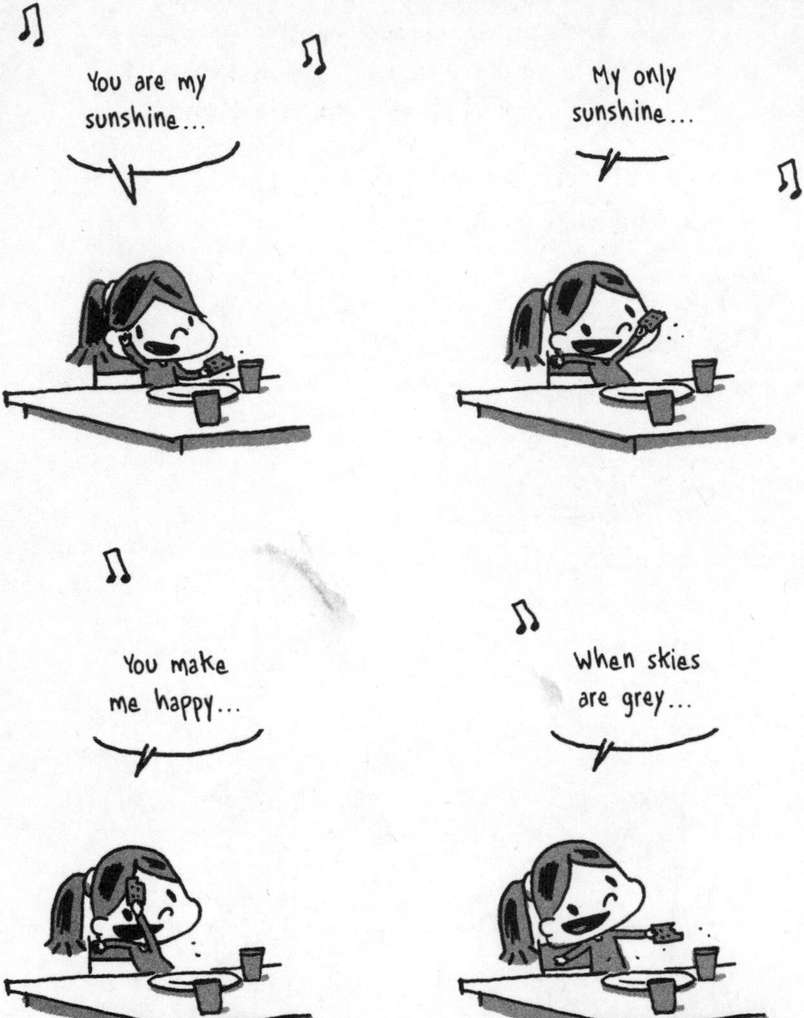
You are my sunshine...
My only sunshine...
You make me happy...
When skies are grey...

Alice, are you trying to make me angry on purpose? Pay attention to what you're doing. You're always spilling crumbs, and before you know it, they're on the floor.
I vacuumed this place yesterday.

It's the same thing every meal... I keep telling you: sit straight and eat over your plate.
I'm sounding like a broken record.

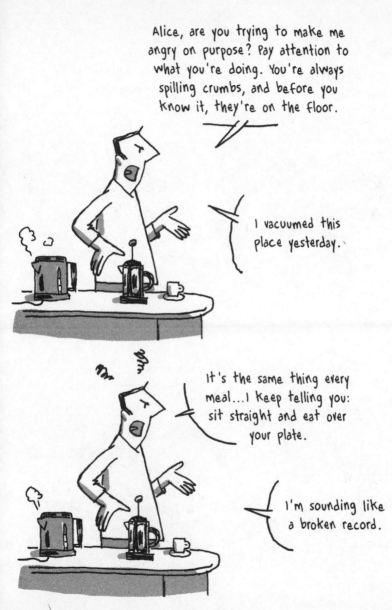

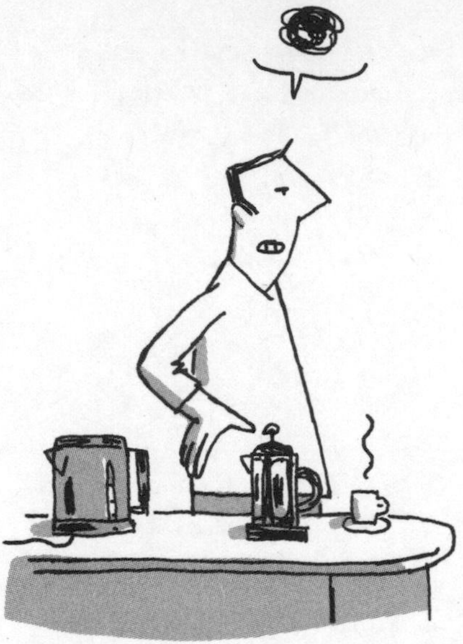

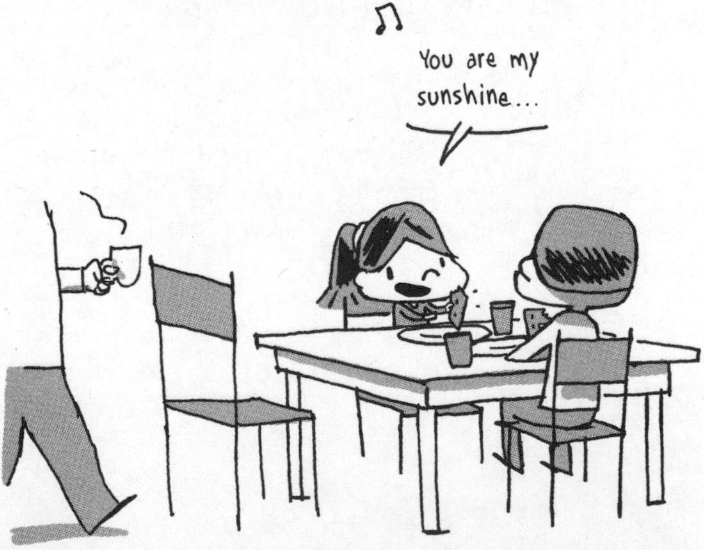

You are my sunshine...

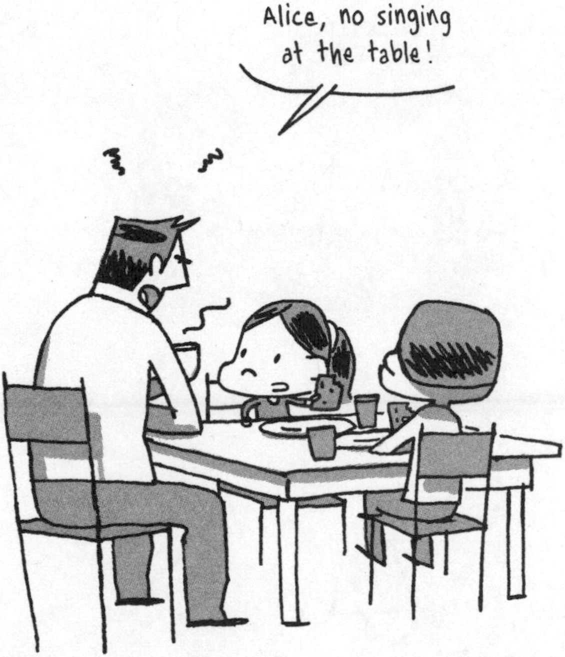
Alice, no singing at the table!

Delisle

- Titch

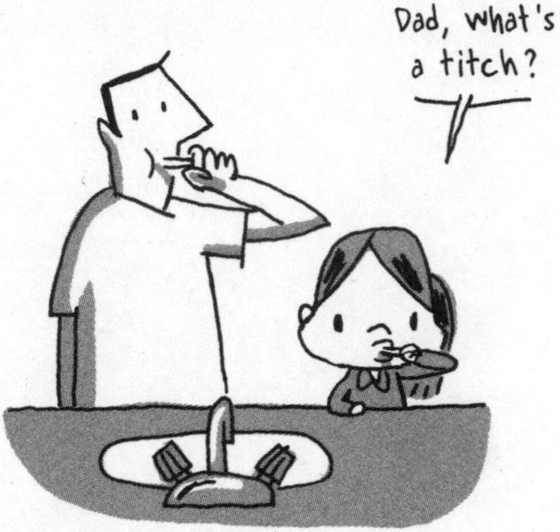
Dad, what's a titch?

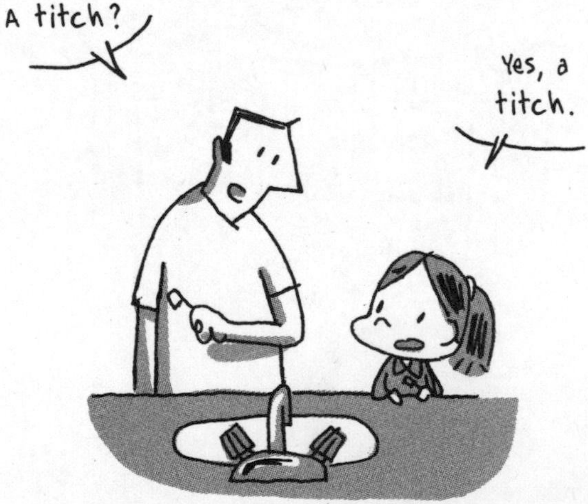
A titch?
Yes, a titch.

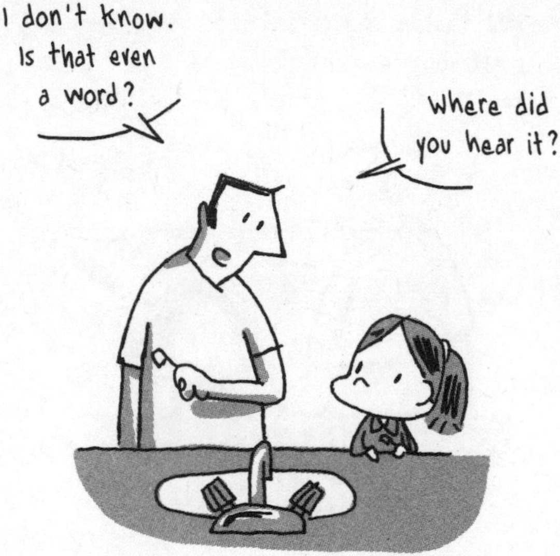
I don't know. Is that even a word?
Where did you hear it?

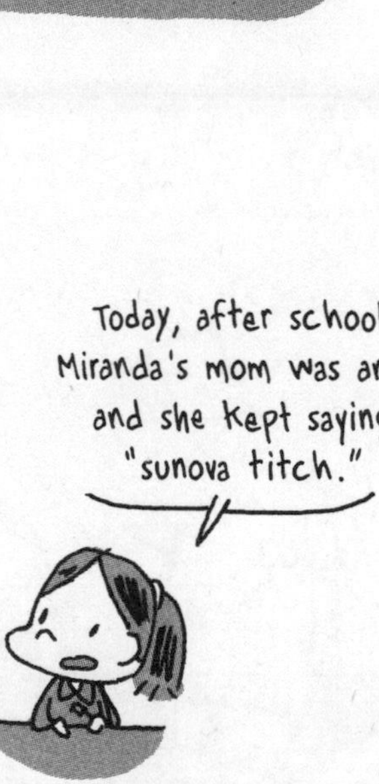
Today, after school. Miranda's mom was angry and she kept saying "sunova titch."

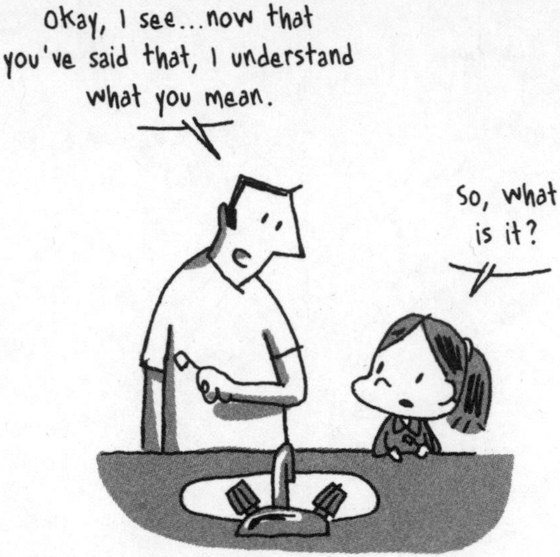
Okay, I see...now that you've said that, I understand what you mean.
So, what is it?

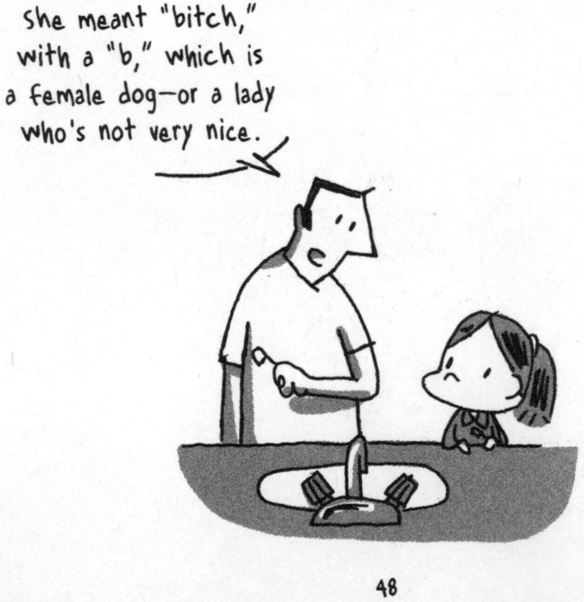
She meant "bitch," with a "b," which is a female dog—or a lady who's not very nice.

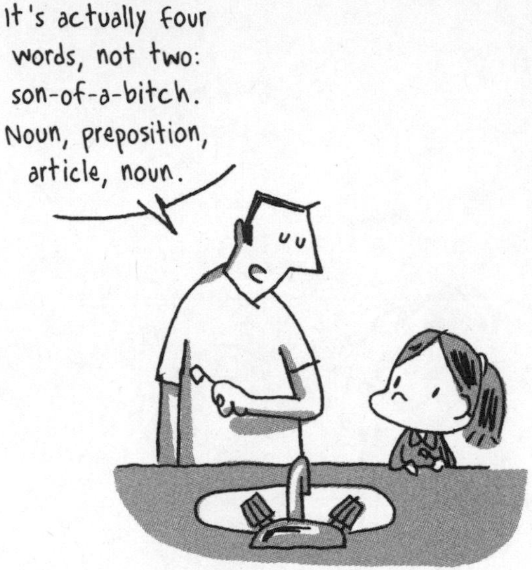
It's actually four words, not two: son-of-a-bitch. Noun, preposition, article, noun.

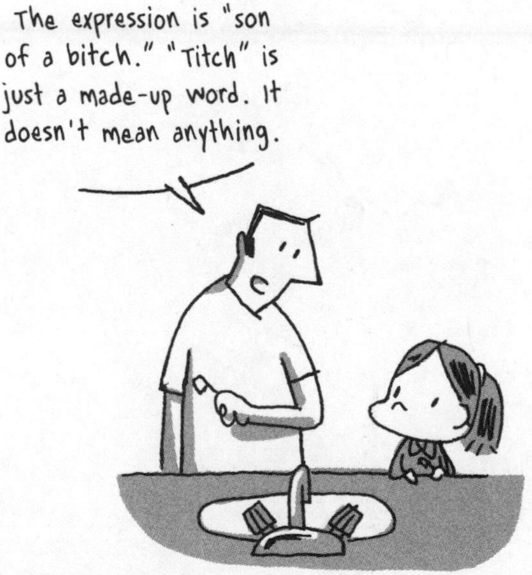
The expression is "son of a bitch." "Titch" is just a made-up word. It doesn't mean anything.

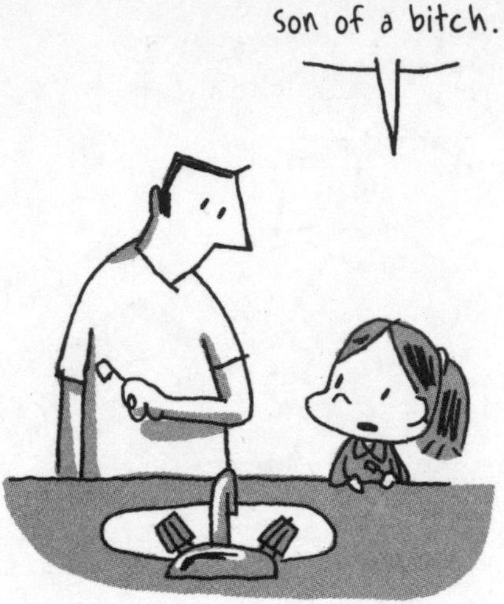
Son of a bitch.

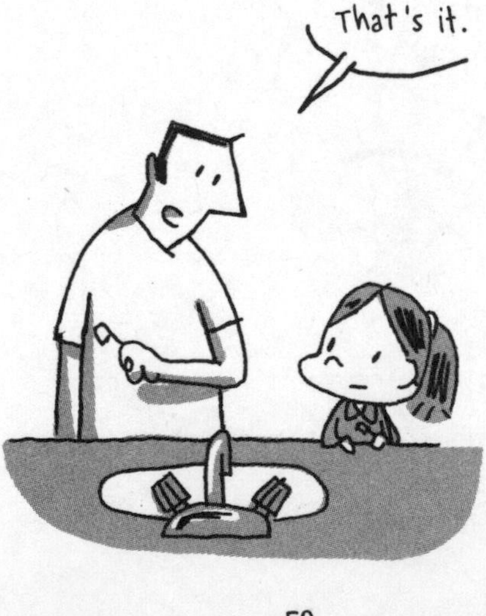
That's it.

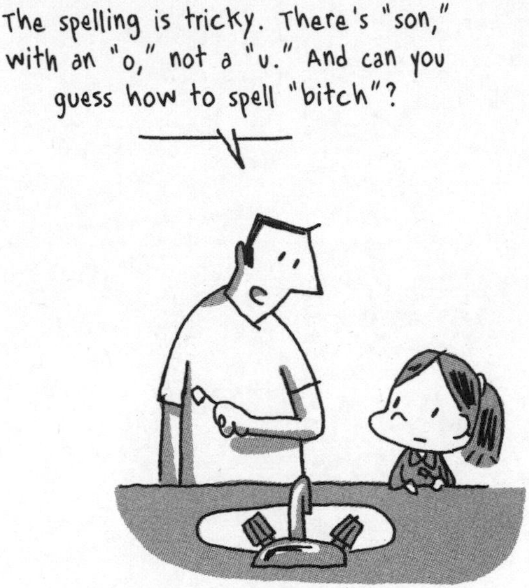
The spelling is tricky. There's "son," with an "o," not a "u." And can you guess how to spell "bitch"?

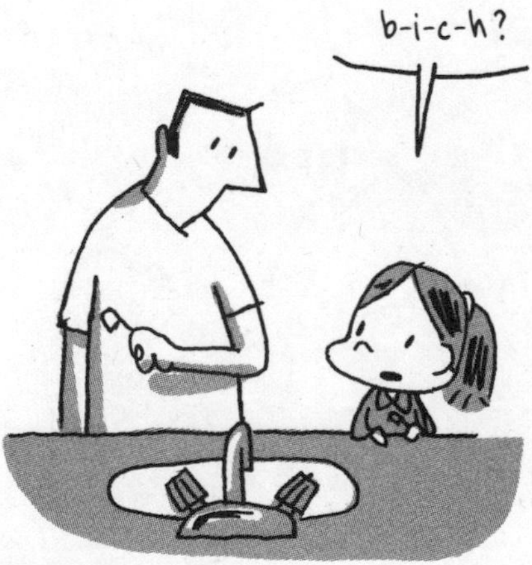
b-i-c-h?

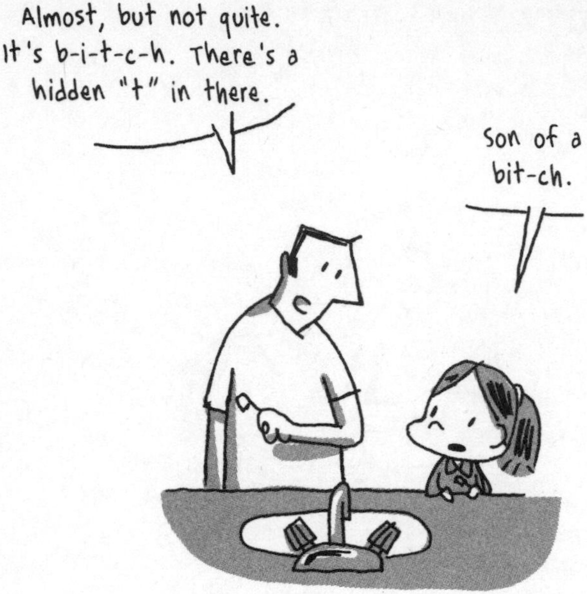
Almost, but not quite. It's b-i-t-c-h. There's a hidden "t" in there.
Son of a bit-ch.

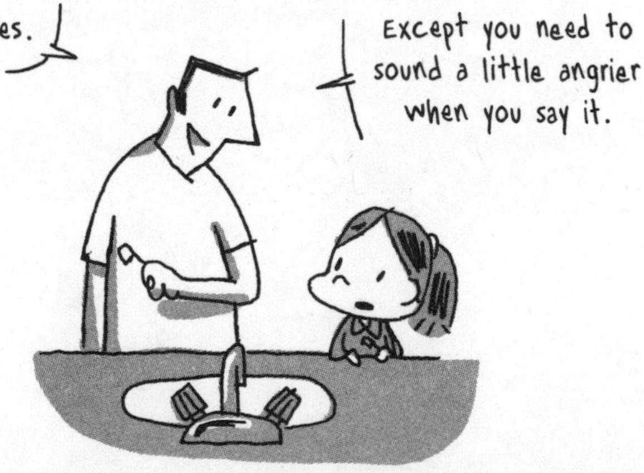
Yes.
Except you need to sound a little angrier when you say it.

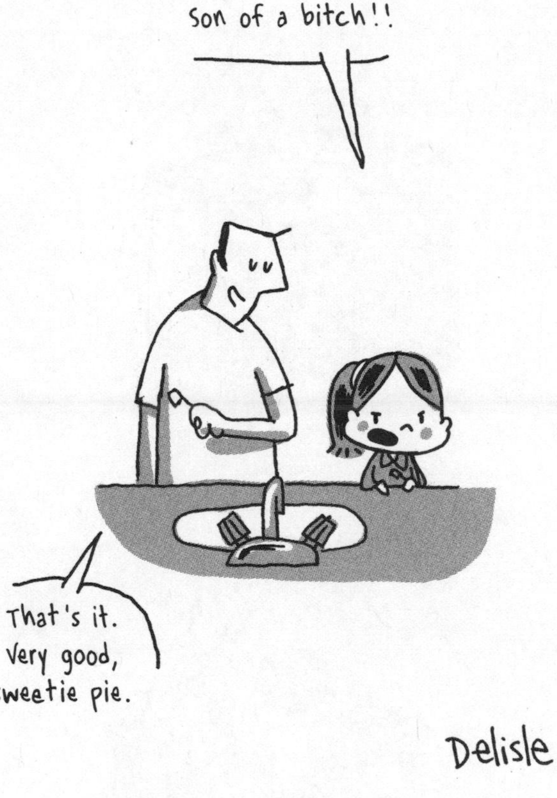
Son of a bitch!!
That's it. Very good, sweetie pie.
Delisle

- Mustard

We did a really stupid contest in the cafeteria today.
What was it?
It was a contest to see who could eat the most mustard.

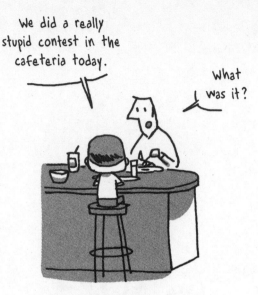

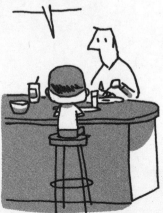

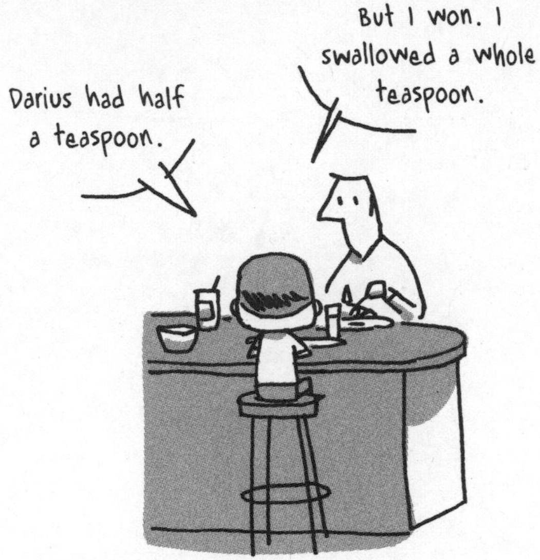
Darius had half a teaspoon.
But I won. I swallowed a whole teaspoon.

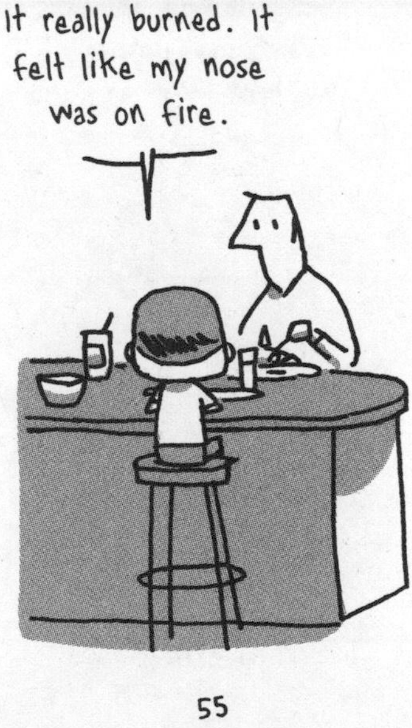
It really burned. It felt like my nose was on fire.

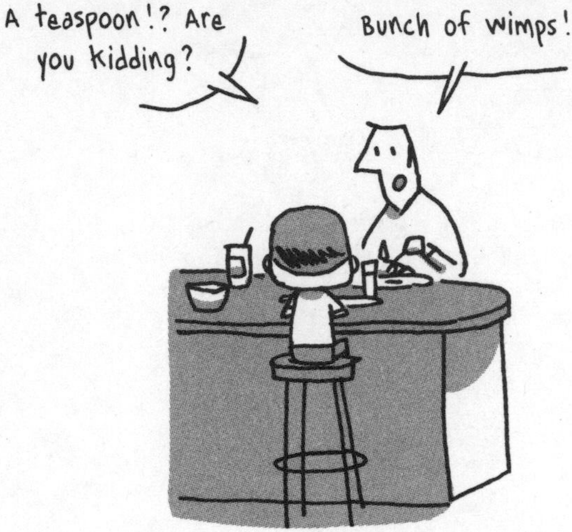
A teaspoon!? Are you kidding?
Bunch of wimps!

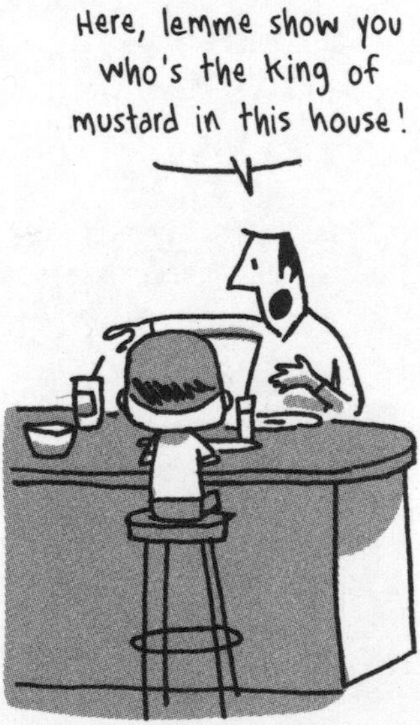
Here, lemme show you who's the king of mustard in this house!

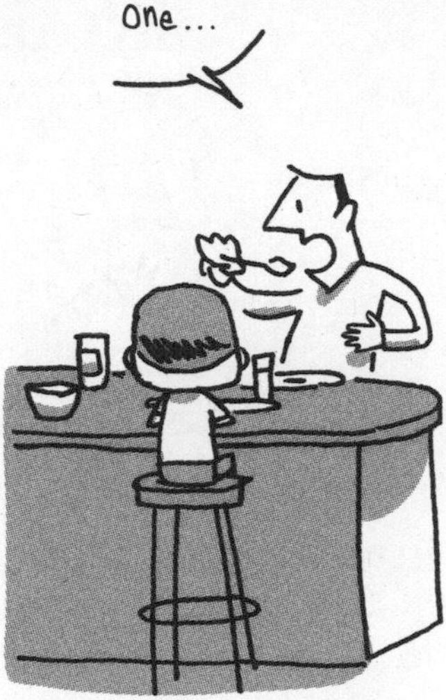
One...

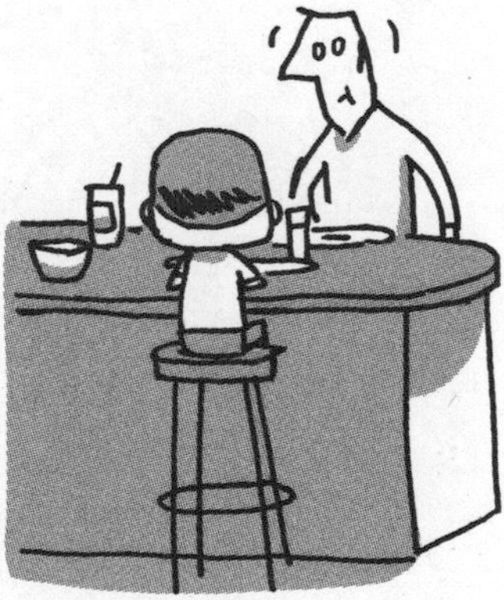

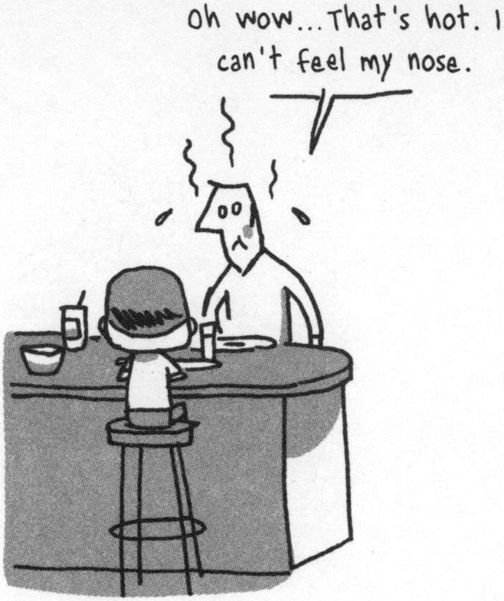
Oh wow... That's hot. I can't feel my nose.

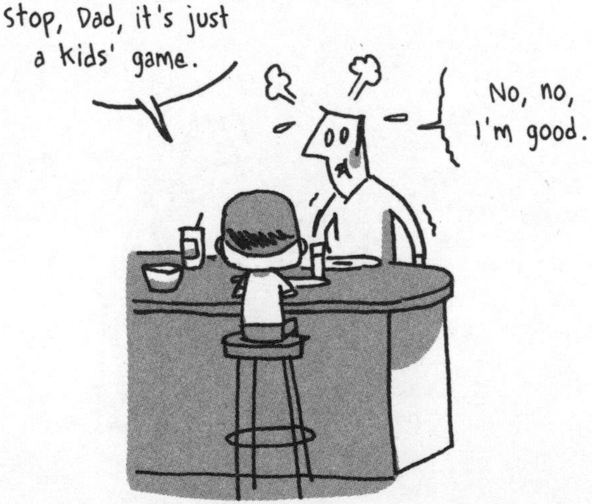
Stop, Dad, it's just a kids' game.
No, no, I'm good.

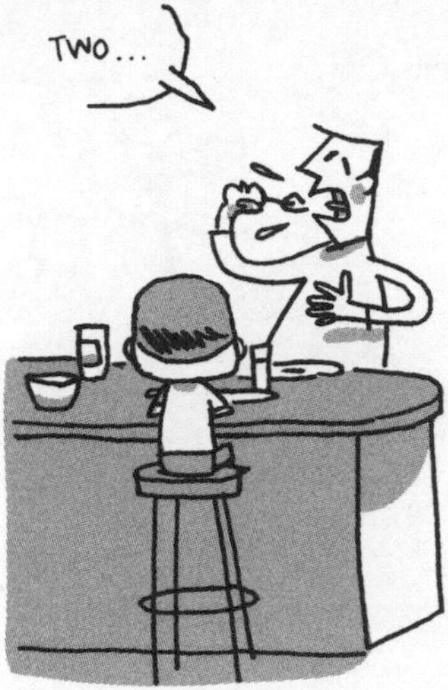
TWO...

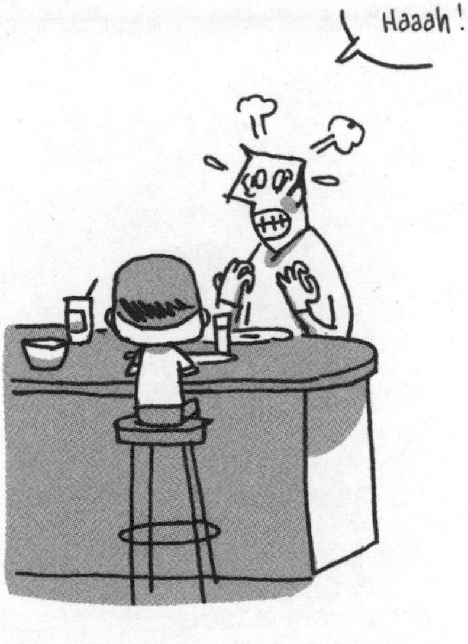
Haaah!

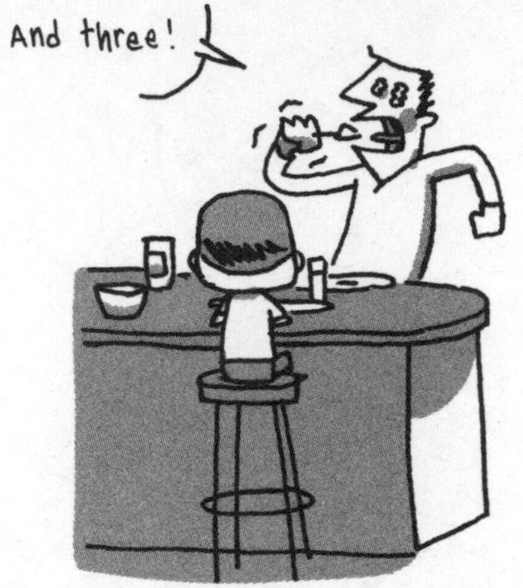
And three!

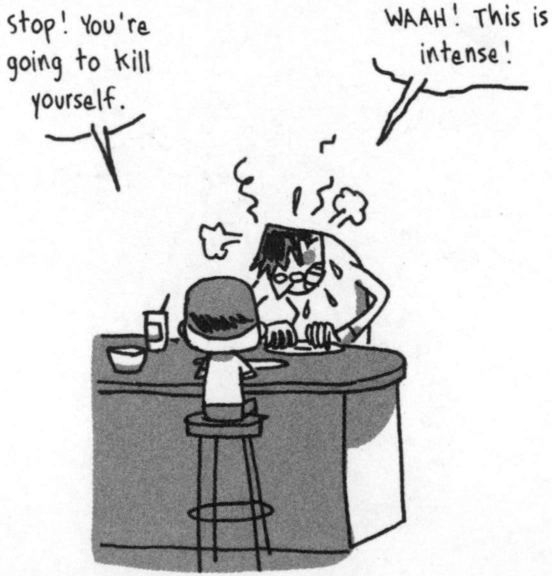
Stop! You're going to kill yourself.
WAAH! This is intense!

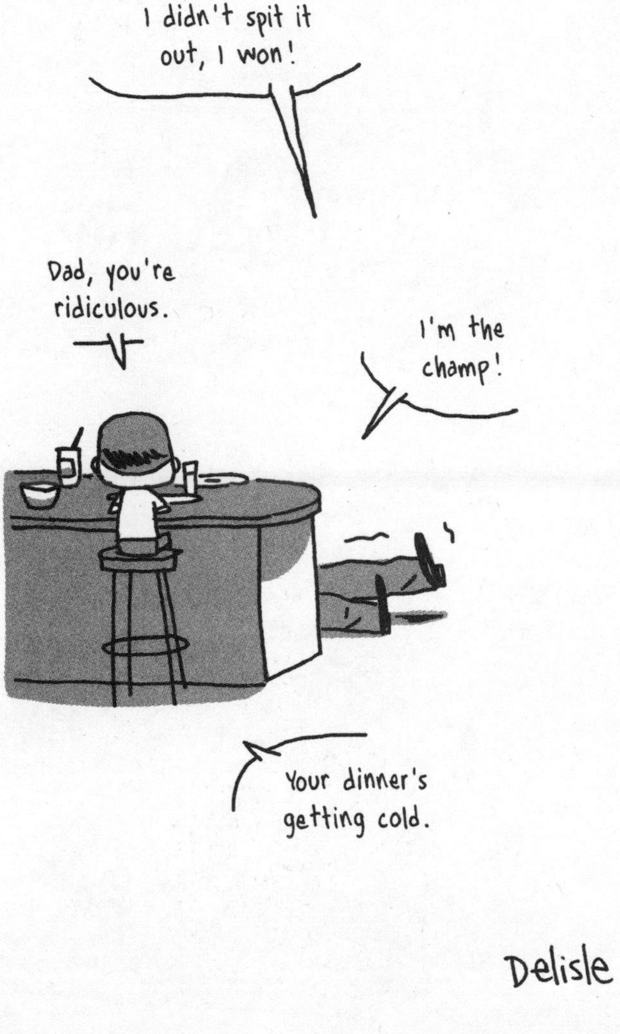
I didn't spit it out, I won!
Dad, you're ridiculous.
I'm the champ!
Your dinner's getting cold.
Delisle

- The executioner

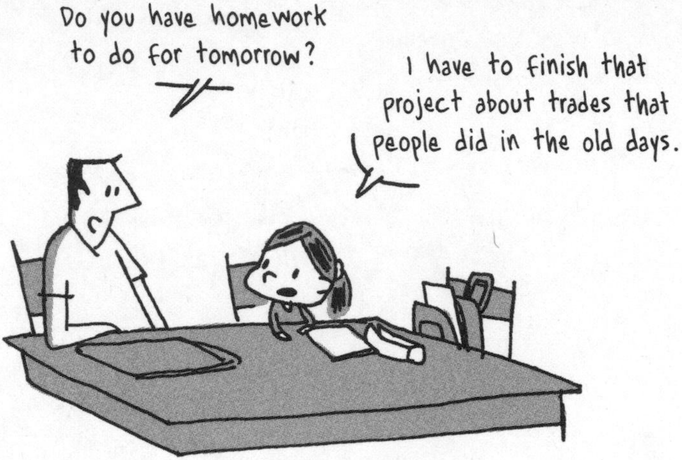

Do you have homework to do for tomorrow?
I have to finish that project about trades that people did in the old days.

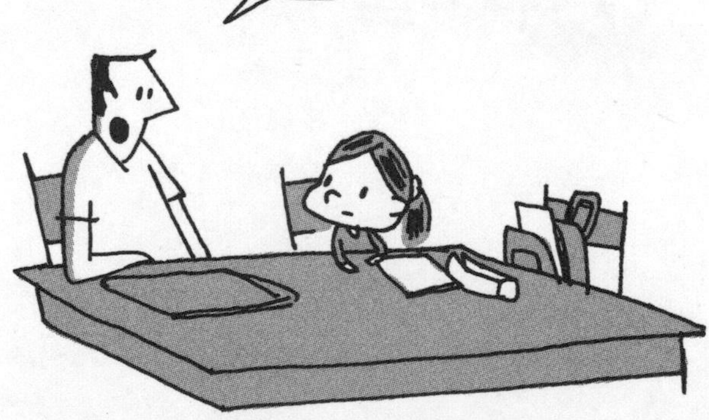

What?
Your teacher assigned that project two weeks ago, and you're only mentioning it now?

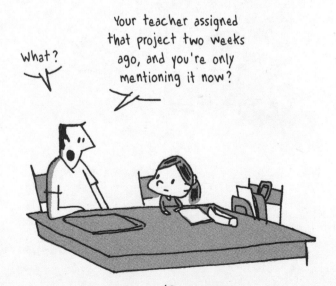

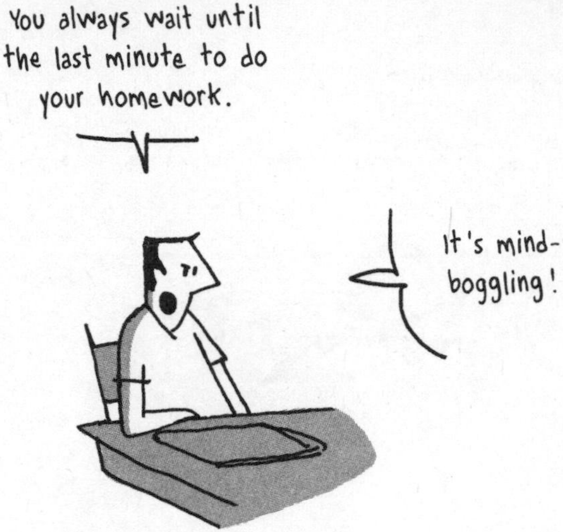
You always wait until the last minute to do your homework.
It's mind-boggling!

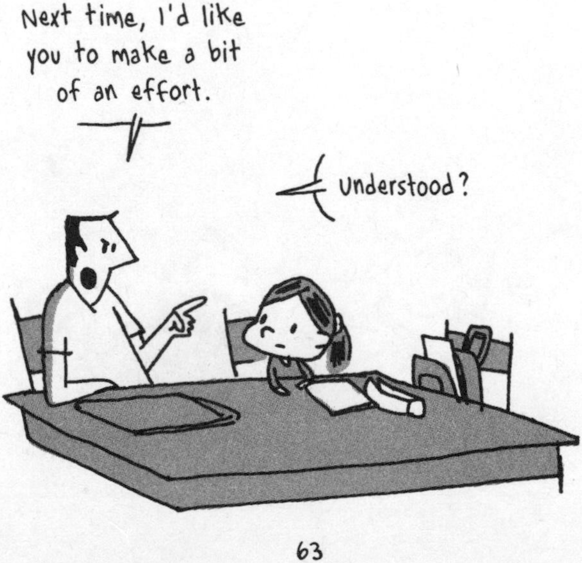
Next time, I'd like you to make a bit of an effort.
Understood?

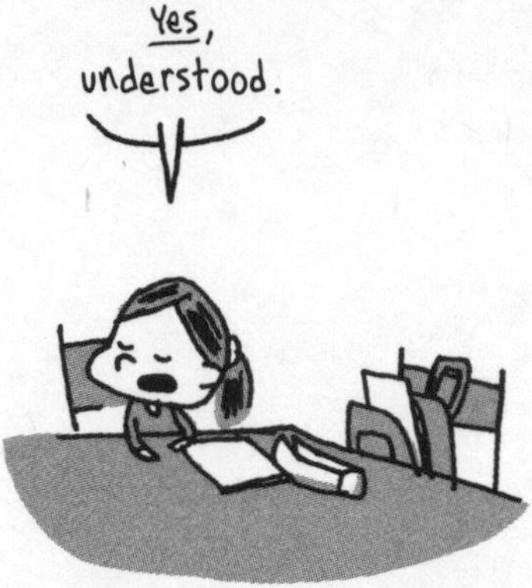
Yes, understood.

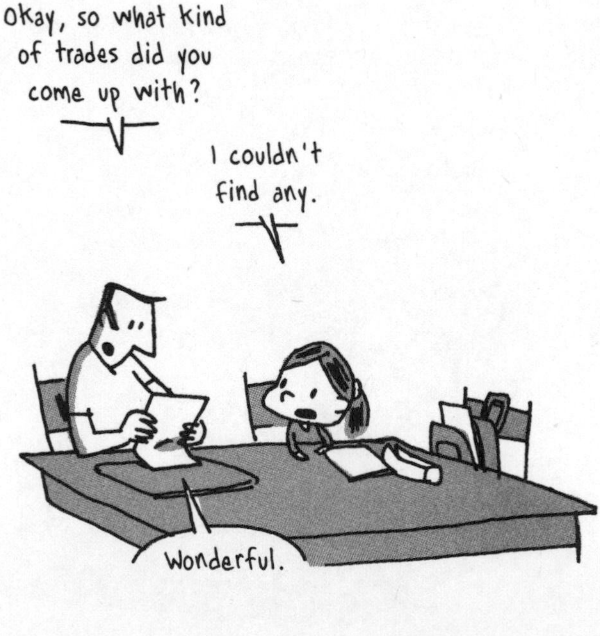
Okay, so what kind of trades did you come up with?
I couldn't find any.
Wonderful.

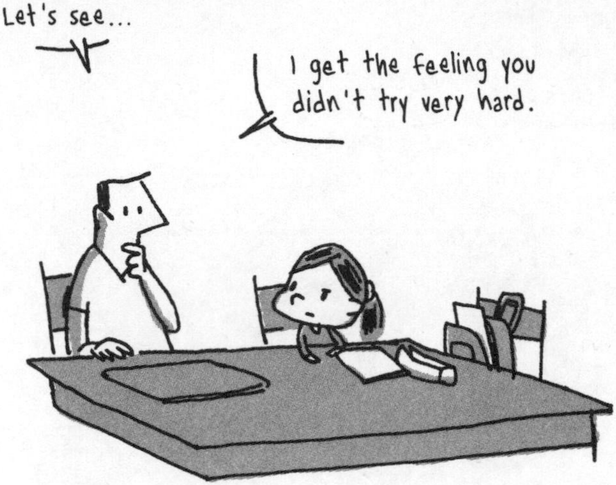
Let's see...
I get the feeling you didn't try very hard.

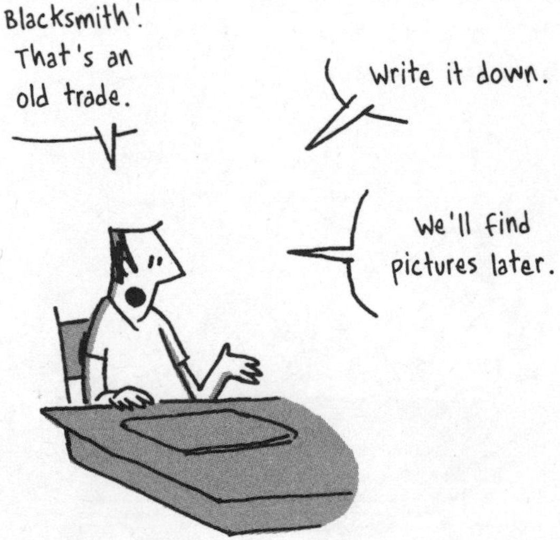
Blacksmith! That's an old trade.
Write it down.
We'll find pictures later.

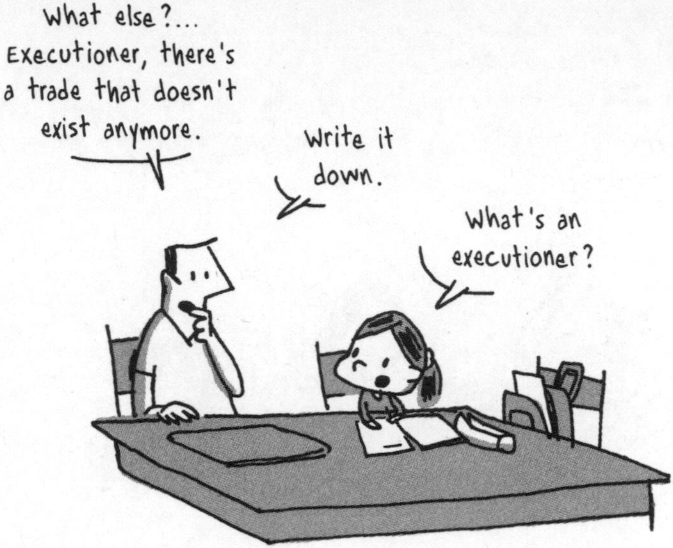
What else?... Executioner, there's a trade that doesn't exist anymore.
Write it down.
What's an executioner?

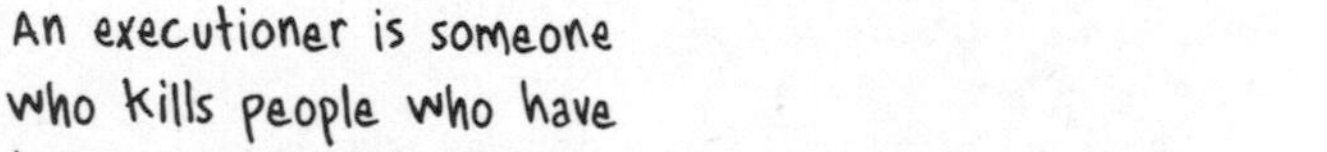
An executioner is someone who kills people who have been sentenced to death.
Sentenced to death? What does that mean?

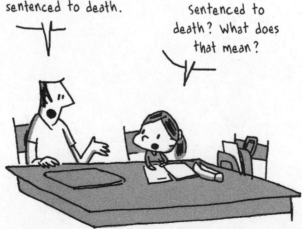

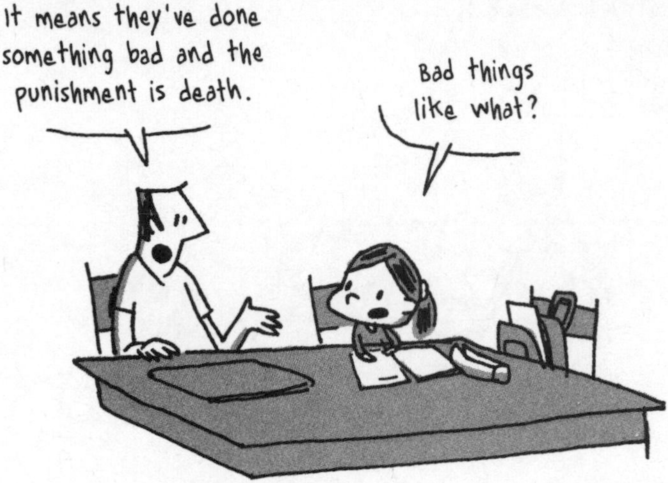
It means they've done something bad and the punishment is death.
Bad things like what?

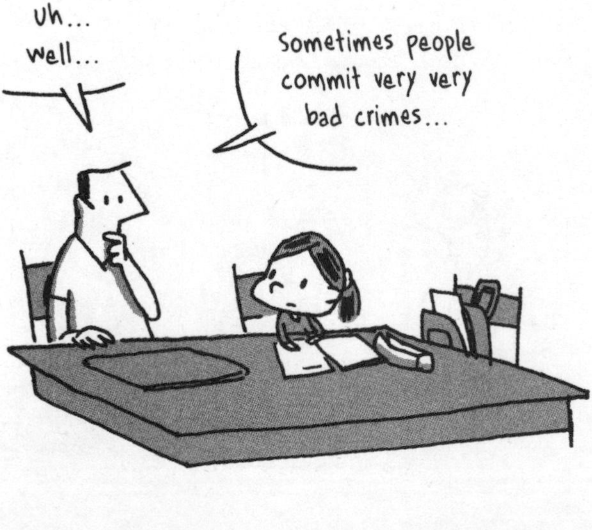
Uh... well...
Sometimes people commit very very bad crimes...

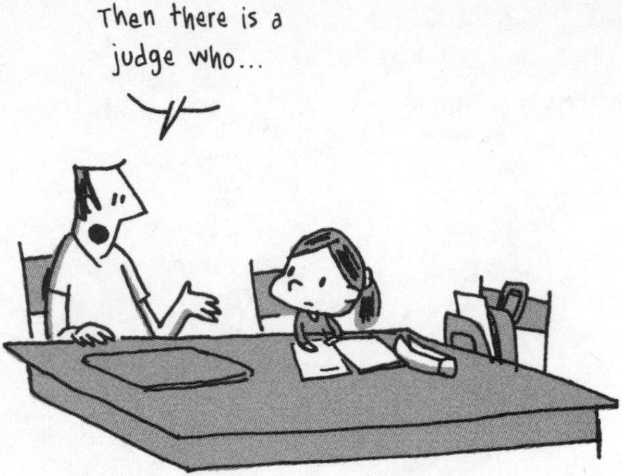
Then there is a judge who...

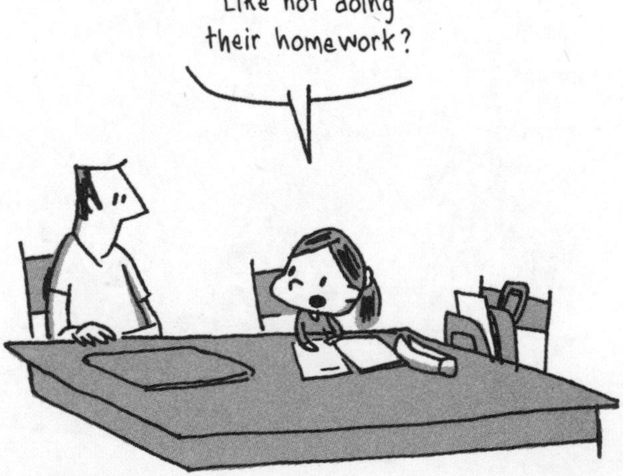
Like not doing their homework?

Well...uh...

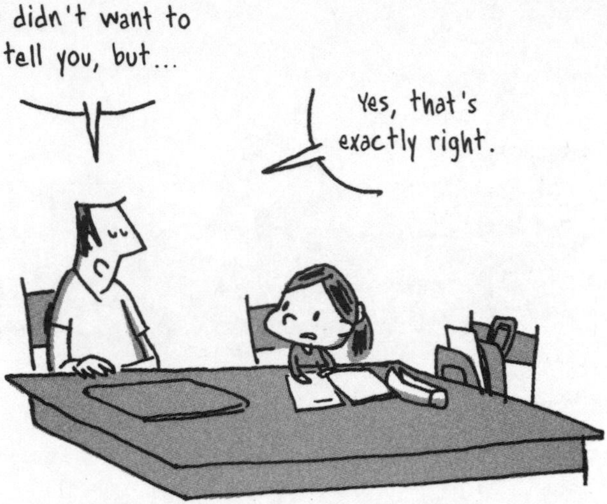
I didn't want to tell you, but...
Yes, that's exactly right.

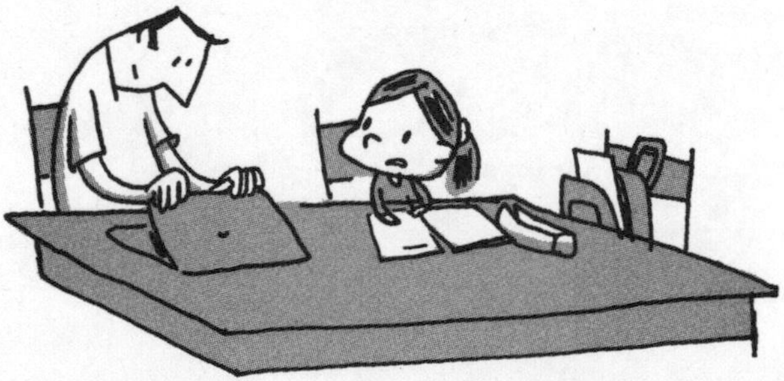

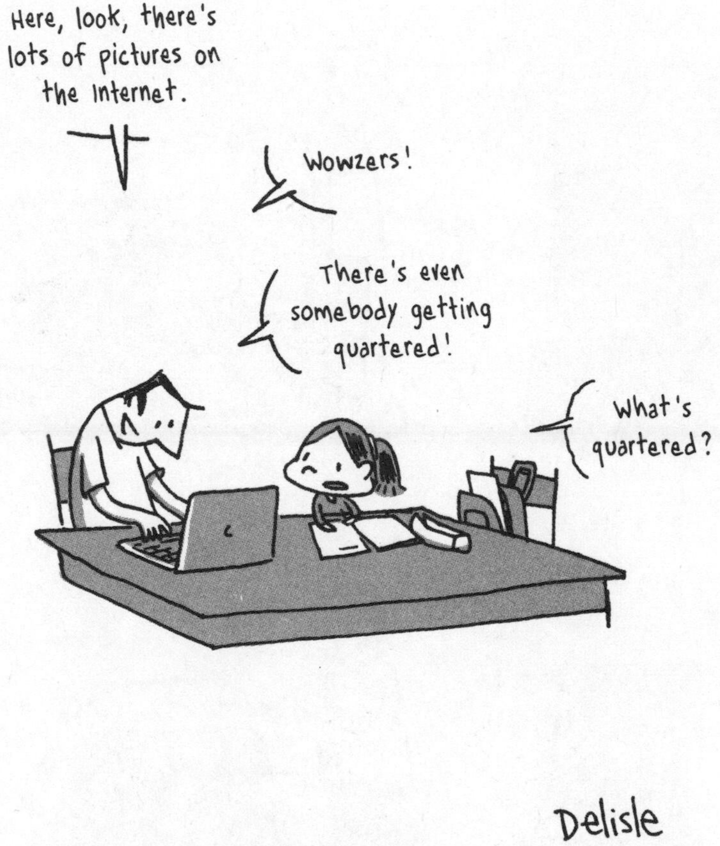
Here, look, there's lots of pictures on the internet.
Wowzers!
There's even somebody getting quartered!
What's quartered?
Delisle

- DVD

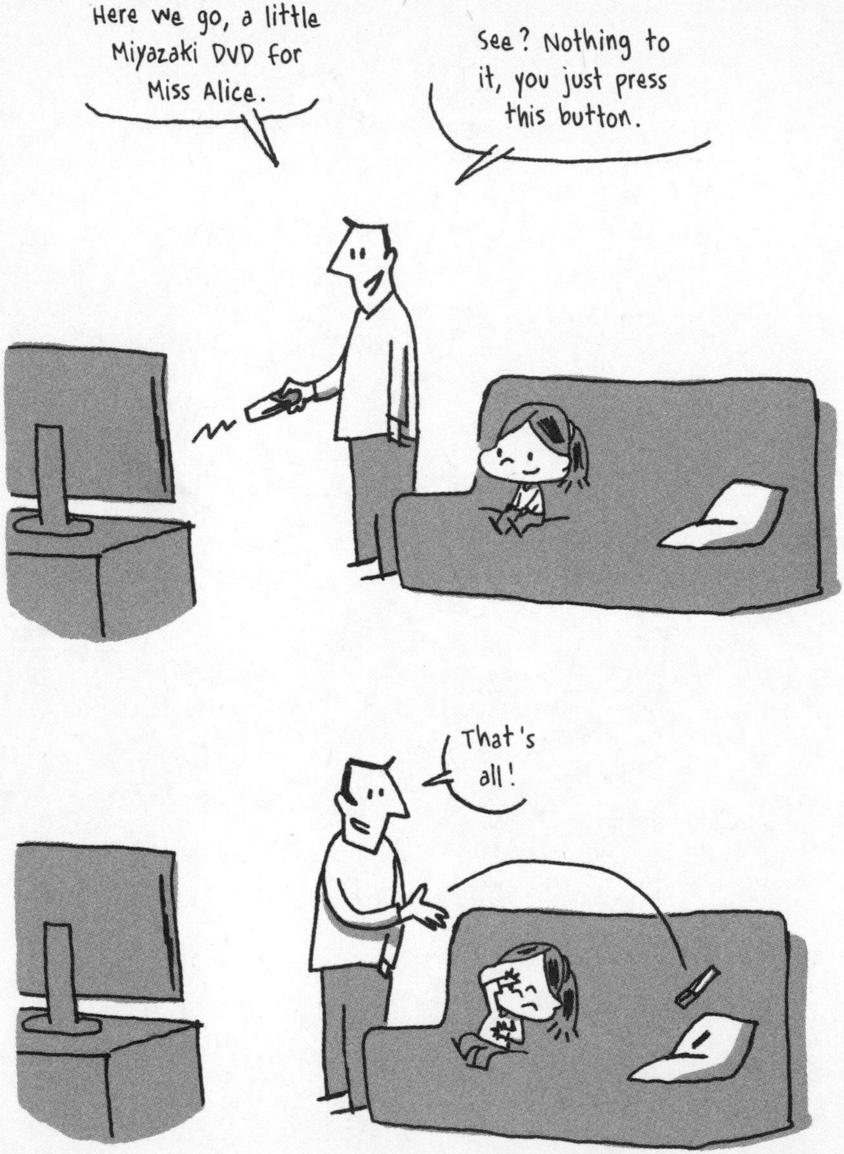

Here we go, a little Miyazaki DVD for Miss Alice.
See? Nothing to it, you just press this button.
That's all!

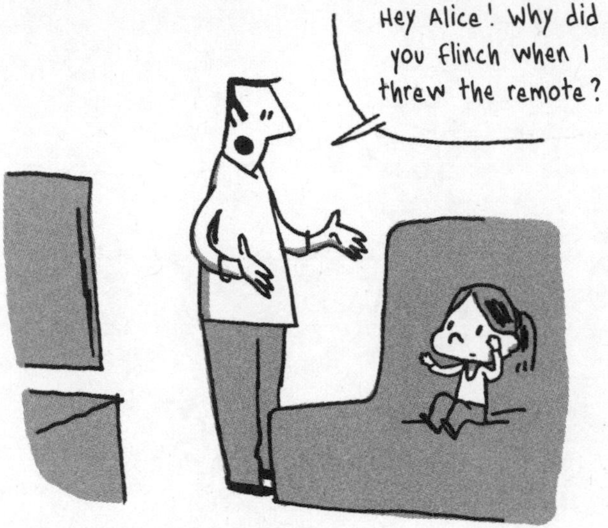
Hey Alice! Why did you flinch when I threw the remote?

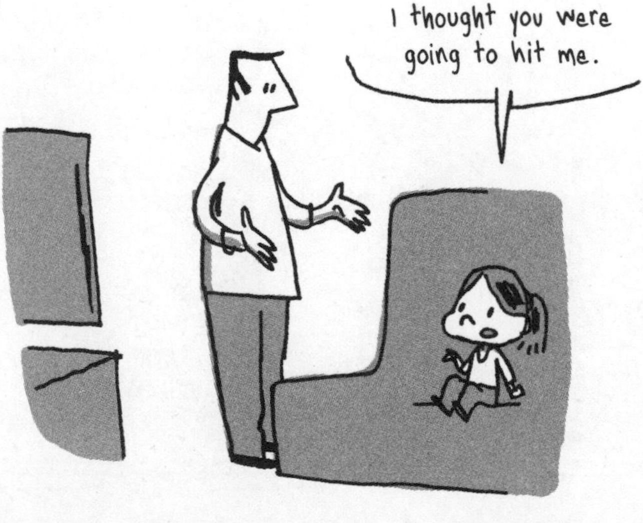
I thought you were going to hit me.

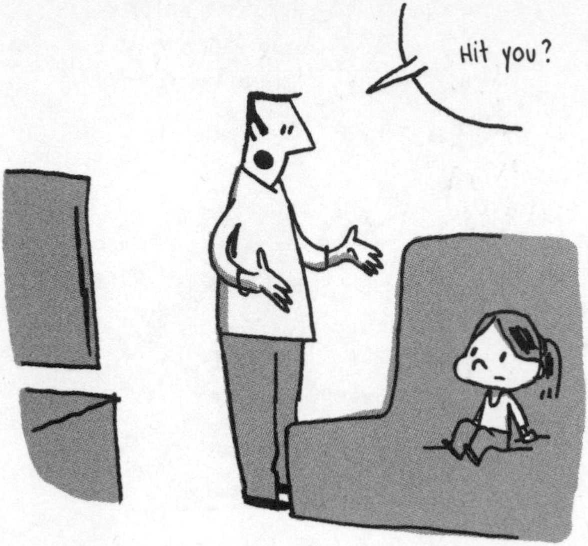
Hit you?

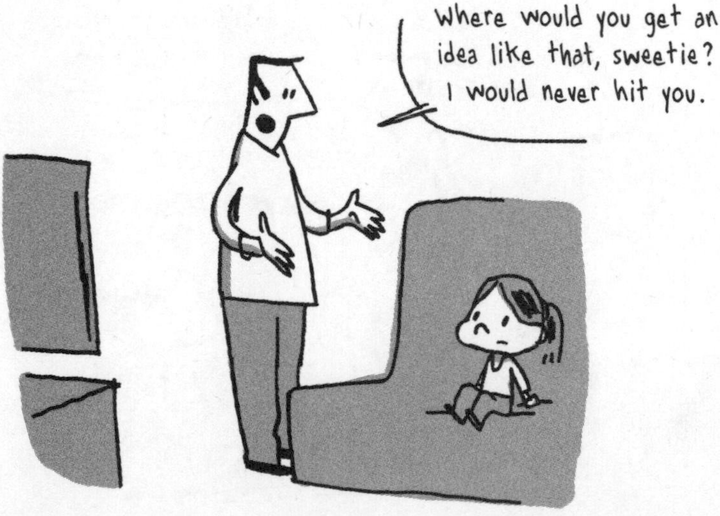
Where would you get an idea like that, sweetie? I would never hit you.

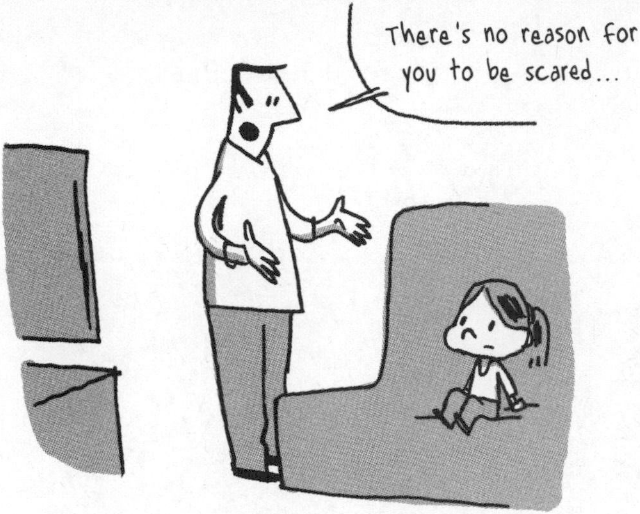
There's no reason for you to be scared...

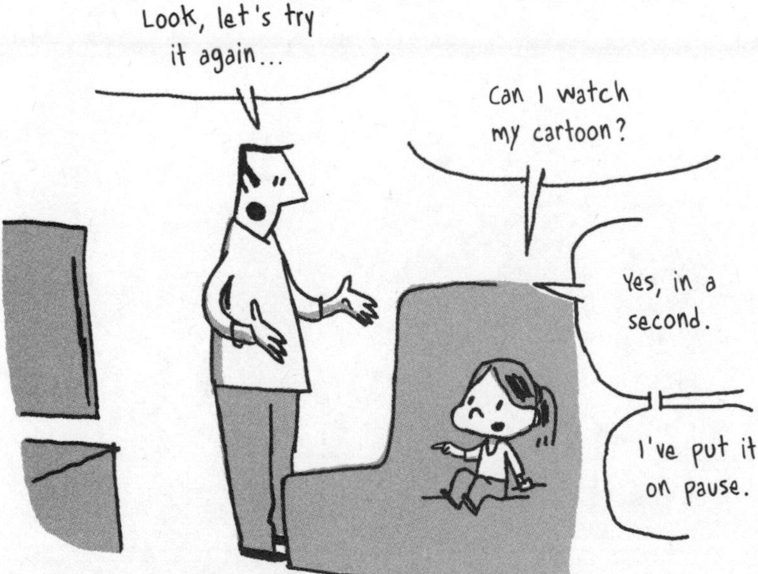
Look, let's try it again...
Can I watch my cartoon?
Yes, in a second.
I've put it on pause.

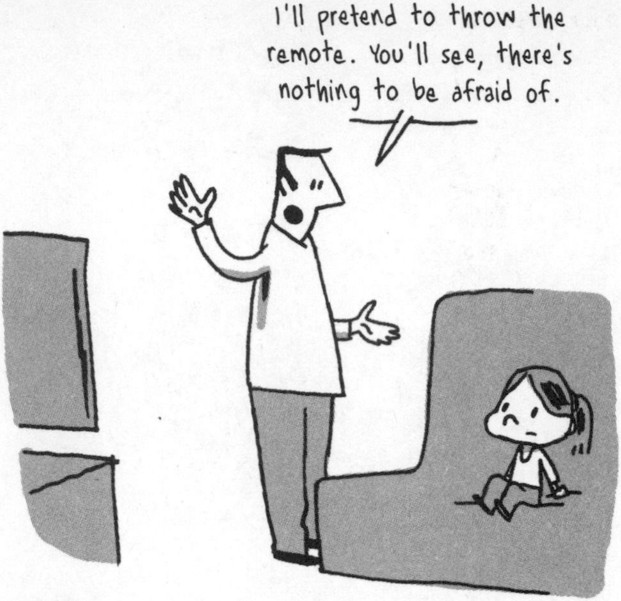
I'll pretend to throw the remote. You'll see, there's nothing to be afraid of.

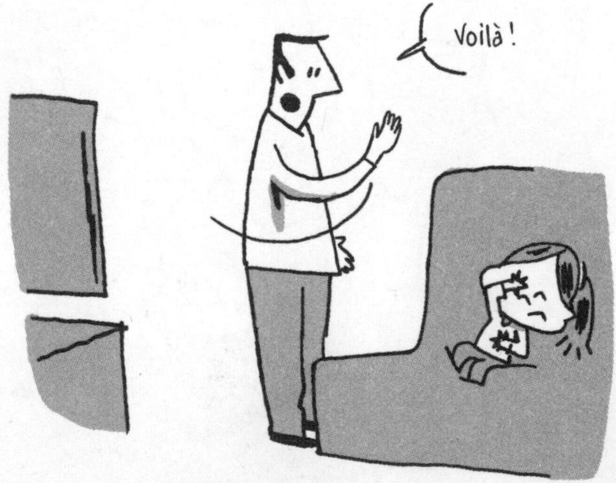
Voilà!

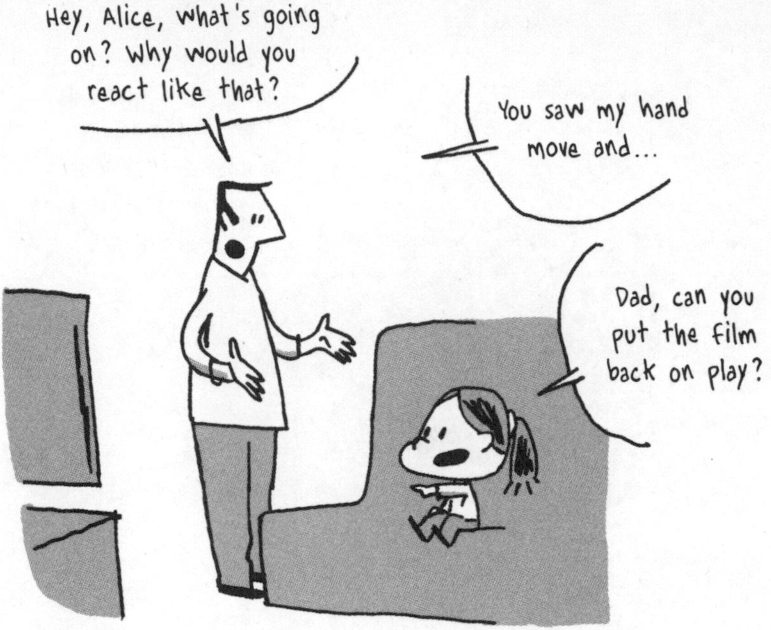
Hey, Alice, what's going on? Why would you react like that?
You saw my hand move and...
Dad, can you put the film back on play?

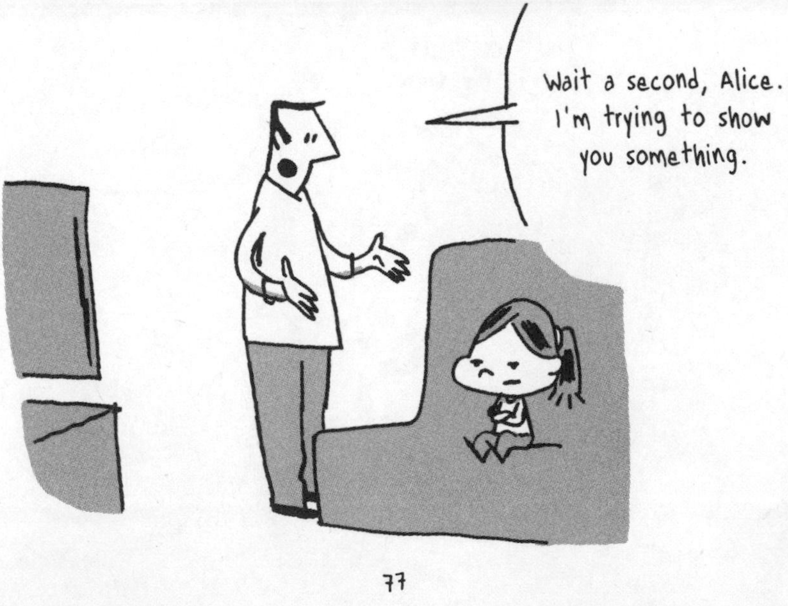
Wait a second, Alice. I'm trying to show you something.

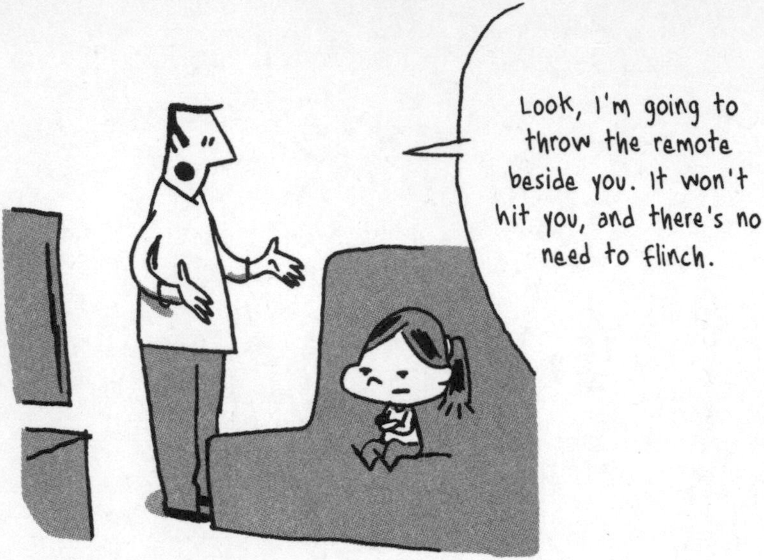
Look, I'm going to throw the remote beside you. It won't hit you, and there's no need to flinch.

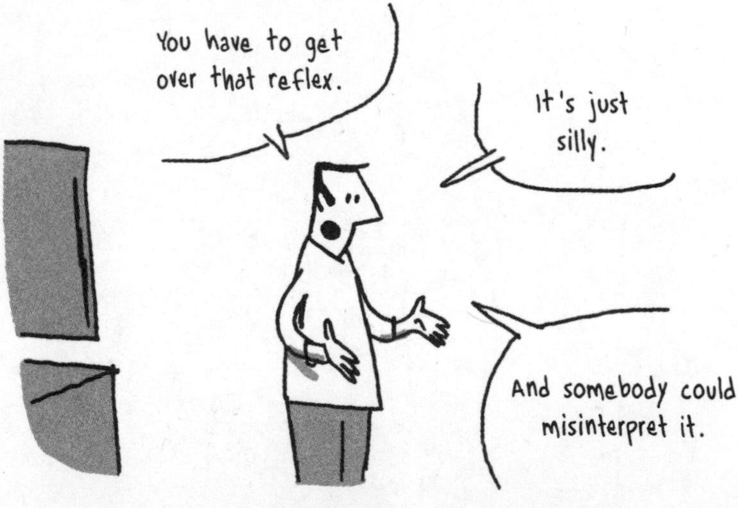
You have to get over that reflex.
It's just silly.
And somebody could misinterpret it.

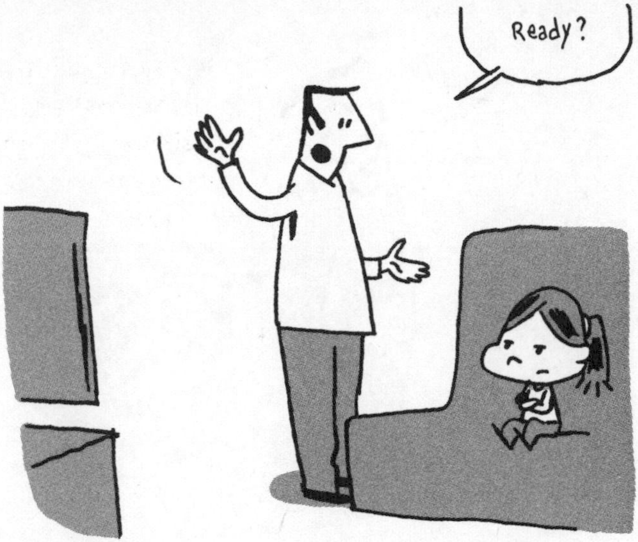
Ready?

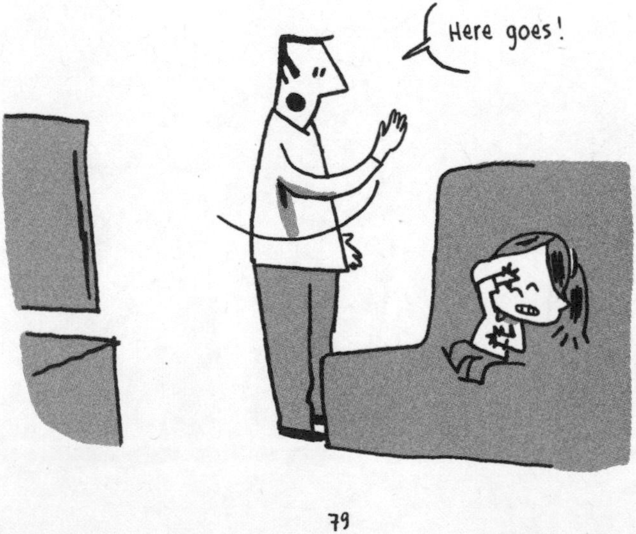
Here goes!

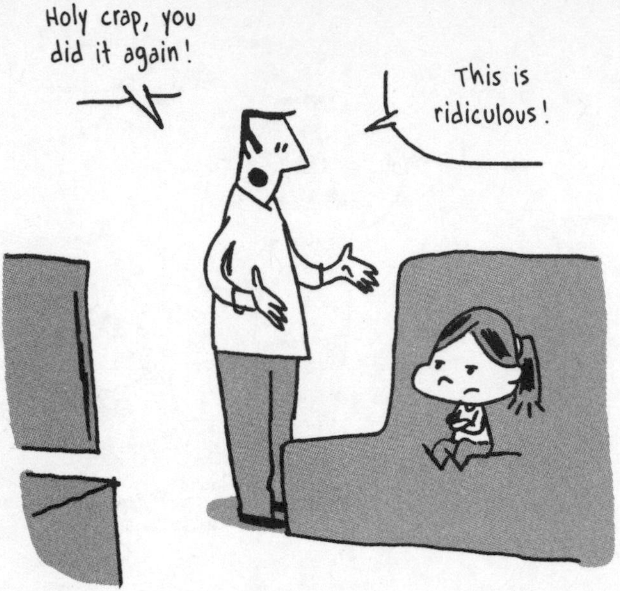
Holy crap, you did it again!
This is ridiculous!

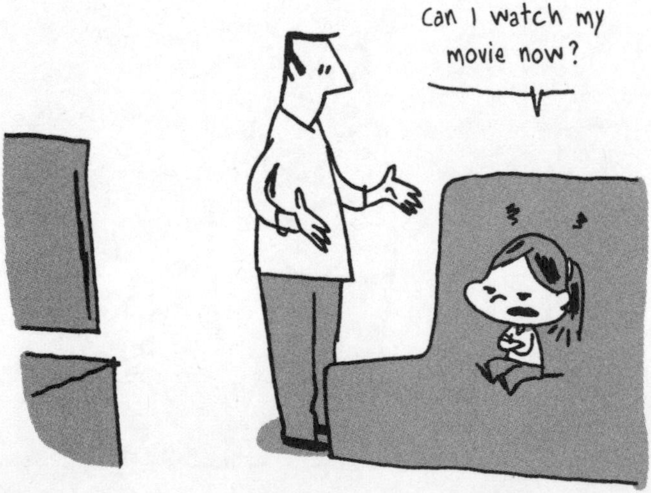
Can I watch my movie now?

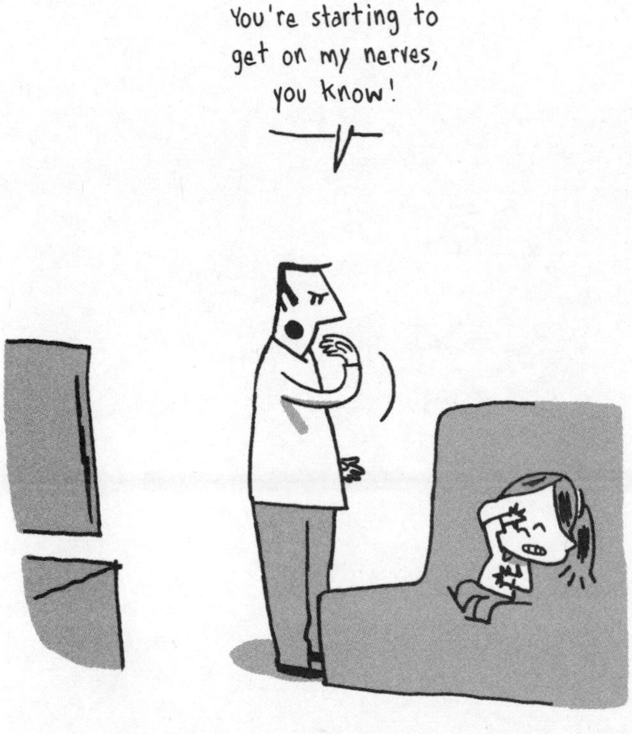
You're starting to get on my nerves, you know!
Delisle

– The birthday present

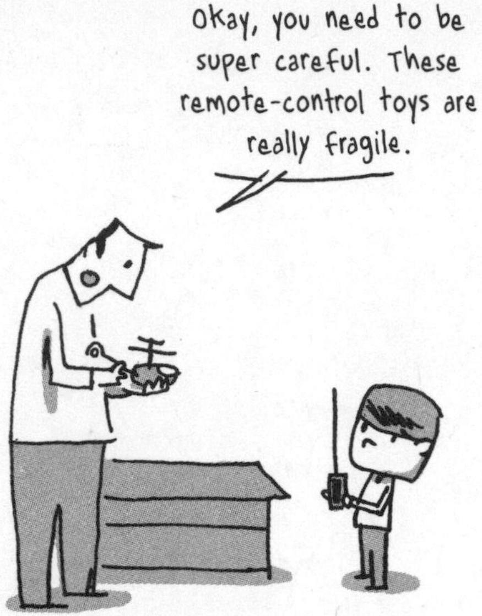
Okay, you need to be super careful. These remote-control toys are really fragile.

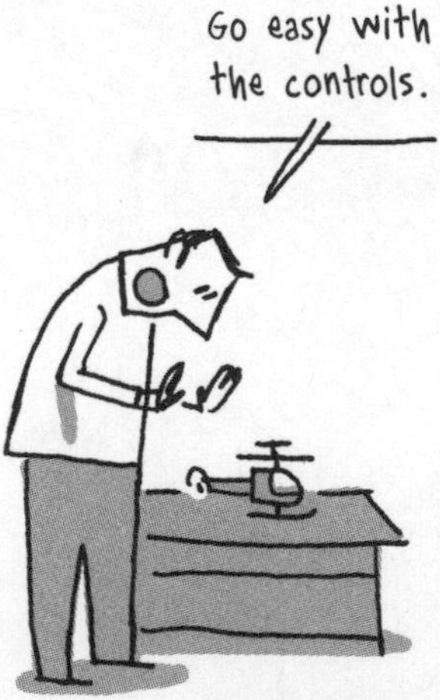
Go easy with the controls.

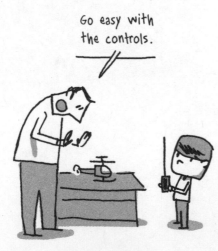

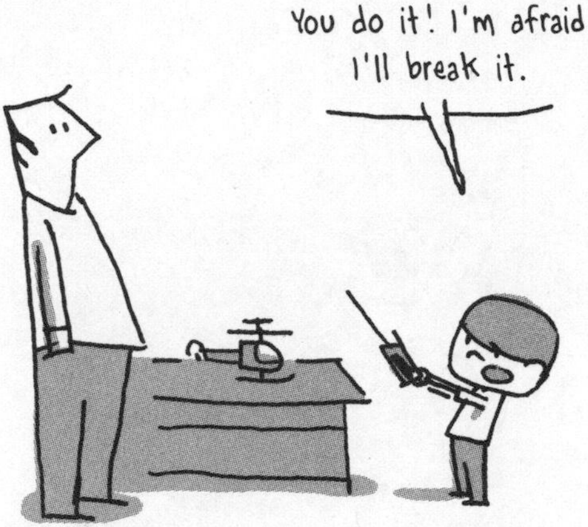
You do it! I'm afraid I'll break it.

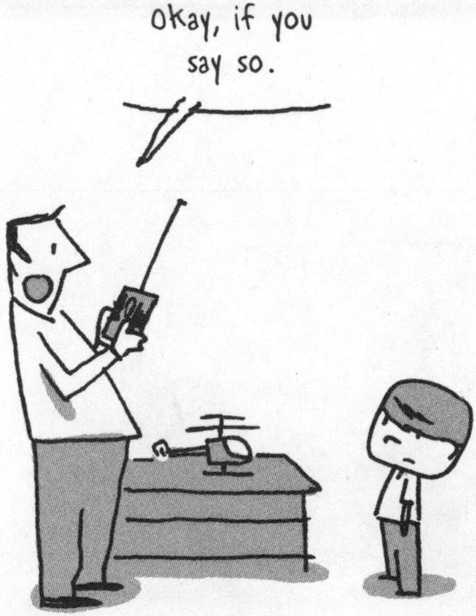
Okay, if you say so.

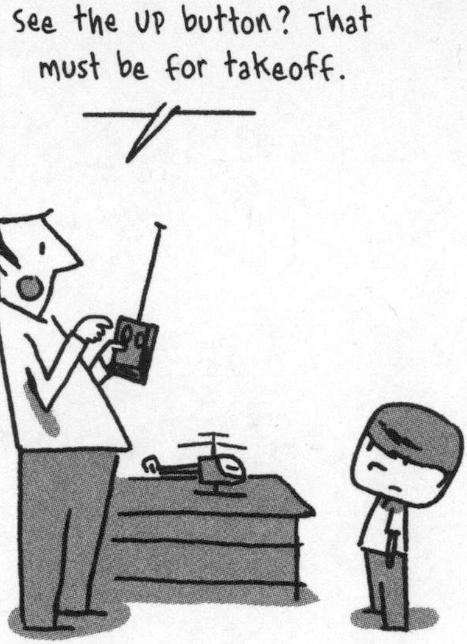
See the UP button? That must be for takeoff.

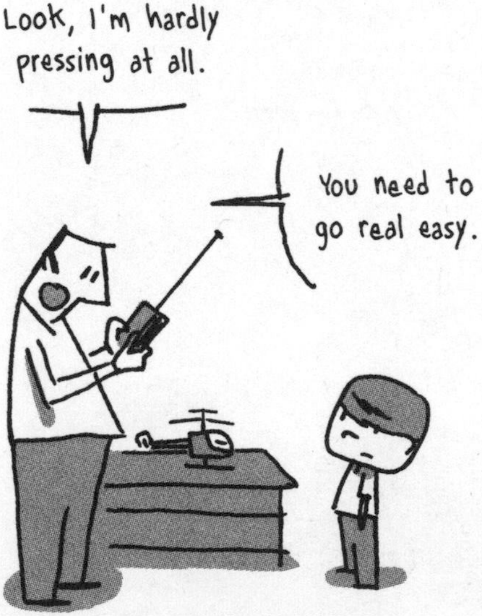
Look, I'm hardly pressing at all.
You need to go real easy.

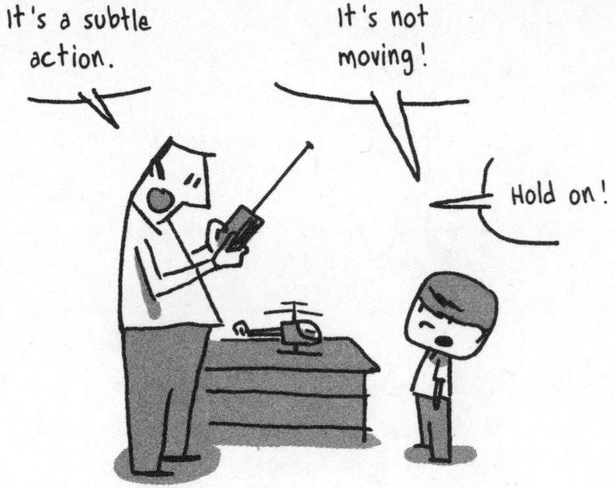
It's a subtle action.
It's not moving!
Hold on!

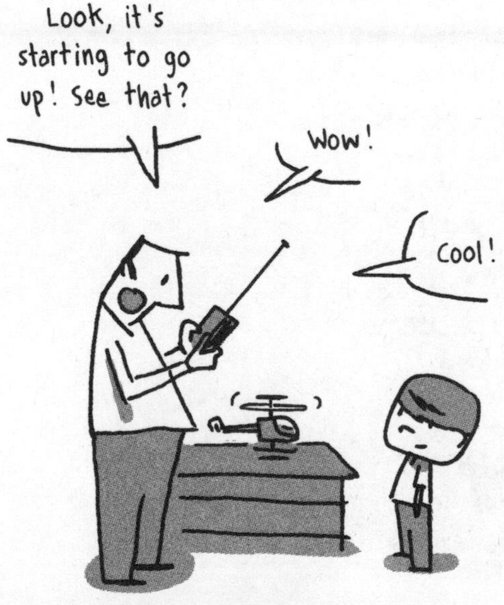
Look, it's starting to go up! See that?
Wow!
Cool!

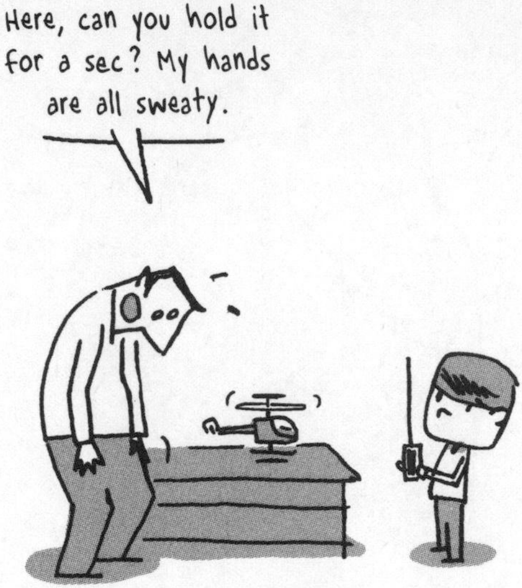
Here, can you hold it for a sec? My hands are all sweaty.

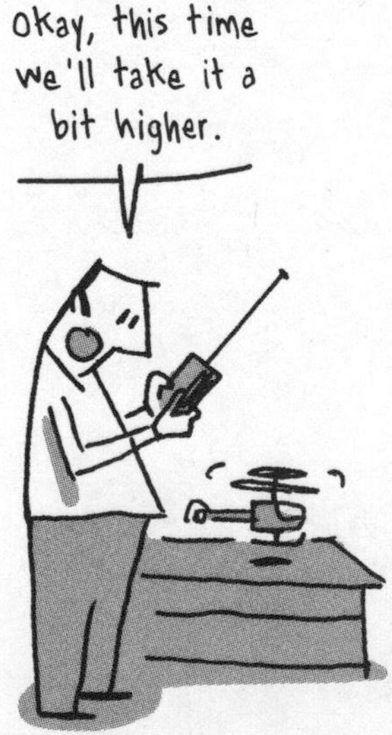
Okay, this time we'll take it a bit higher.

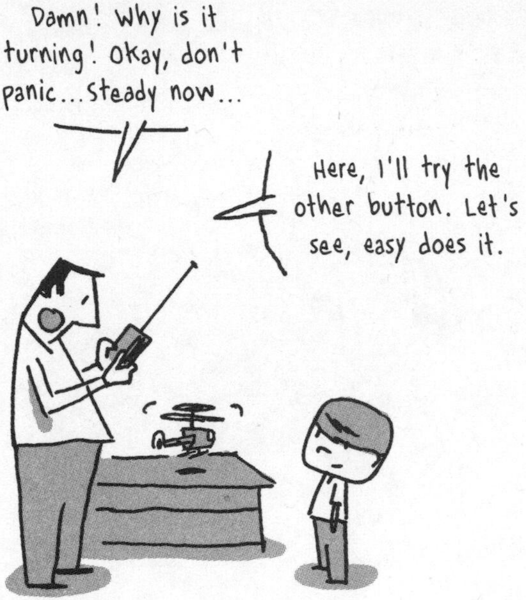
Damn! Why is it turning! Okay, don't panic... Steady now...
Here, I'll try the other button. Let's see, easy does it.

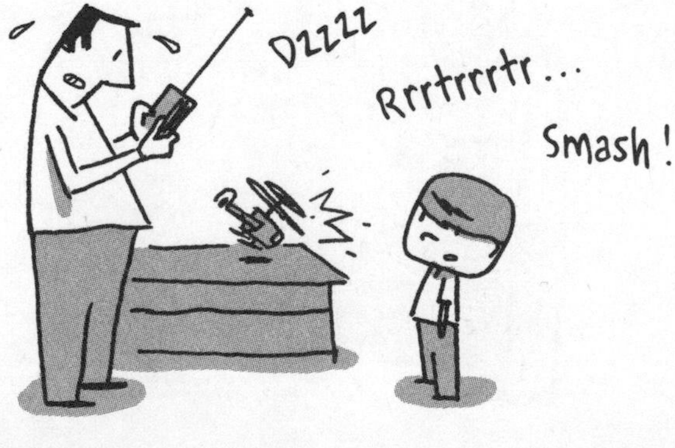
DZZZZ
Rrrtrrrtr...
Smash!

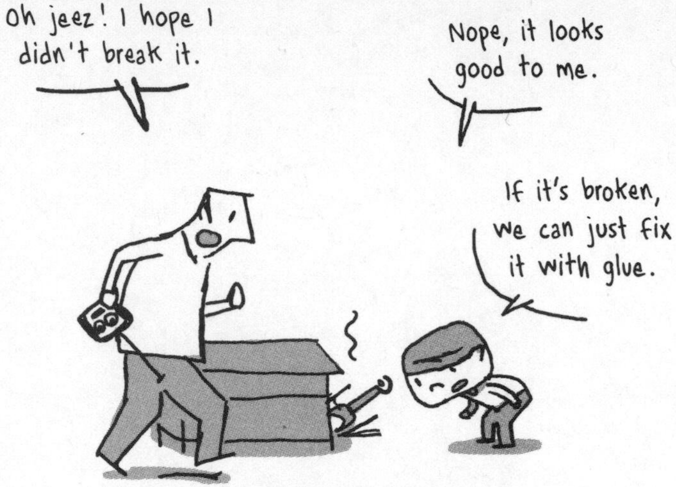
Oh jeez! I hope I didn't break it.
Nope, it looks good to me.
If it's broken, we can just fix it with glue.

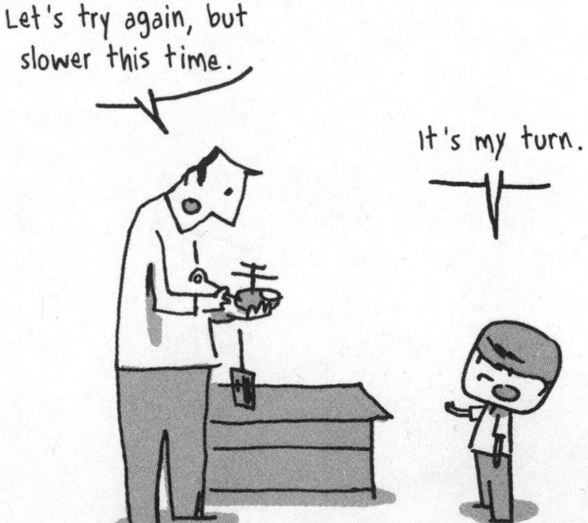
Let's try again, but slower this time.
It's my turn.

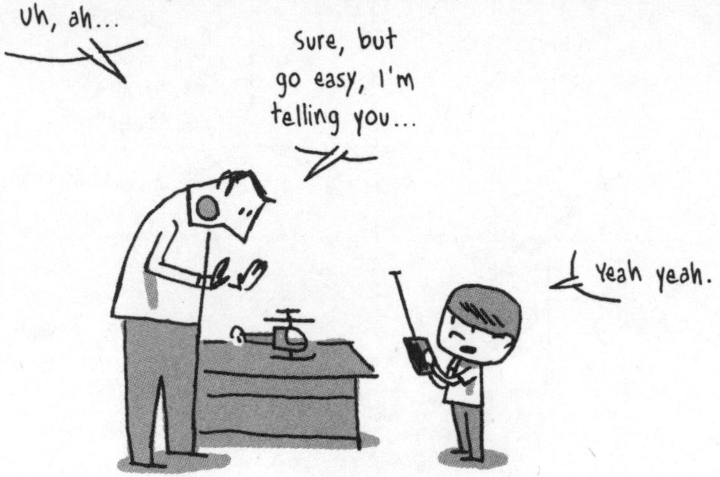
Uh, ah...
Sure, but go easy, I'm telling you...
Yeah yeah.

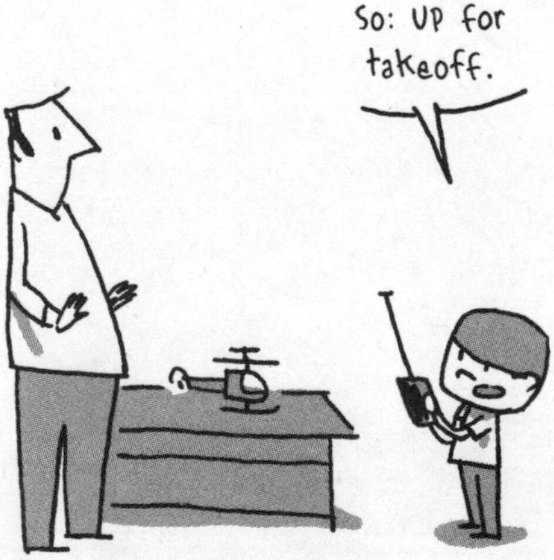
So: Up for takeoff.

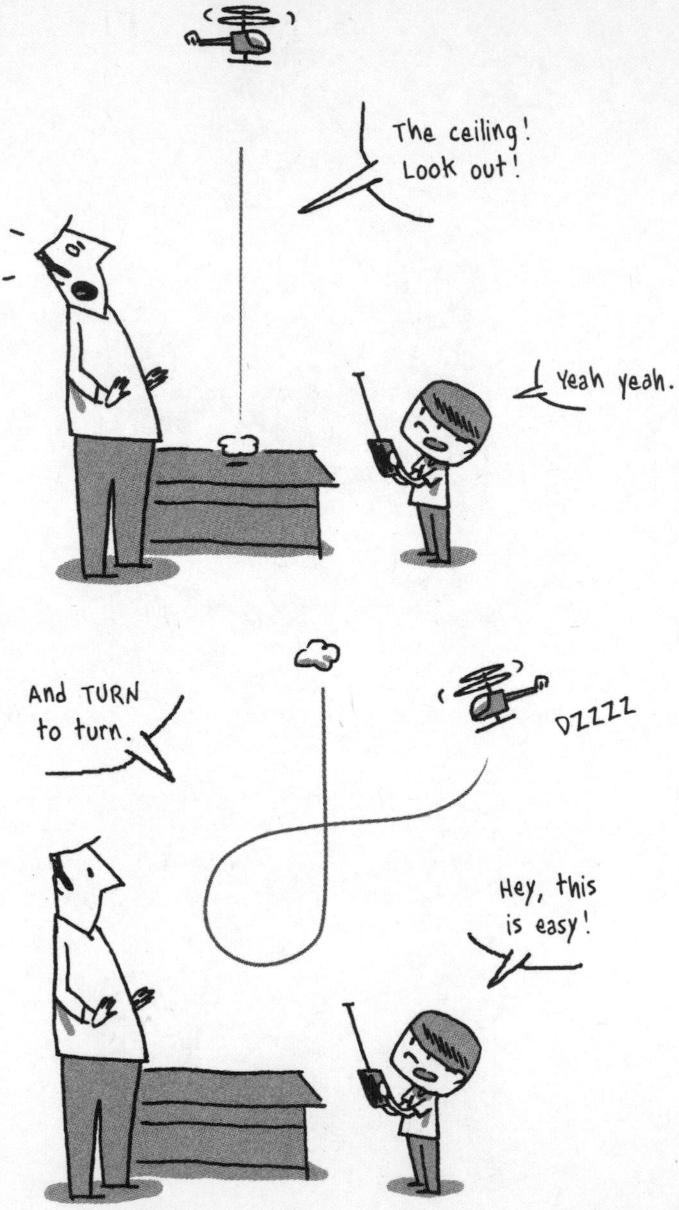
The ceiling! Look out!
Yeah yeah.
And TURN to turn.
DZZZZ
Hey, this is easy!

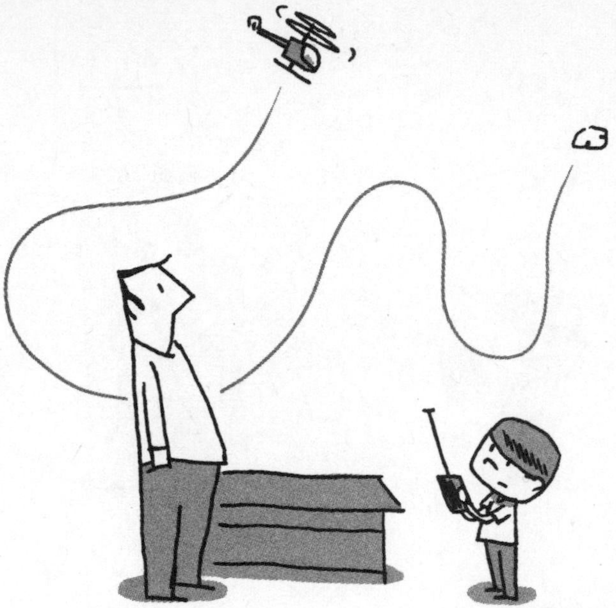

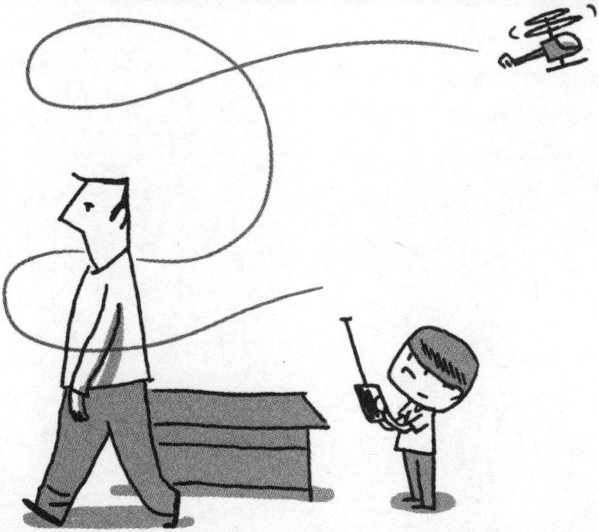

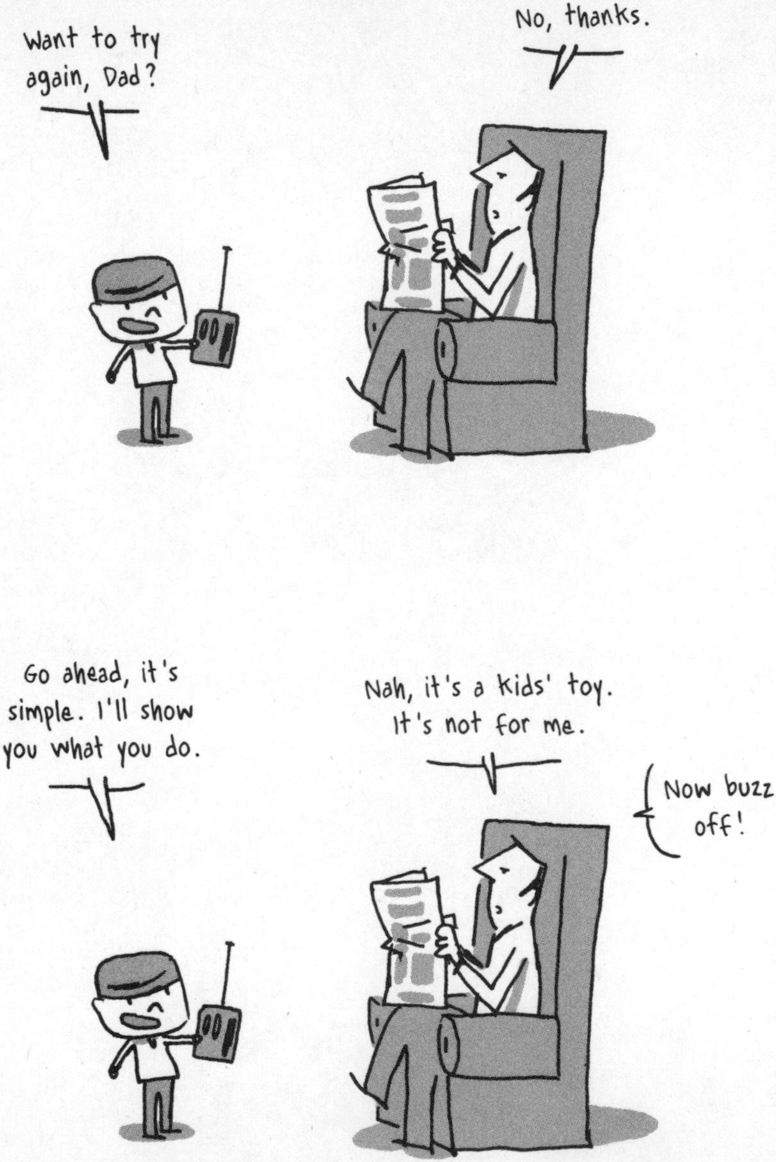
Want to try again, Dad?
No, thanks.
Go ahead, it's simple. I'll show you what you do.
Nah, it's a kids' toy. It's not for me.
Now buzz off!

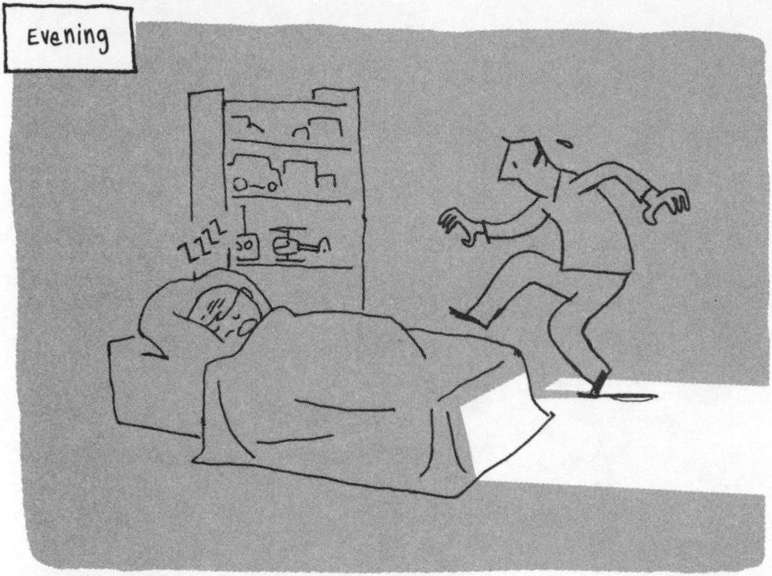
Evening
ZZZZ

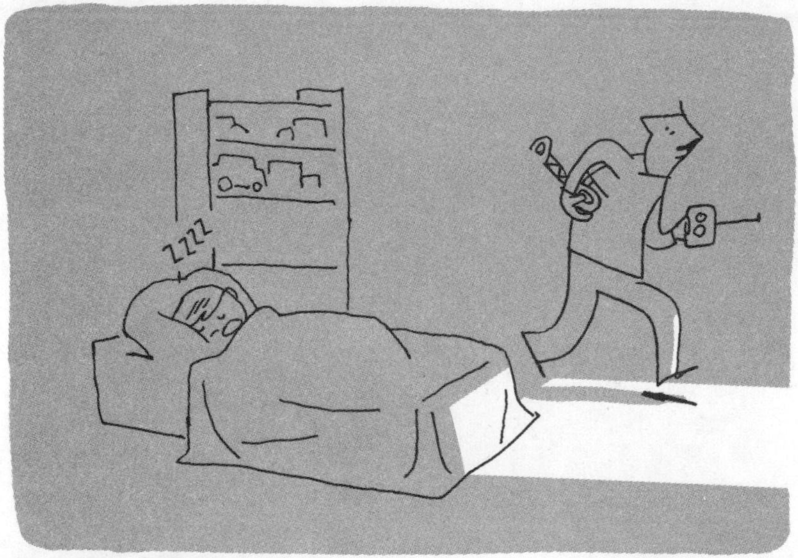
ZZZZ

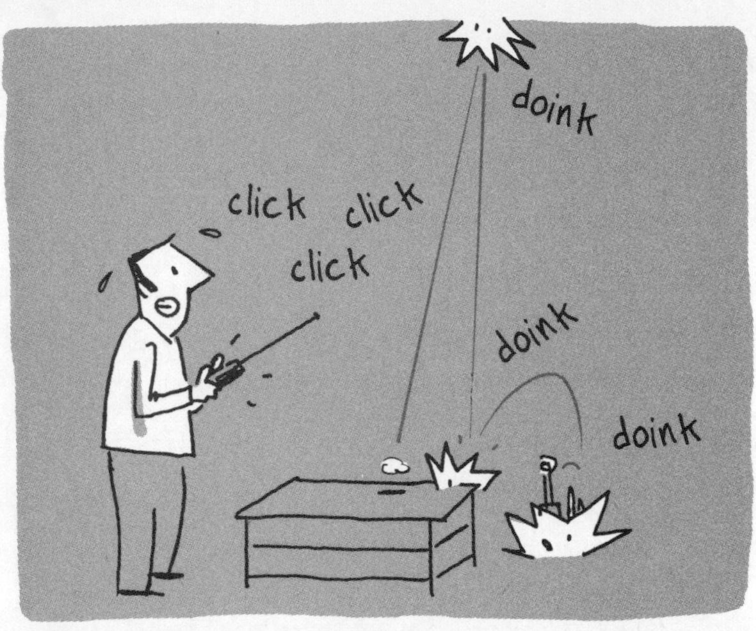
doink
click click
click
doink
doink

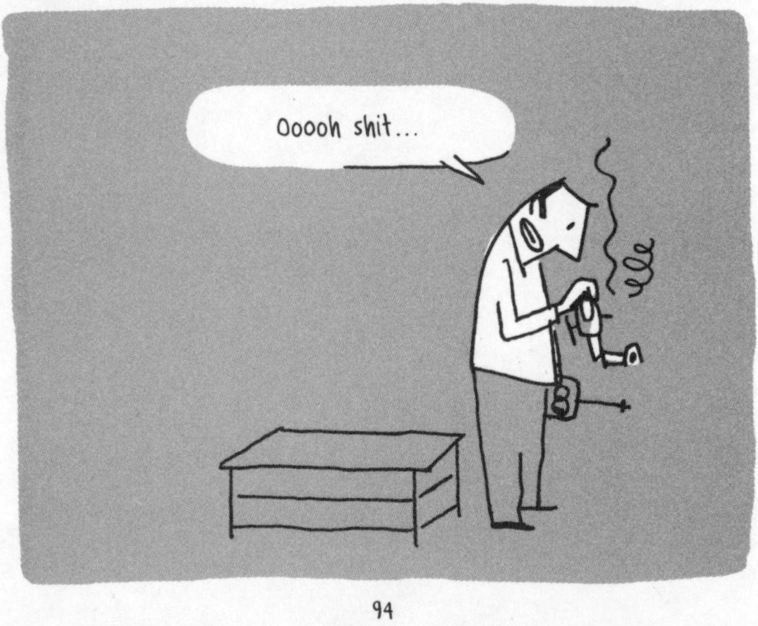
Ooooh shit...

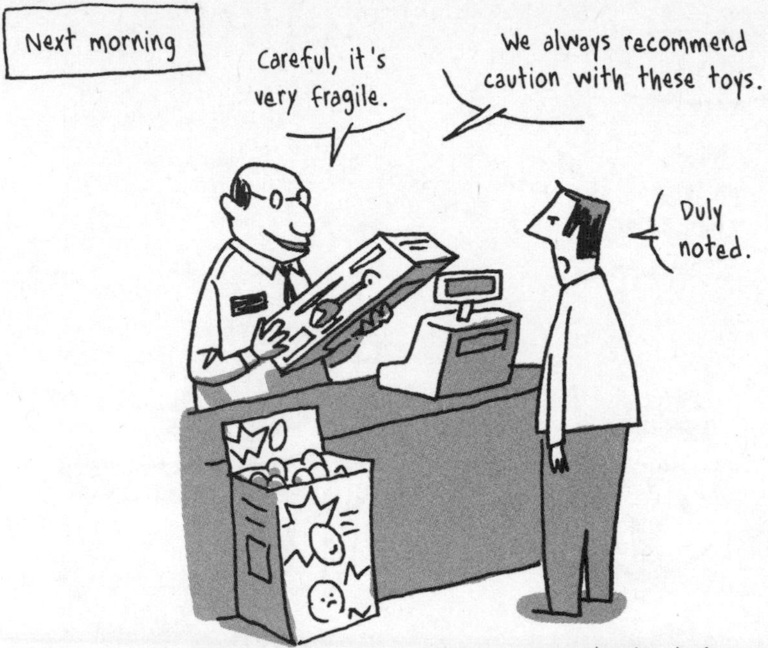
Next morning
Careful, it's very fragile.
We always recommend caution with these toys.
Duly noted.

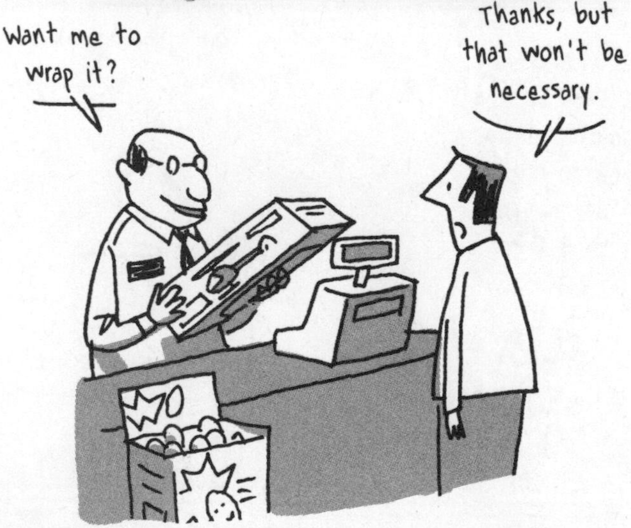
Want me to wrap it?
Thanks, but that won't be necessary.

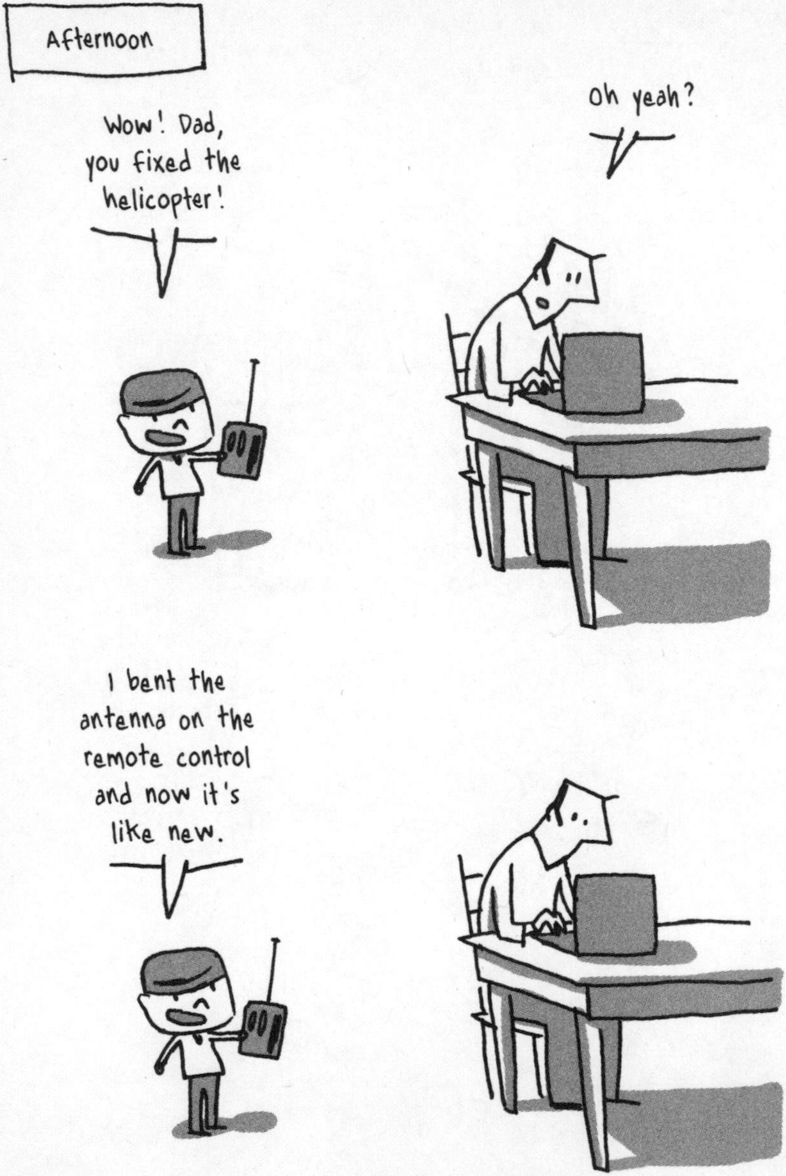
Afternoon
Wow! Dad, you fixed the helicopter!
Oh yeah?
I bent the antenna on the remote control and now it's like new.

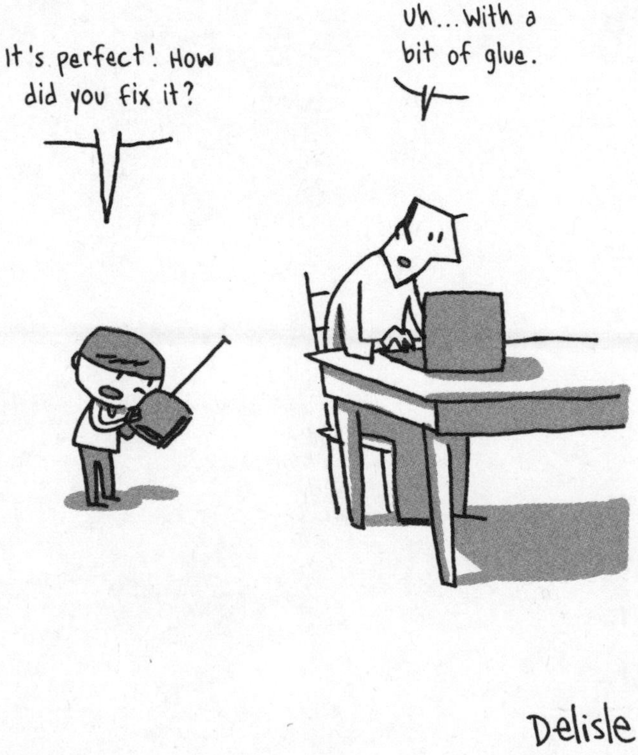
It's perfect! How did you fix it?
Uh... With a bit of glue.
Delisle

- Quality time

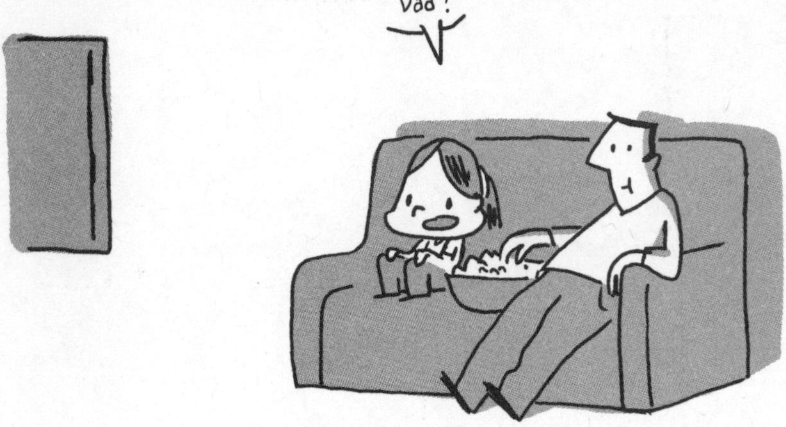
Dad?

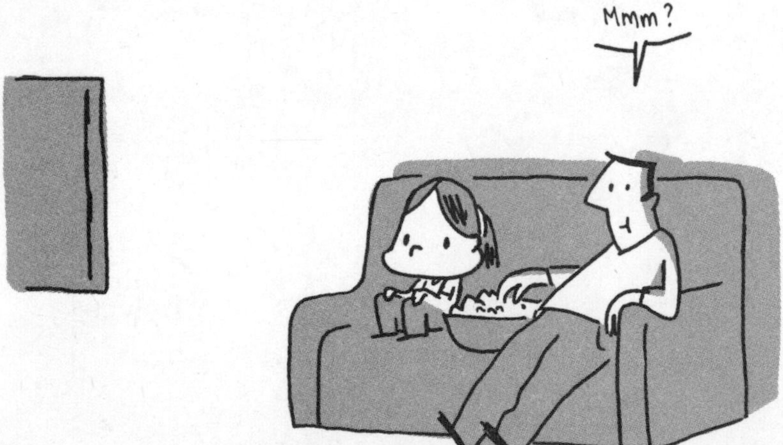
Mmm?

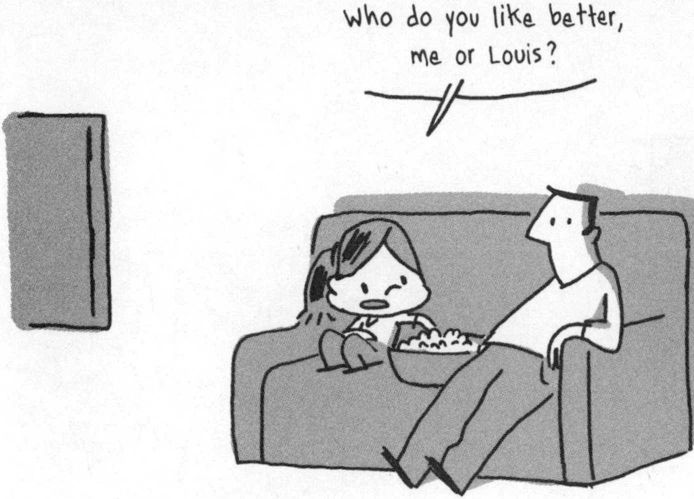
Who do you like better, me or Louis?

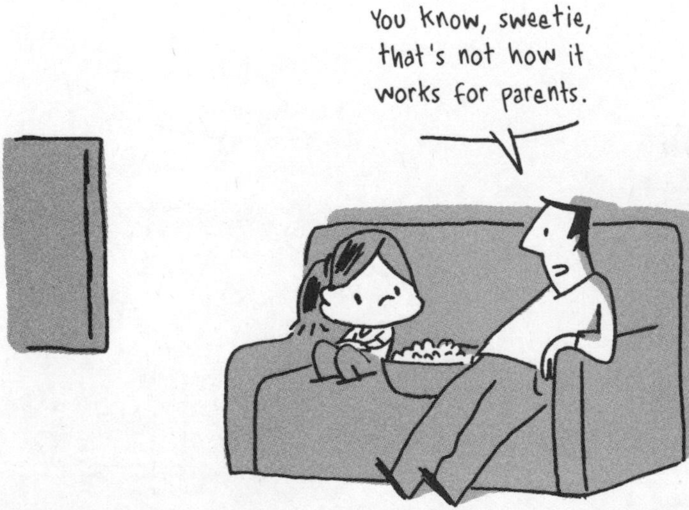
You know, sweetie, that's not how it works for parents.

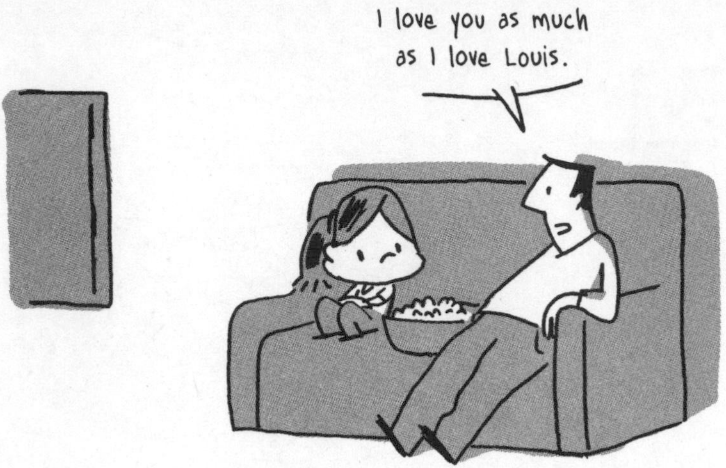
I love you as much as I love Louis.

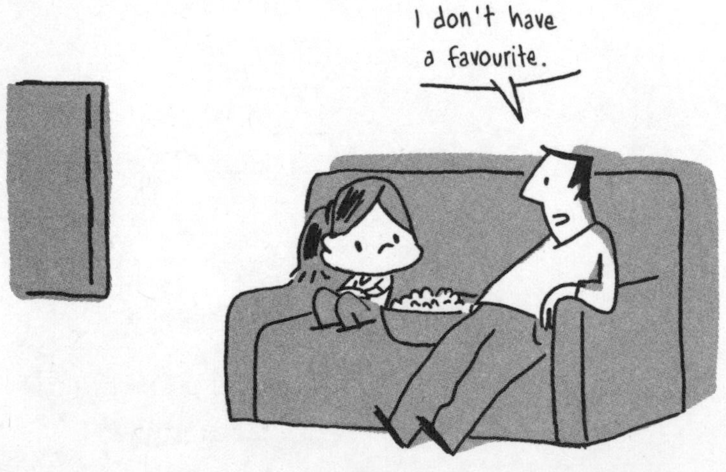
I don't have a favourite.

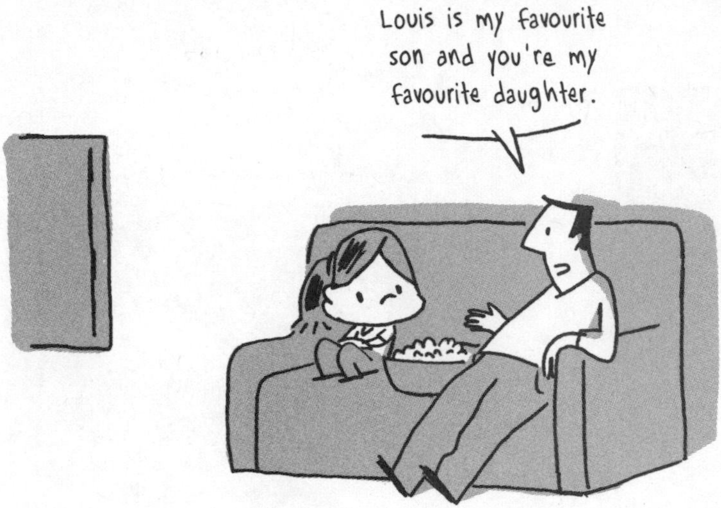
Louis is my favourite son and you're my favourite daughter.

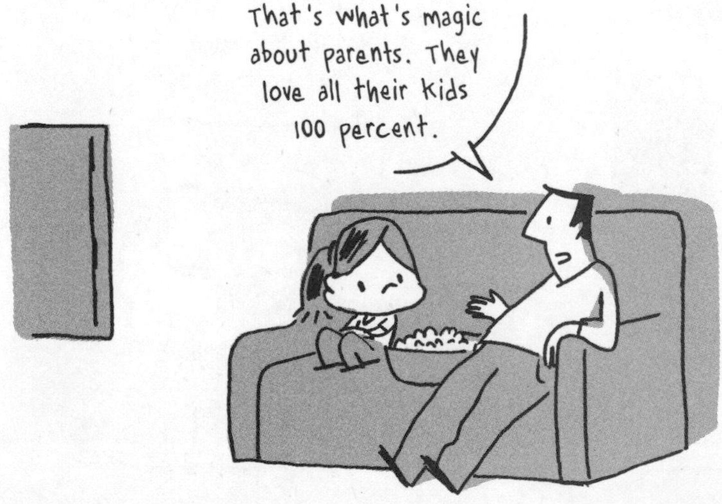
That's what's magic about parents. They love all their kids 100 percent.

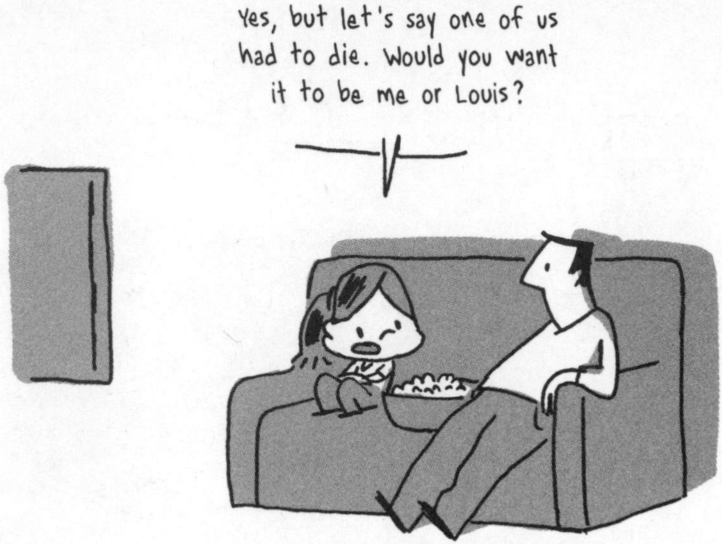
Yes, but let's say one of us had to die. Would you want it to be me or Louis?

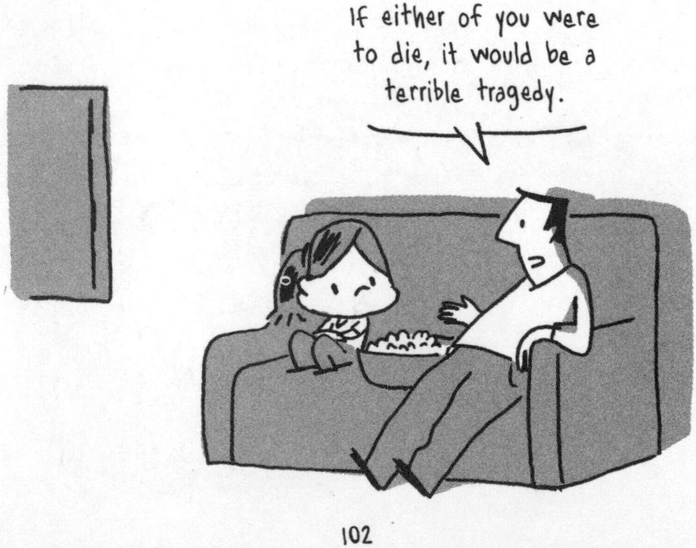
If either of you were to die, it would be a terrible tragedy.

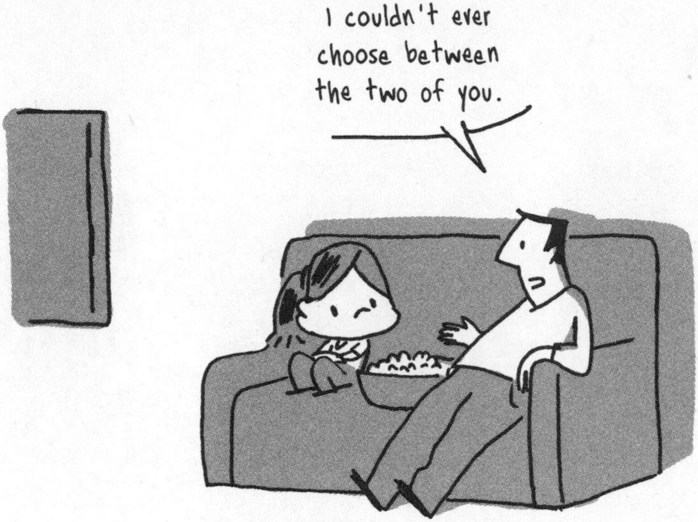
I couldn't ever choose between the two of you.

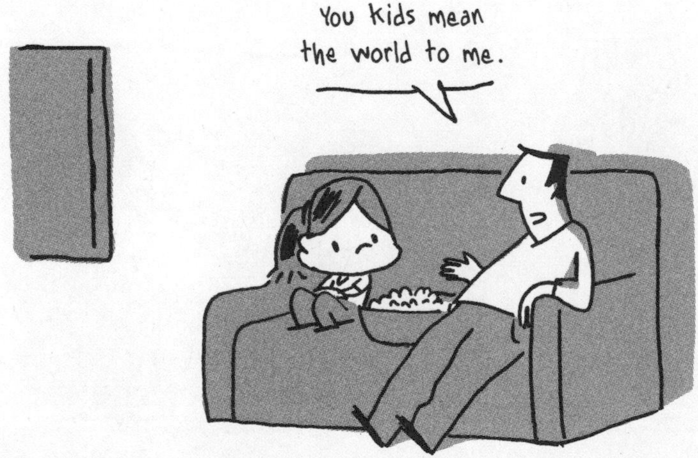
You kids mean the world to me.

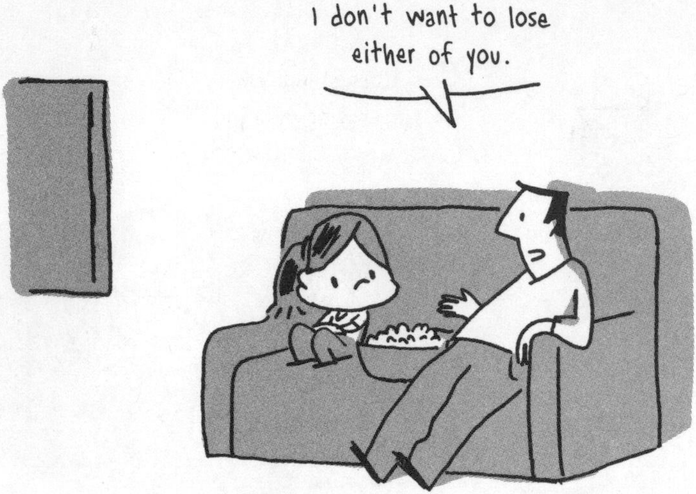
I don't want to lose either of you.

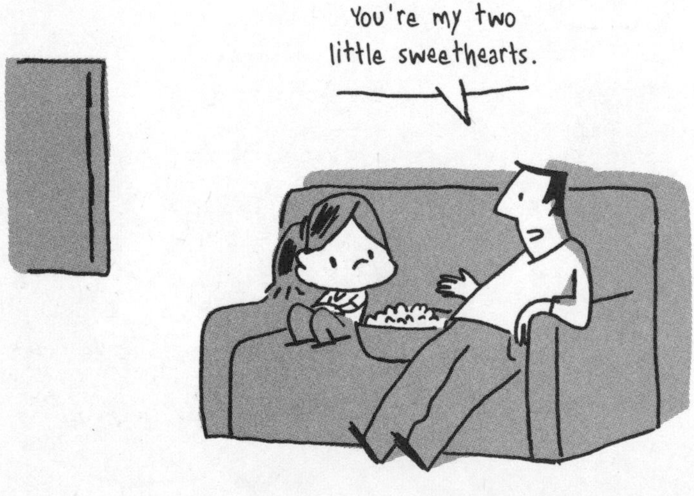
You're my two little sweethearts.

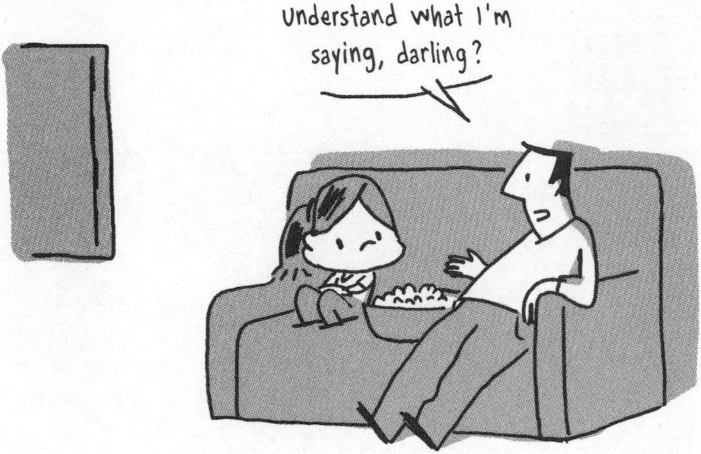
Understand what I'm saying, darling?

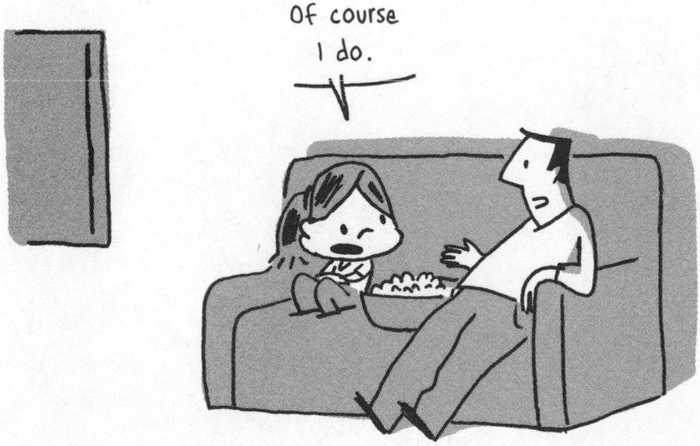
Of course I do.

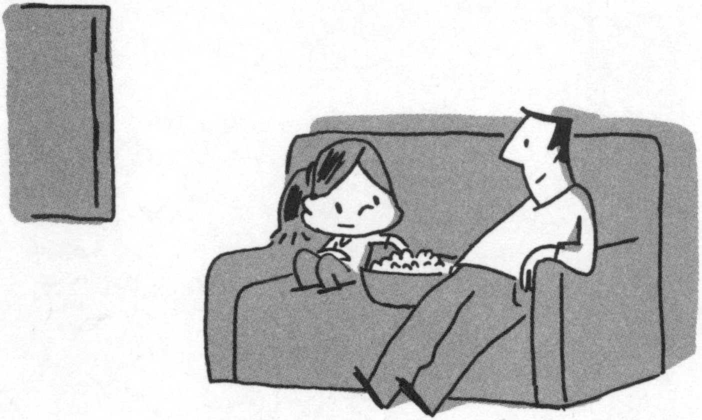

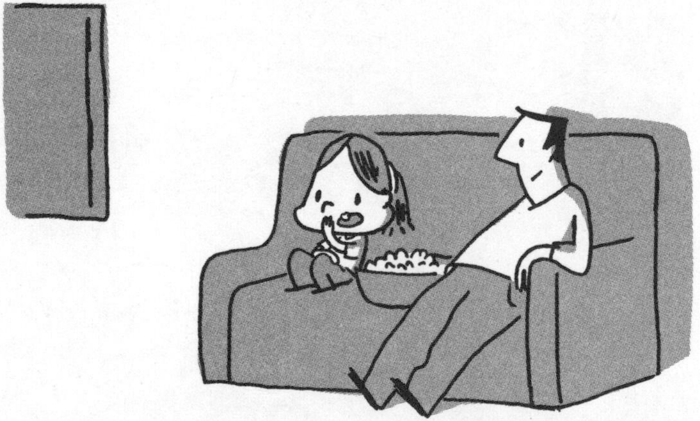

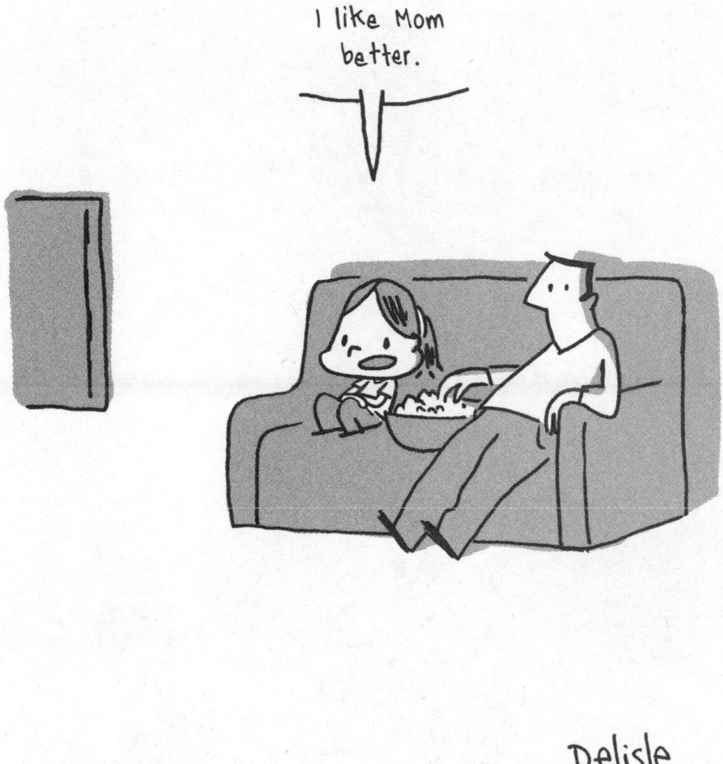
I like Mom
better.
Delisle

- The magic trick

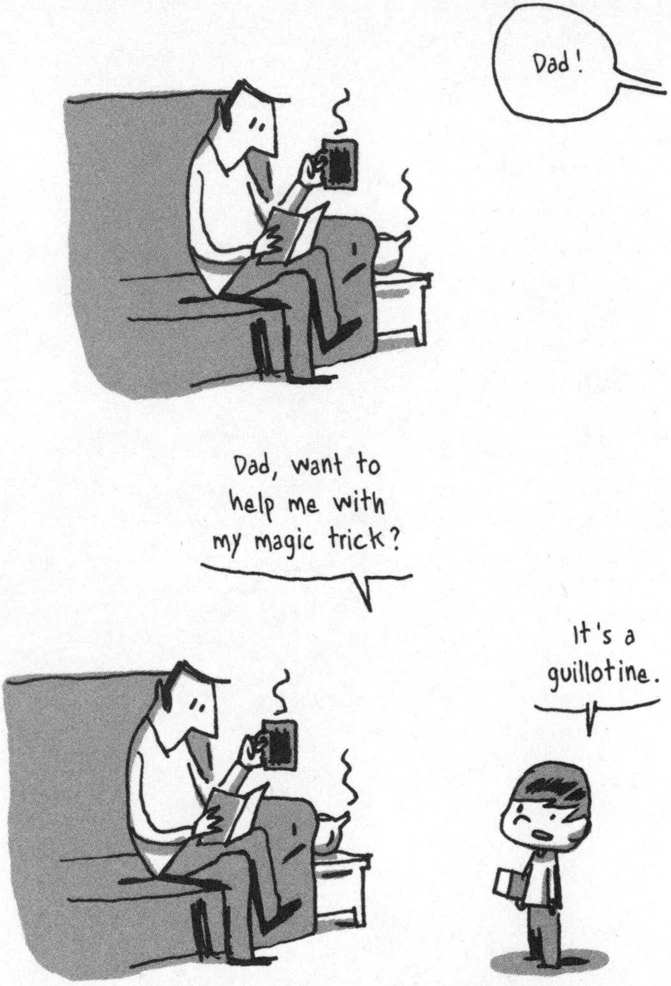
Dad!
Dad, want to help me with my magic trick?
It's a guillotine.

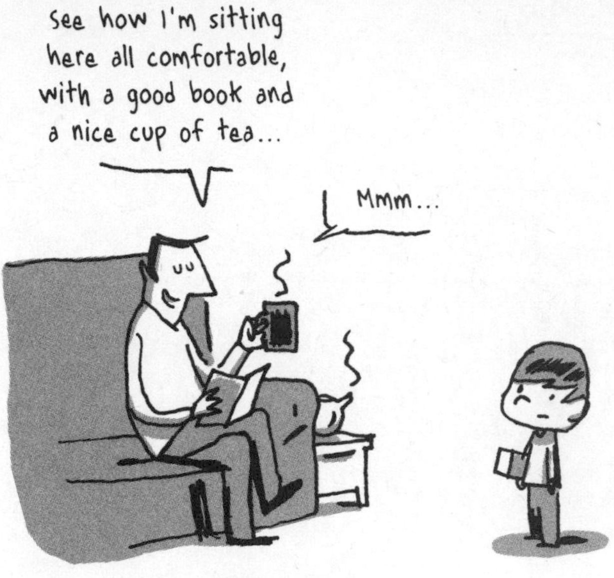
See how I'm sitting here all comfortable, with a good book and a nice cup of tea...
Mmm...

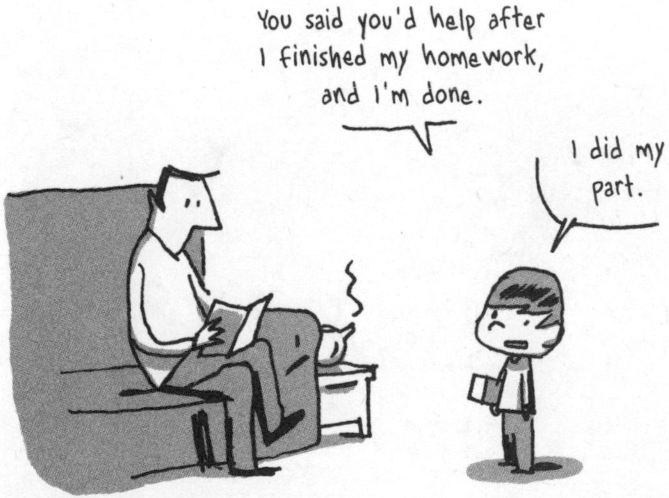
You said you'd help after I finished my homework, and I'm done.
I did my part.

Slurp!

Fine, hand it over...How tricky can it be?
Yay!

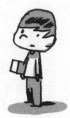

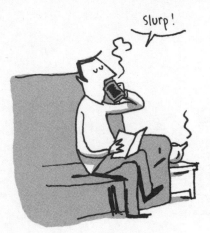

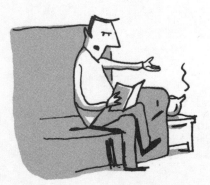

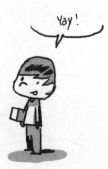

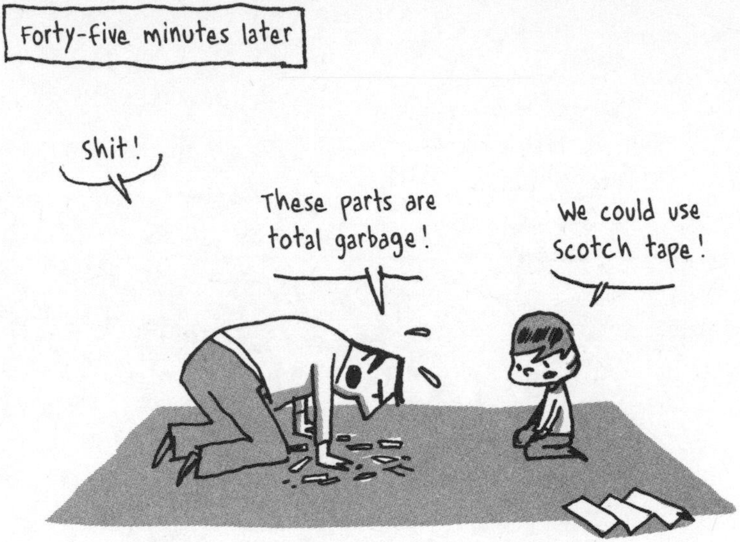
Forty-five minutes later
Shit!
These parts are total garbage!
We could use Scotch tape!

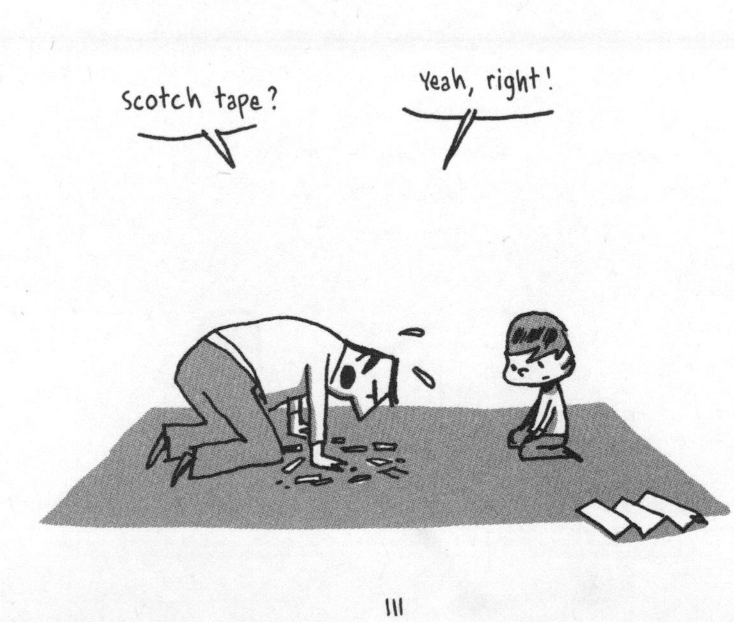
Scotch tape?
Yeah, right!

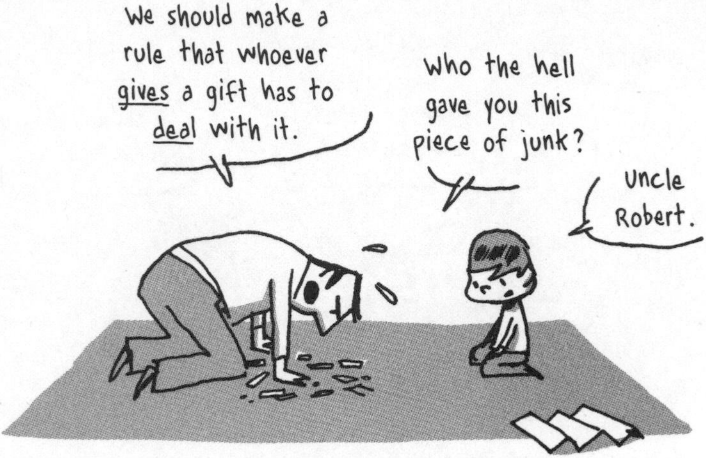
We should make a rule that whoever gives a gift has to deal with it.
Who the hell gave you this piece of junk?
Uncle Robert.

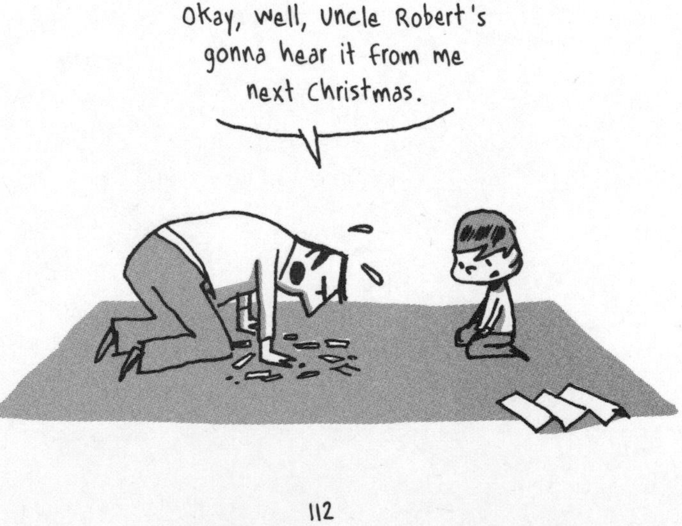
Okay, well, Uncle Robert's gonna hear it from me next Christmas.

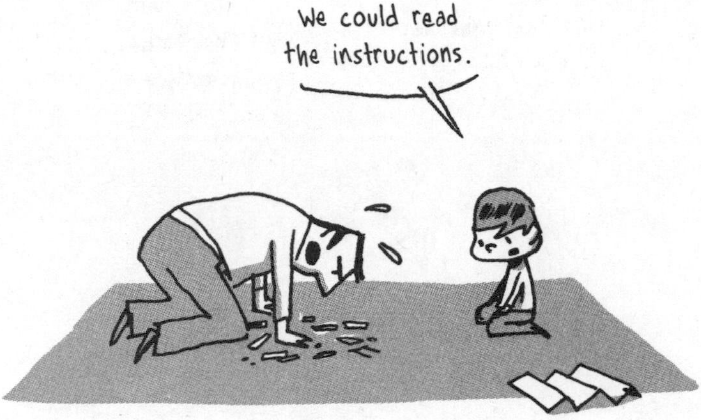
We could read the instructions.

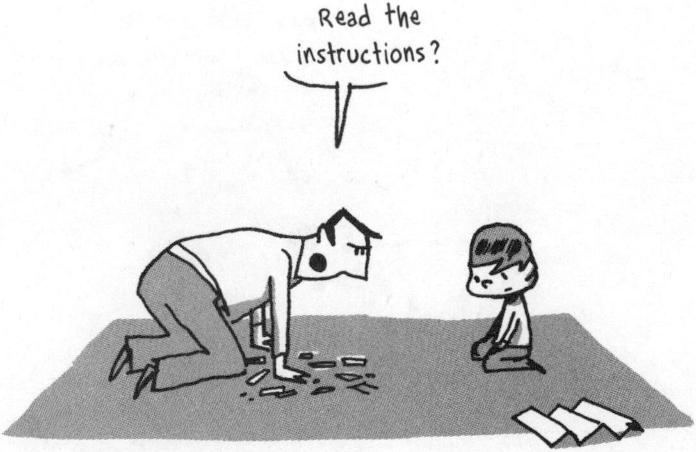
Read the instructions?

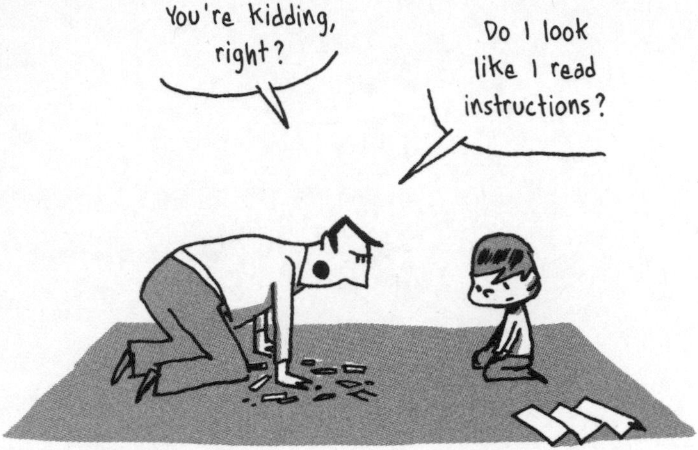
You're kidding, right?
Do I look like I read instructions?

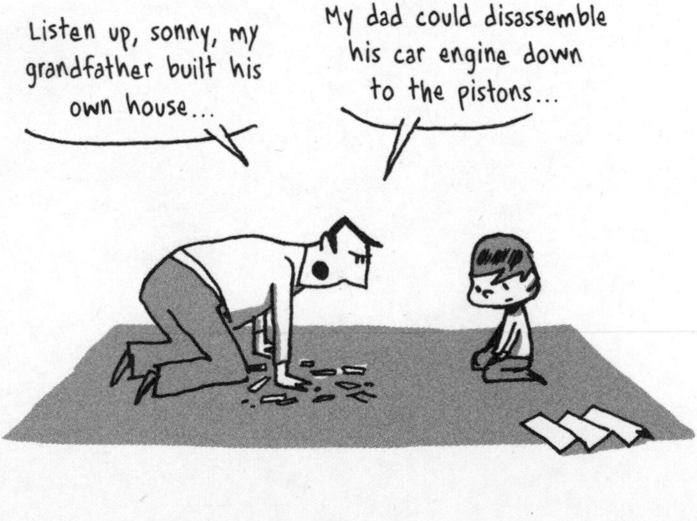
Listen up, sonny, my grandfather built his own house...
My dad could disassemble his car engine down to the pistons...

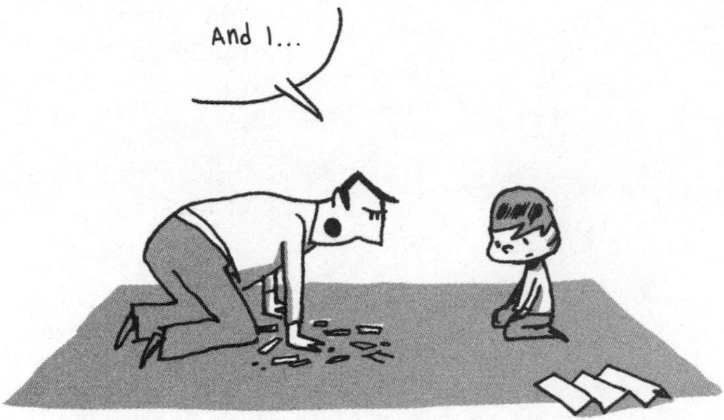
And I...

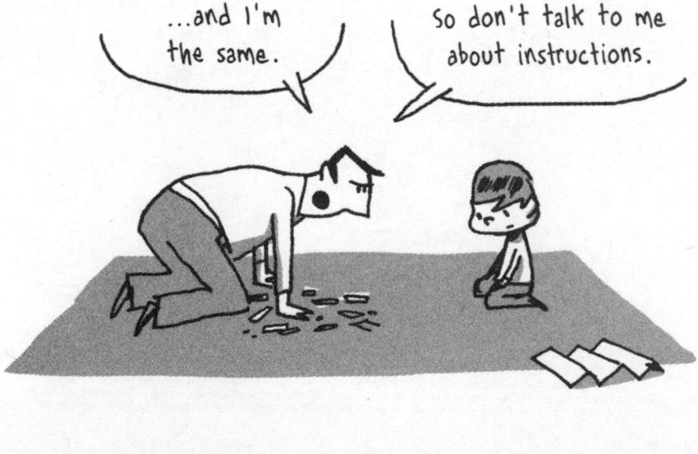
...and I'm the same.
So don't talk to me about instructions.

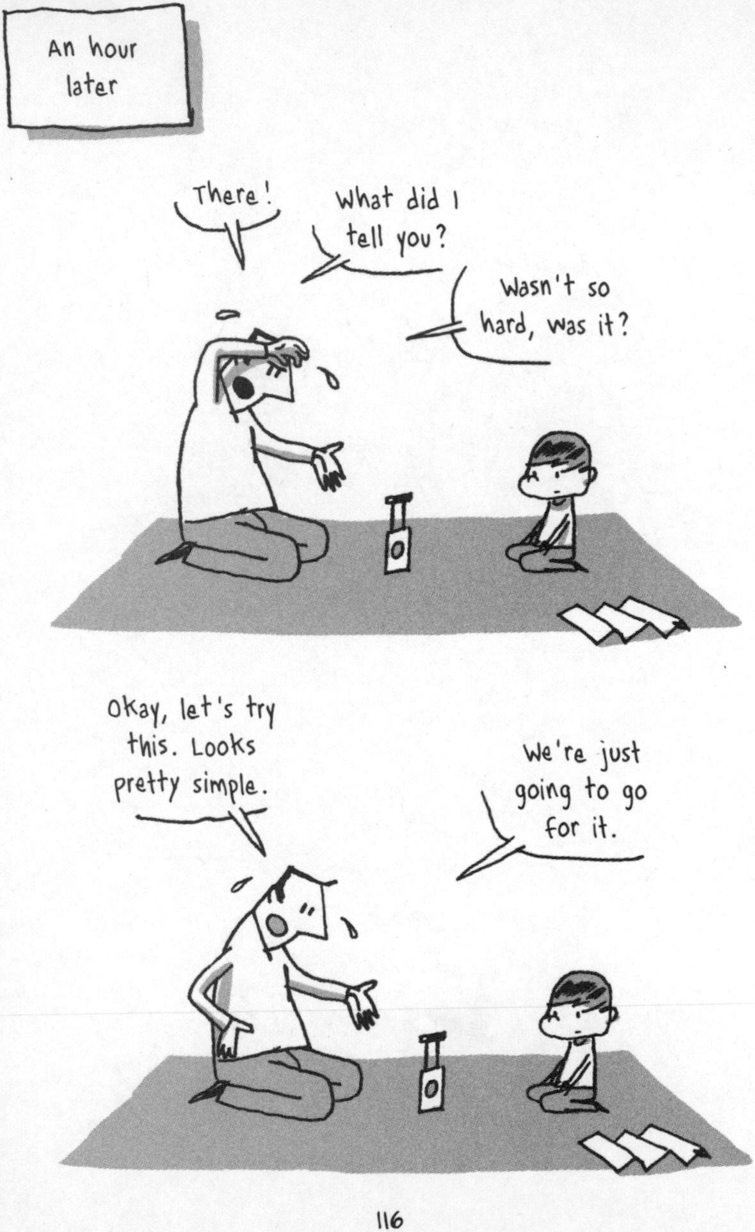
An hour later
There!
What did I tell you?
Wasn't so hard, was it?
Okay, let's try this. Looks pretty simple.
We're just going to go for it.

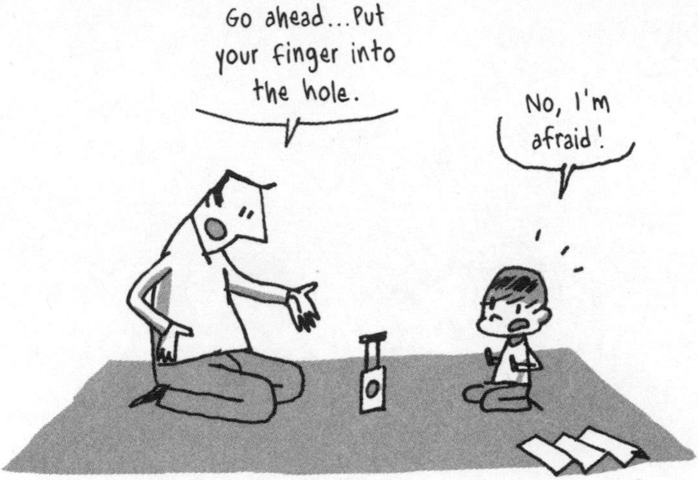
Go ahead...Put your finger into the hole.
No, I'm afraid!

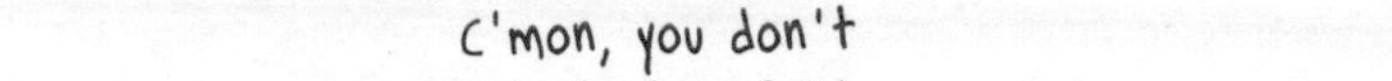
C'mon, you don't have to be afraid, it's just a toy!

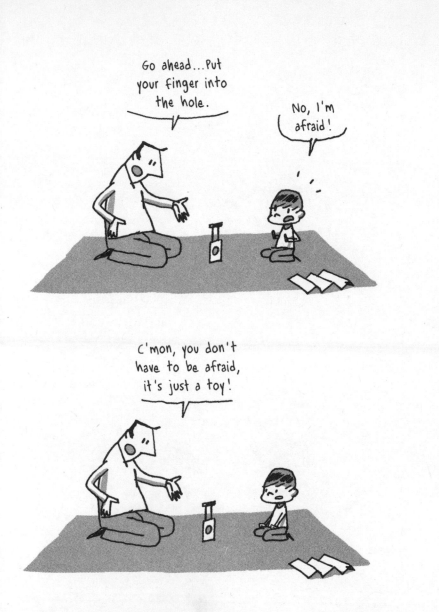

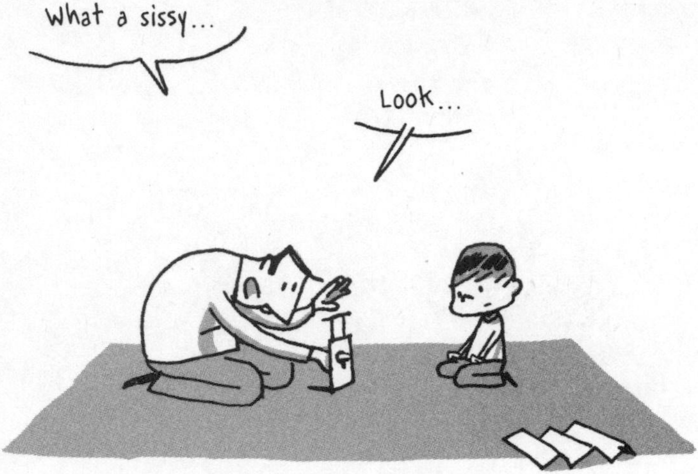
What a sissy...
Look...

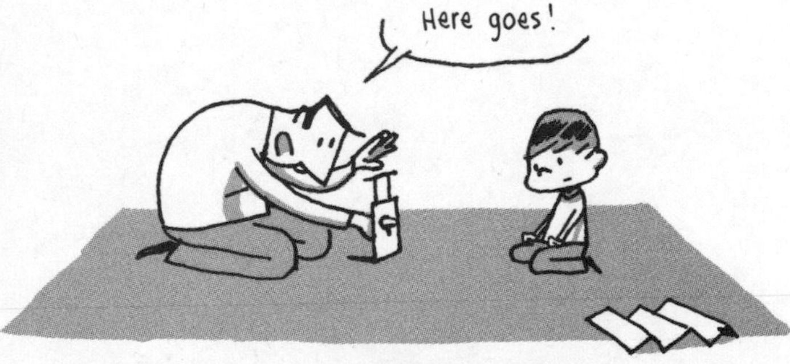
Here goes!

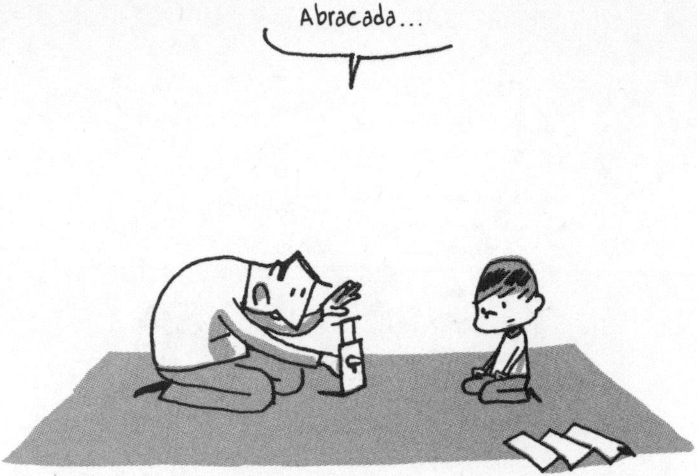
Abracada...

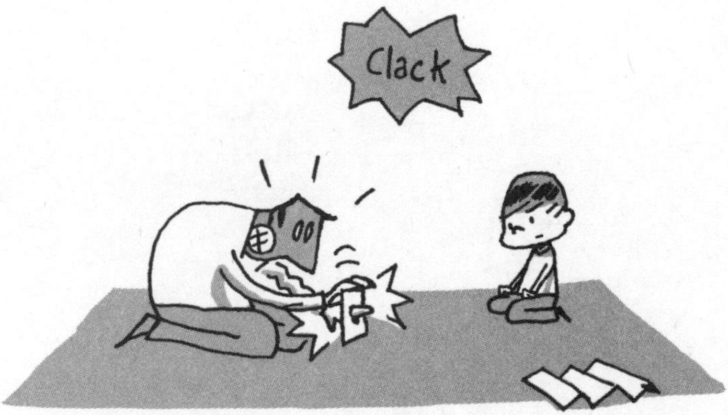
Clack

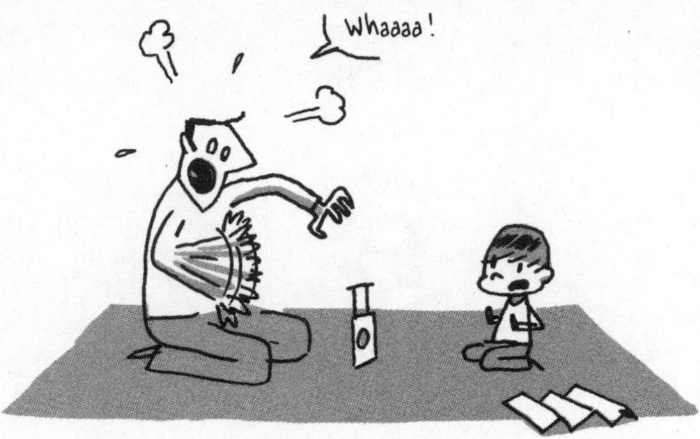
Whaaaa!

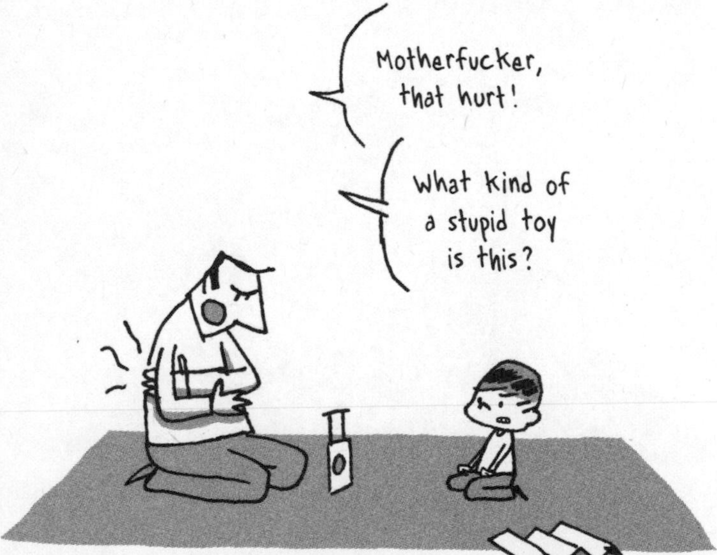
Motherfucker, that hurt!
What kind of a stupid toy is this?

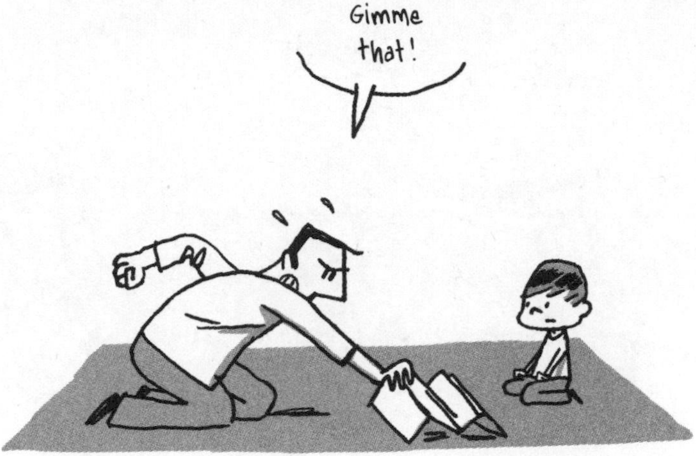
Gimme that!

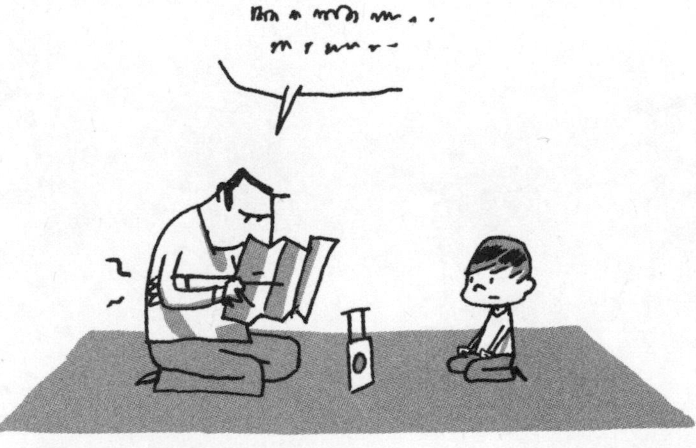

The ⭐ magic ⭐ guillotine

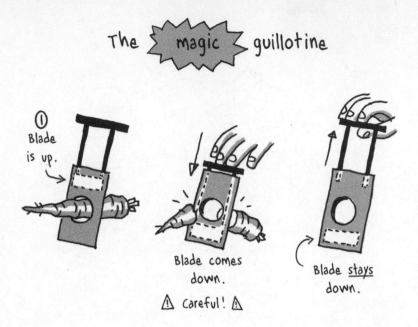

① Blade is up.

Blade comes down.

⚠ Careful! ⚠

Blade _stays_ down.

②

CLACK

Blade goes back up.

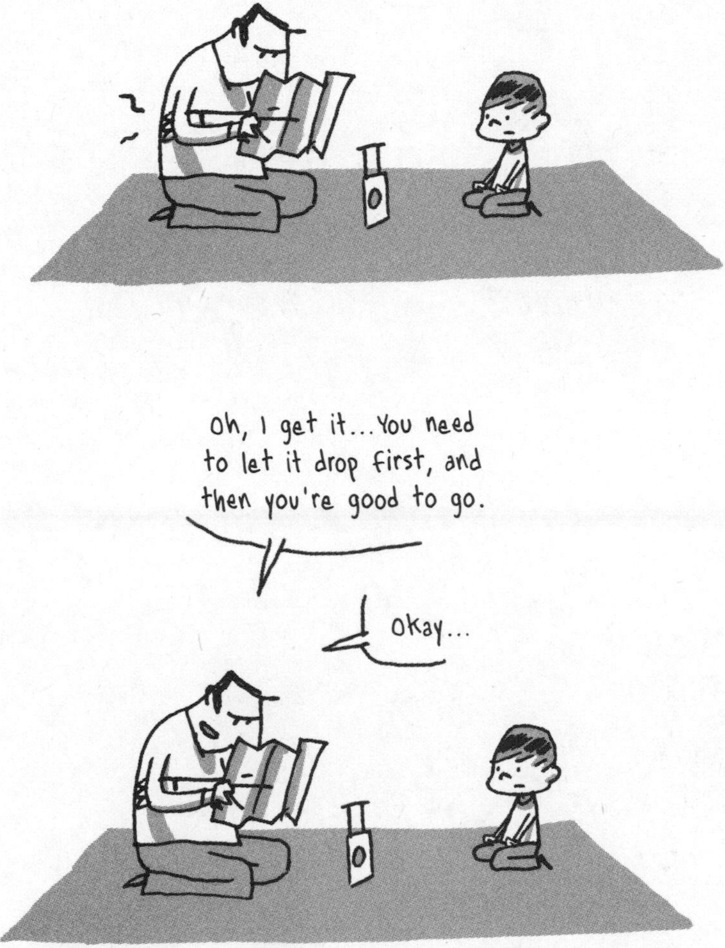
Oh, I get it... You need to let it drop first, and then you're good to go.
Okay...

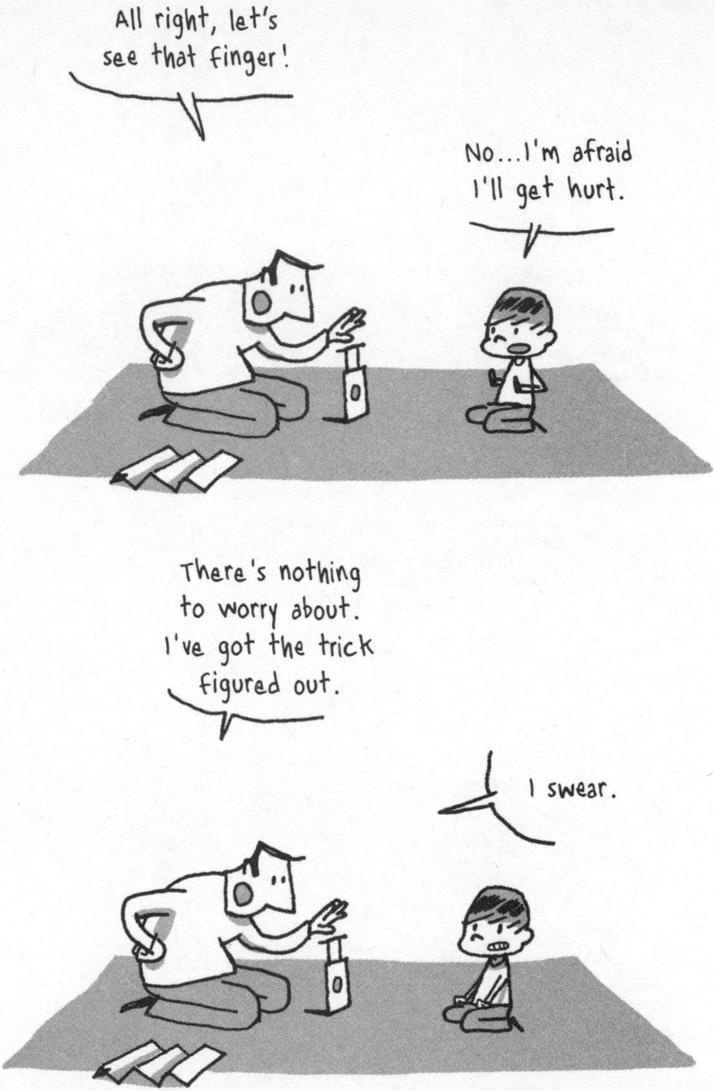

All right, let's see that finger!
No...I'm afraid I'll get hurt.
There's nothing to worry about. I've got the trick figured out.
I swear.

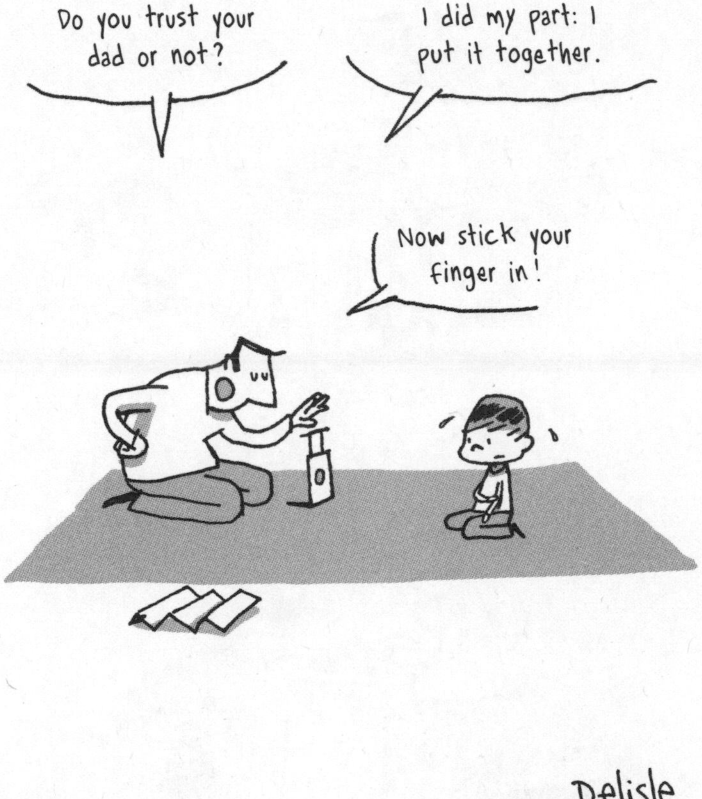
Do you trust your dad or not?
I did my part: I put it together.
Now stick your finger in!
Delisle

- The penguin

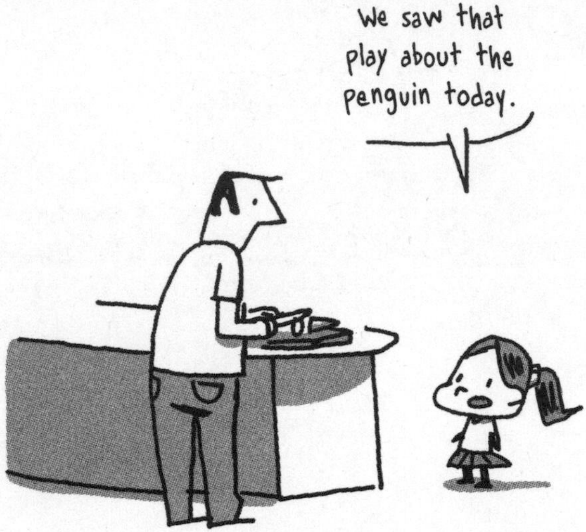
We saw that play about the penguin today.

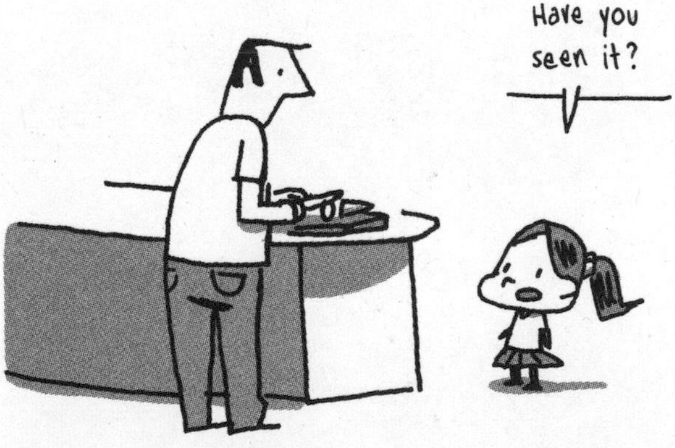
Have you seen it?

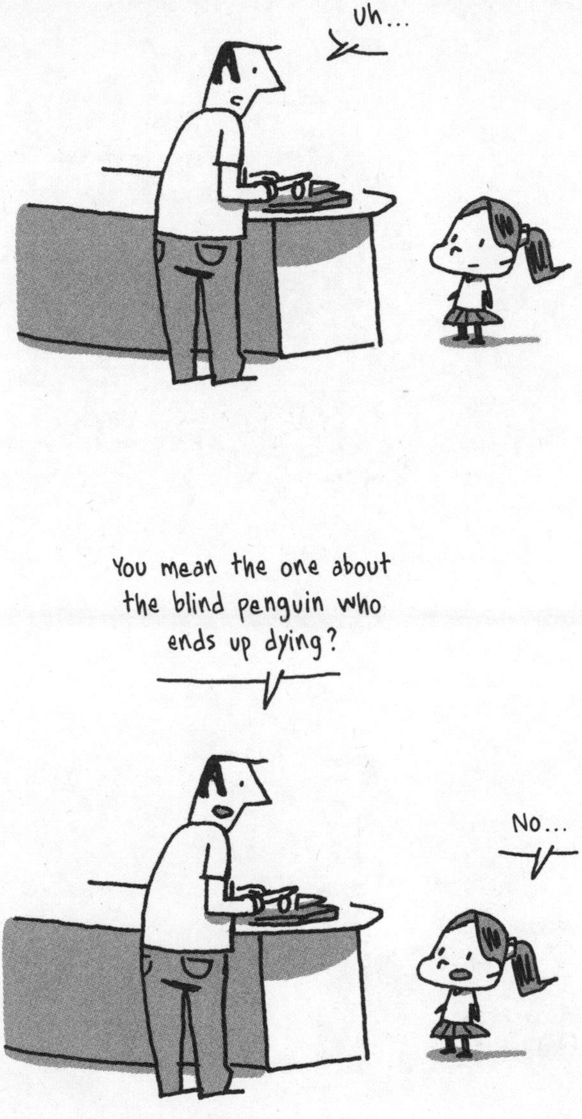
Uh...
You mean the one about the blind penguin who ends up dying?
No...

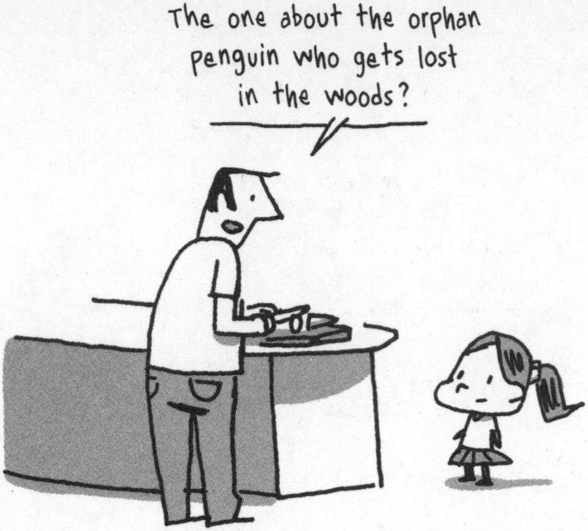
The one about the orphan penguin who gets lost in the woods?

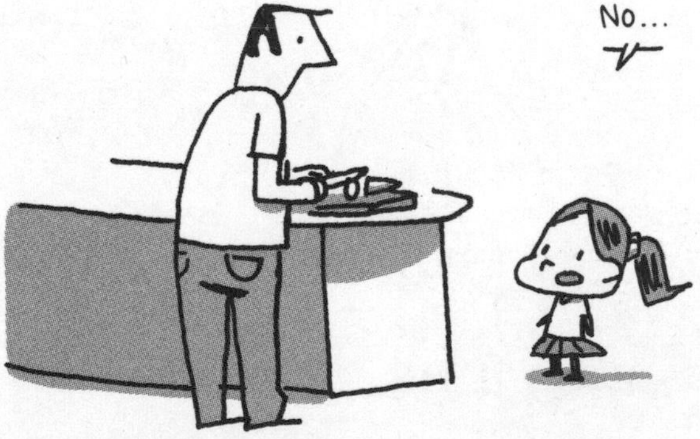
No...

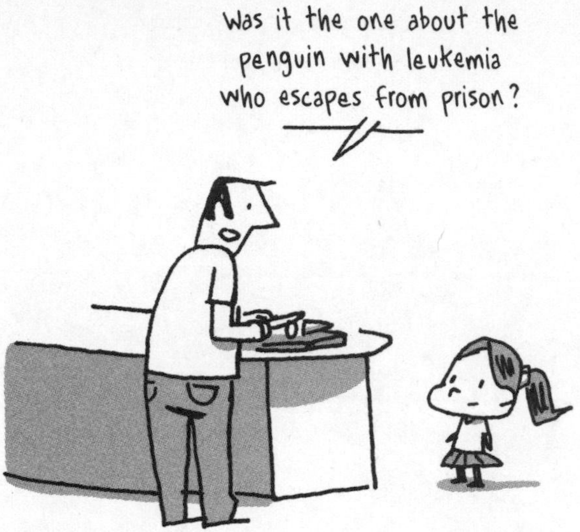
Was it the one about the penguin with leukemia who escapes from prison?

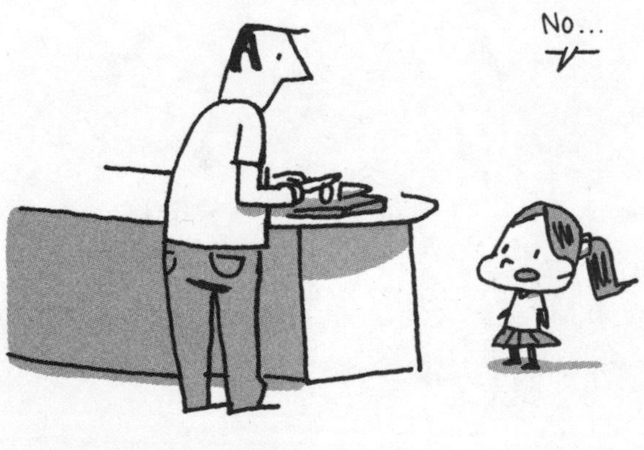
No...

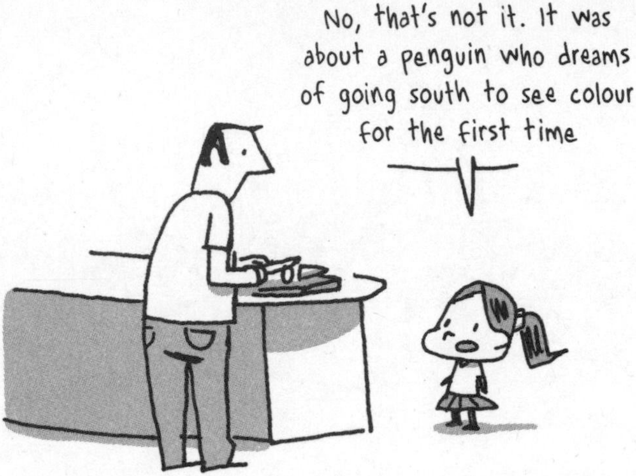
No, that's not it. It was about a penguin who dreams of going south to see colour for the first time

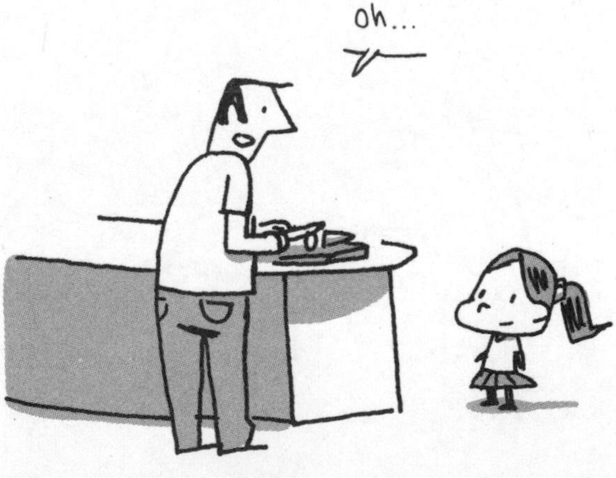
oh...

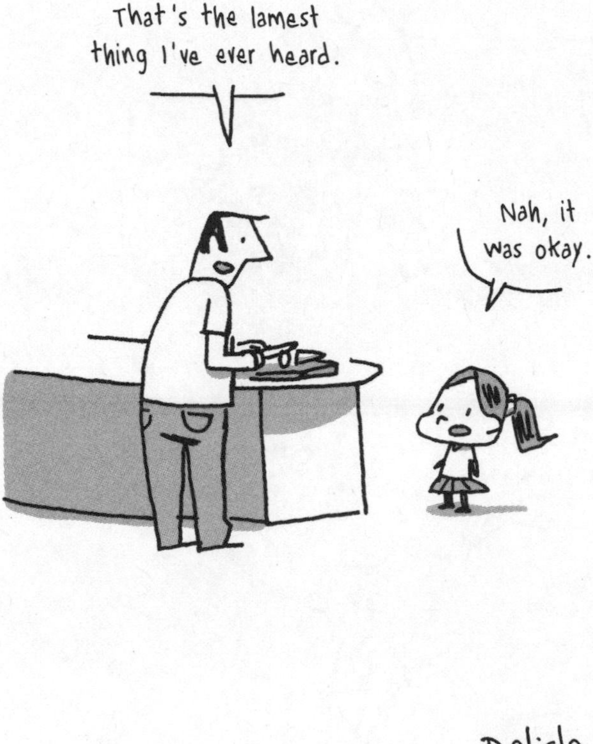
That's the lamest thing I've ever heard.
Nah, it was okay.
Delisle

- Life

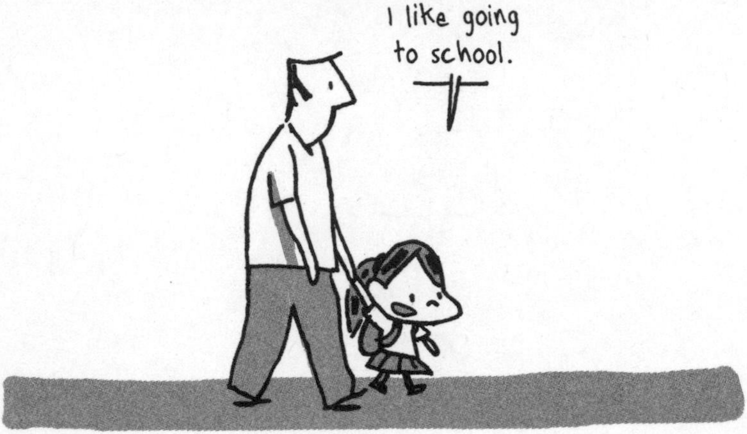
I like going to school.

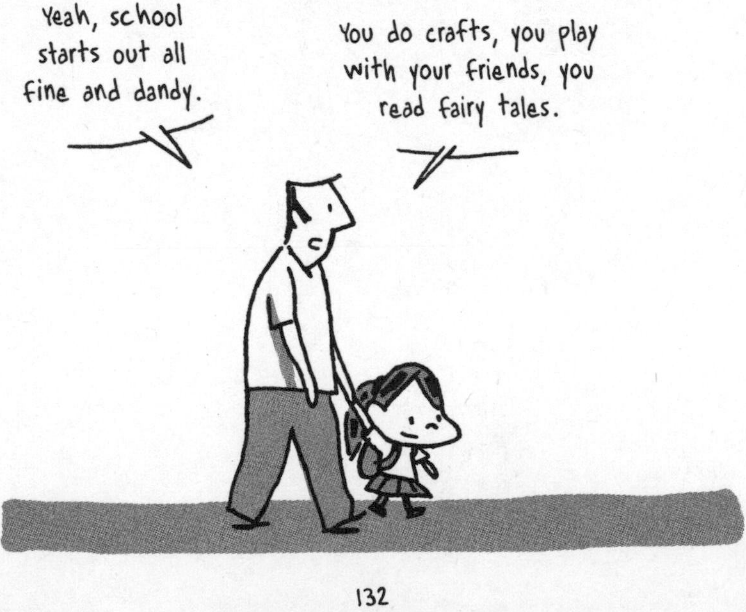
Yeah, school starts out all fine and dandy.
You do crafts, you play with your friends, you read fairy tales.

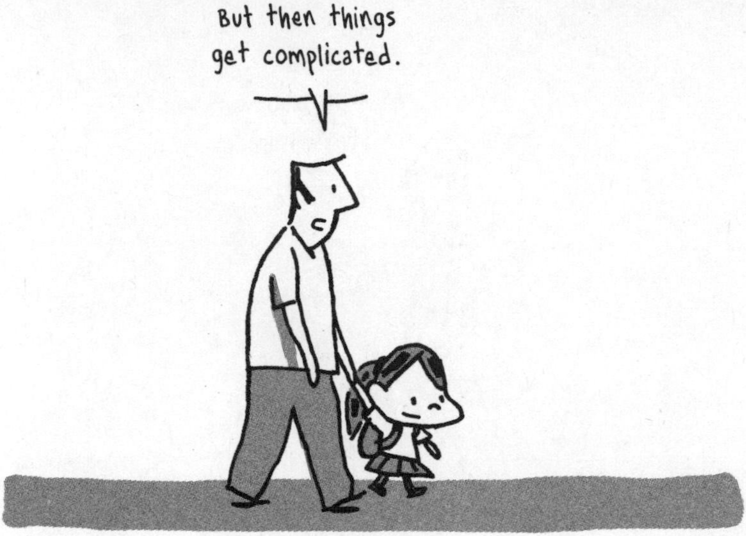
But then things get complicated.

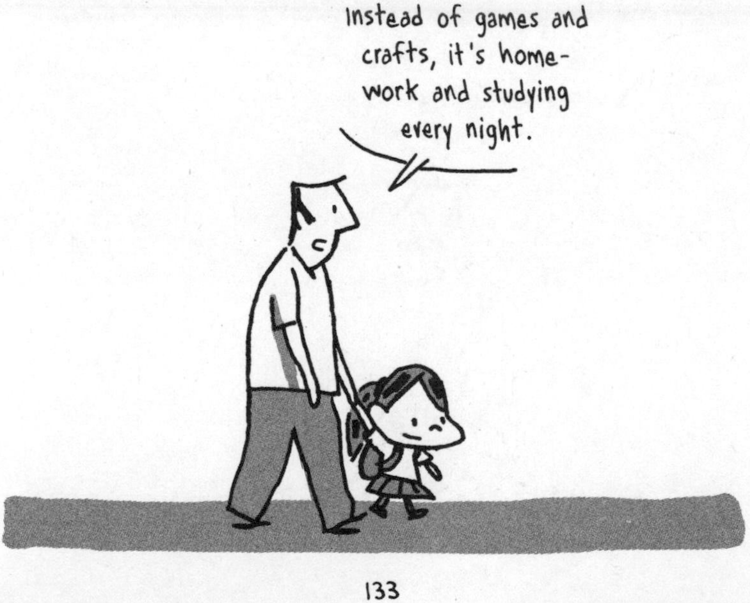
Instead of games and crafts, it's home-work and studying every night.

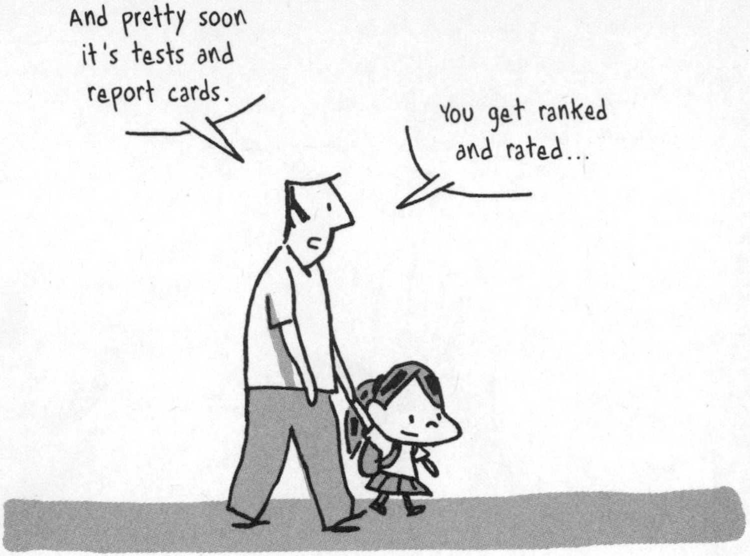

And pretty soon it's tests and report cards.
You get ranked and rated...

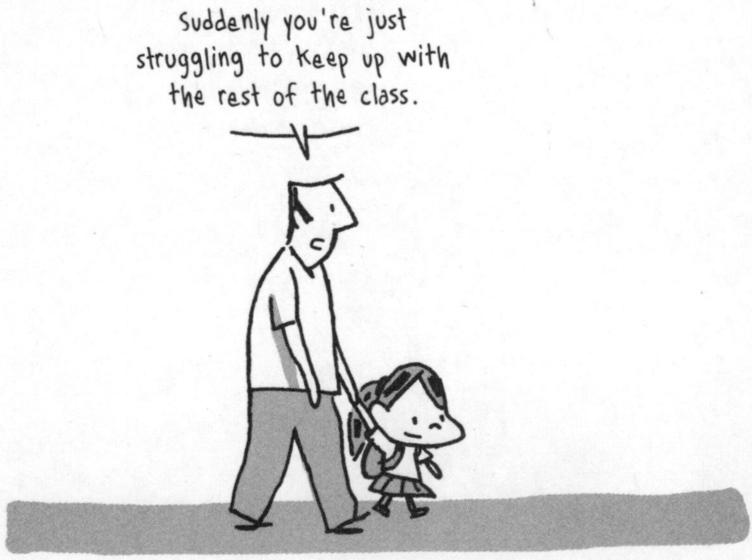

Suddenly you're just struggling to keep up with the rest of the class.

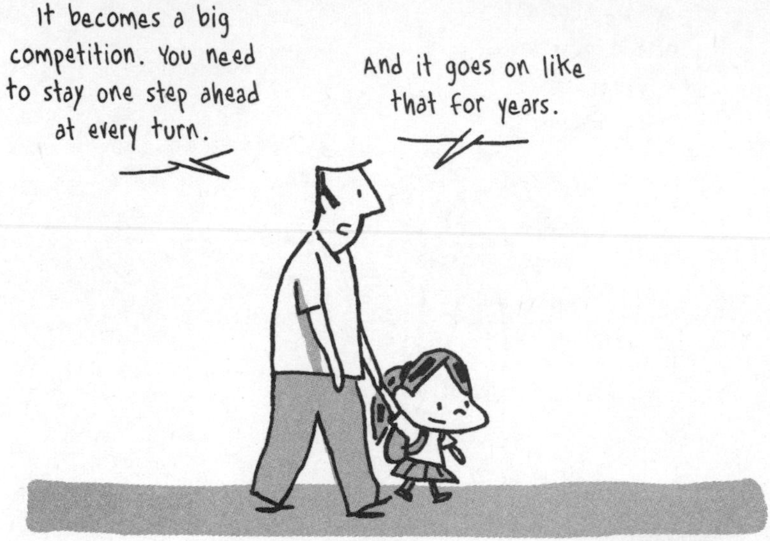
It becomes a big competition. You need to stay one step ahead at every turn.
And it goes on like that for years.

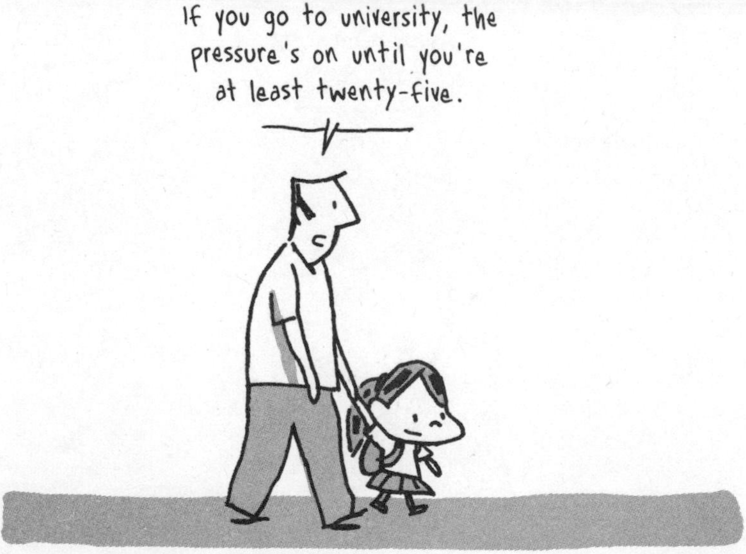
If you go to university, the pressure's on until you're at least twenty-five.

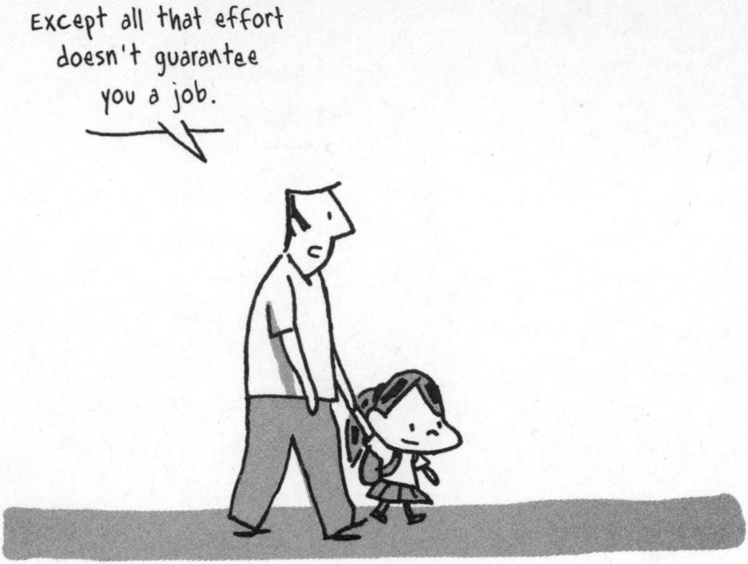
Except all that effort doesn't guarantee you a job.

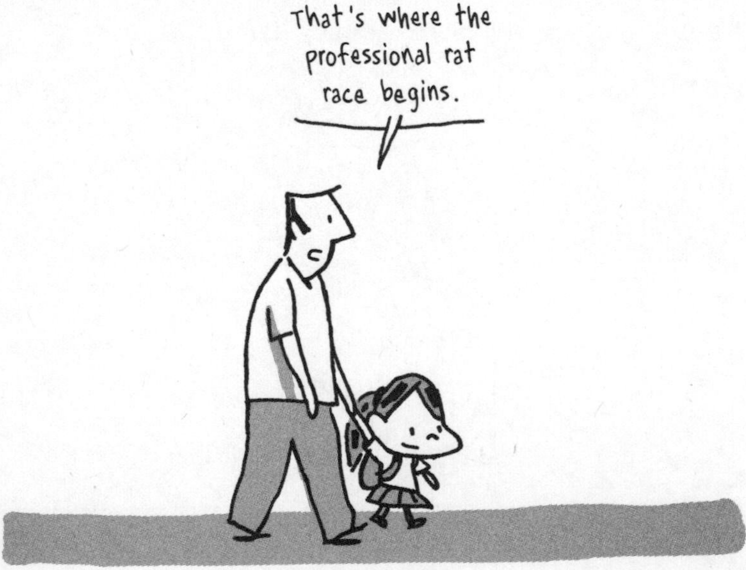
That's where the professional rat race begins.

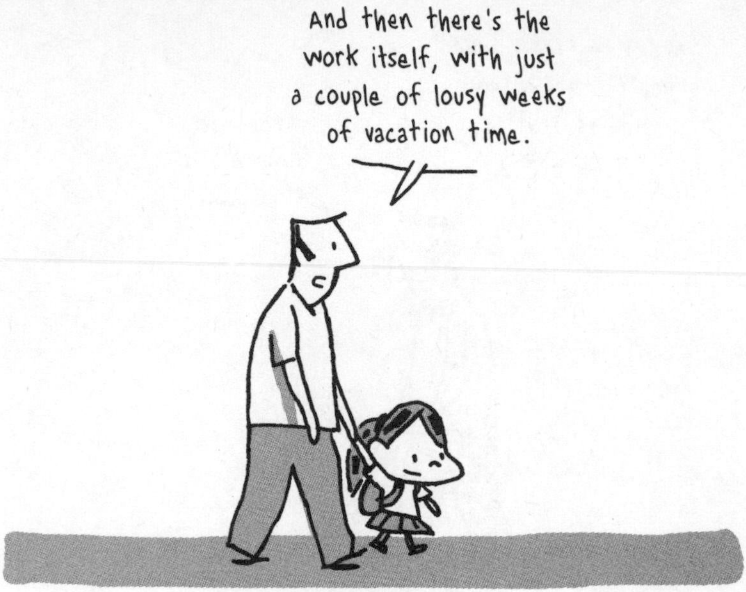
And then there's the work itself, with just a couple of lousy weeks of vacation time.

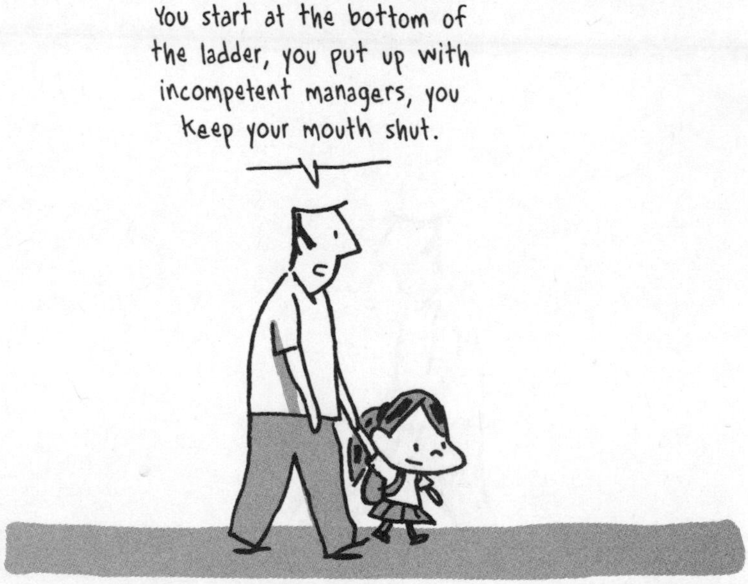
You start at the bottom of the ladder, you put up with incompetent managers, you keep your mouth shut.

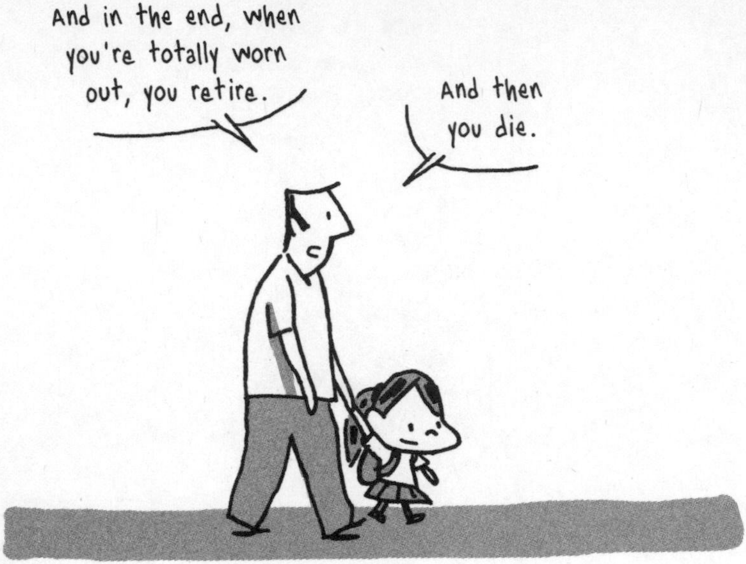
And in the end, when you're totally worn out, you retire.
And then you die.

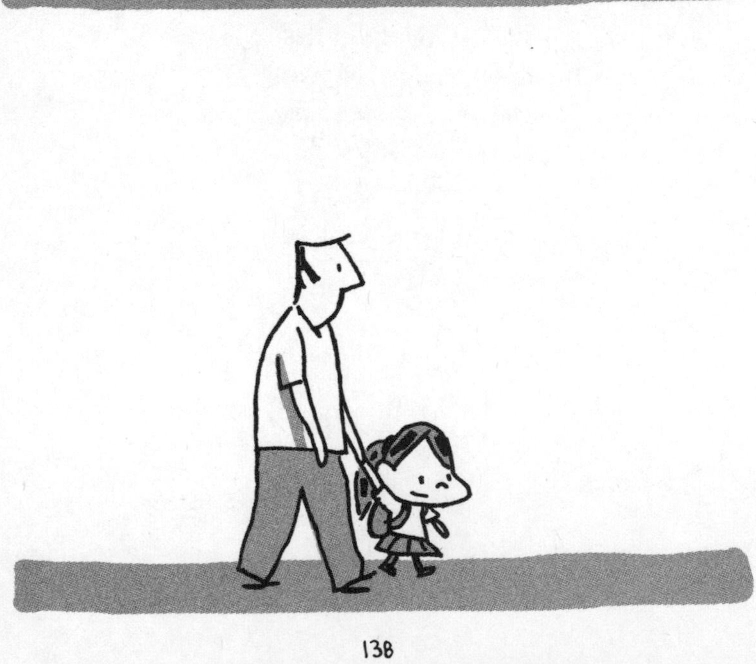

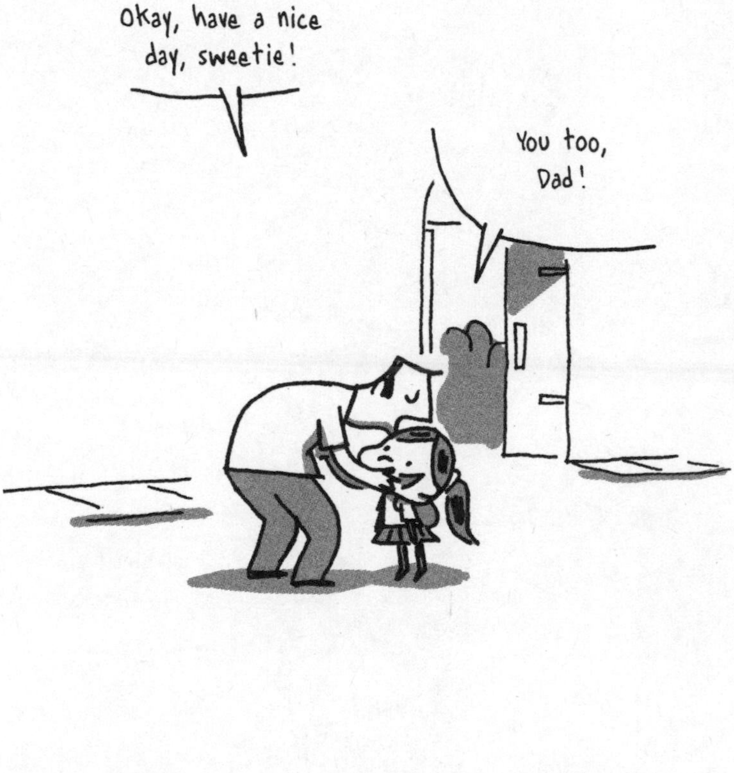
Okay, have a nice day, sweetie!
You too, Dad!
Delisle

- Goldilocks

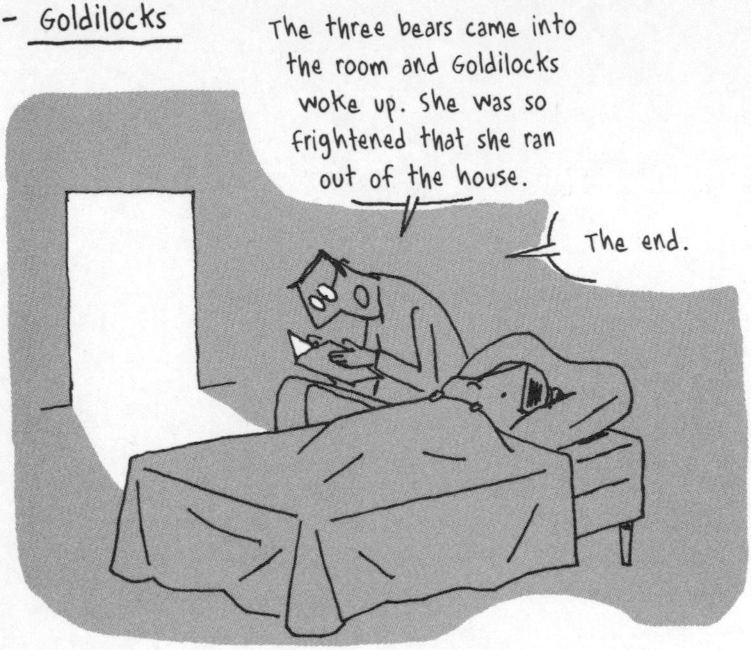
The three bears came into the room and Goldilocks woke up. She was so frightened that she ran out of the house.
The end.

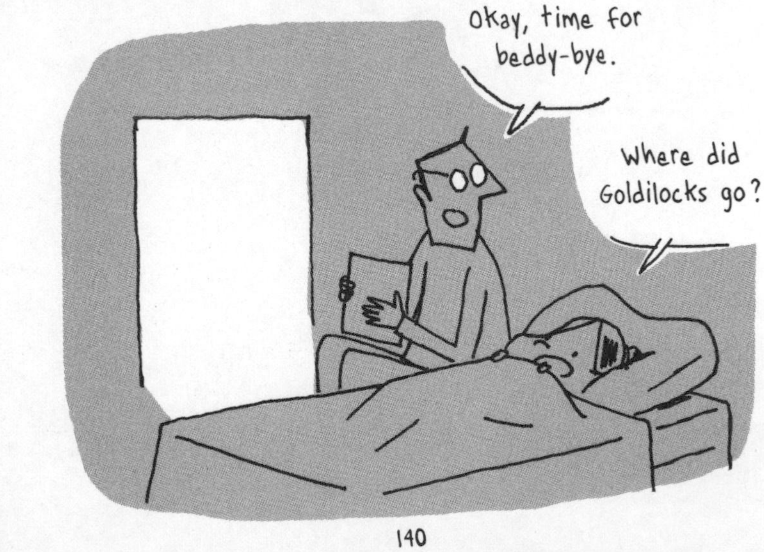
Okay, time for beddy-bye.
Where did Goldilocks go?

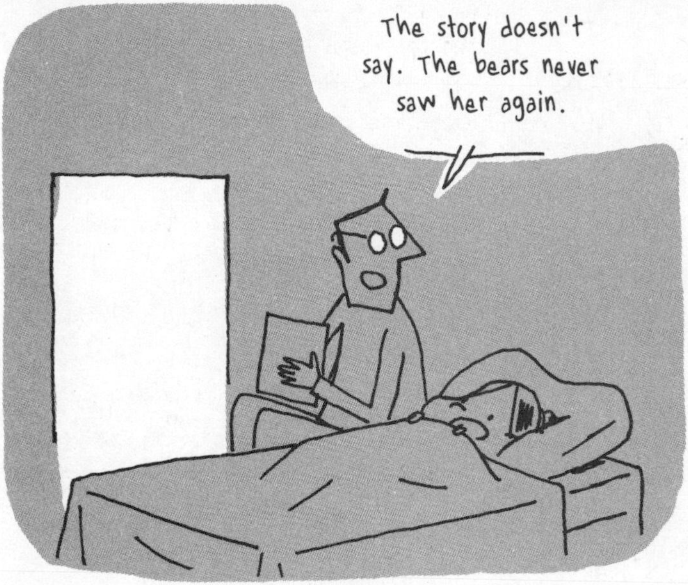
The story doesn't say. The bears never saw her again.

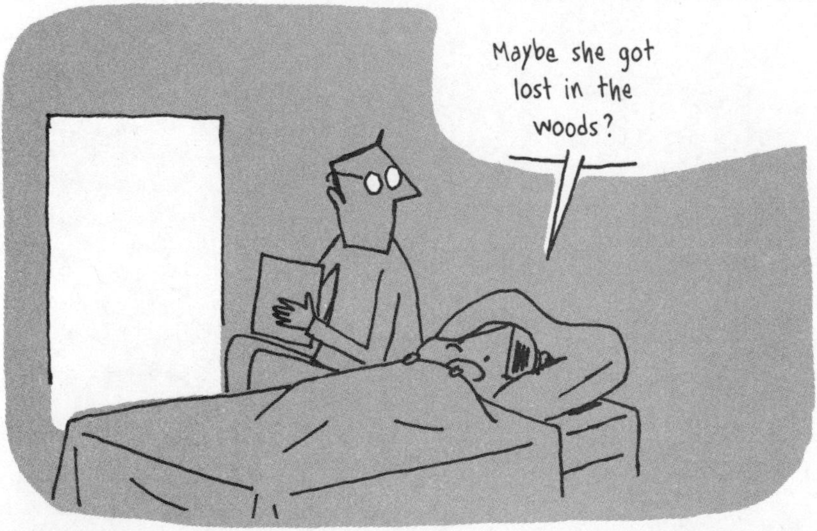
Maybe she got lost in the woods?

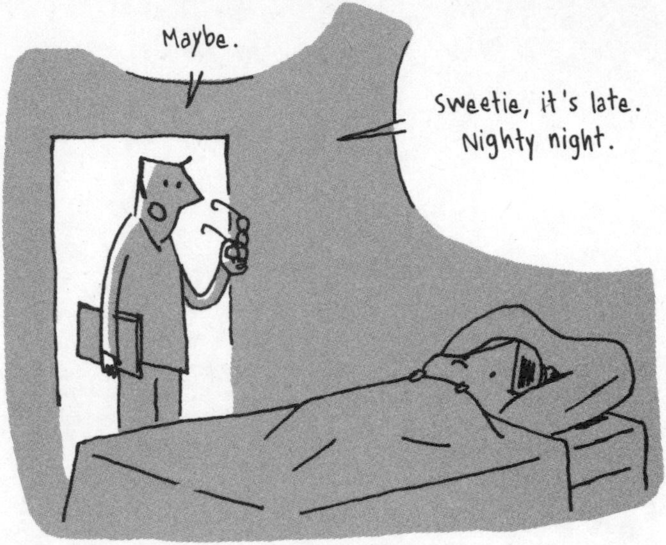
Maybe.
Sweetie, it's late. Nighty night.

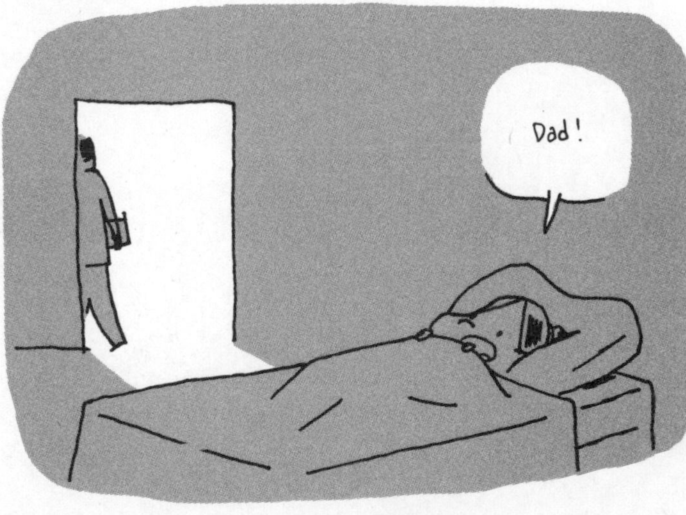
Dad!

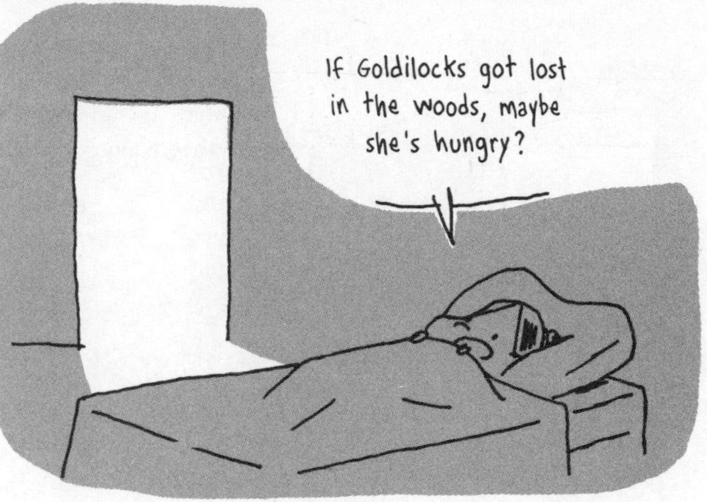
If Goldilocks got lost in the woods, maybe she's hungry?

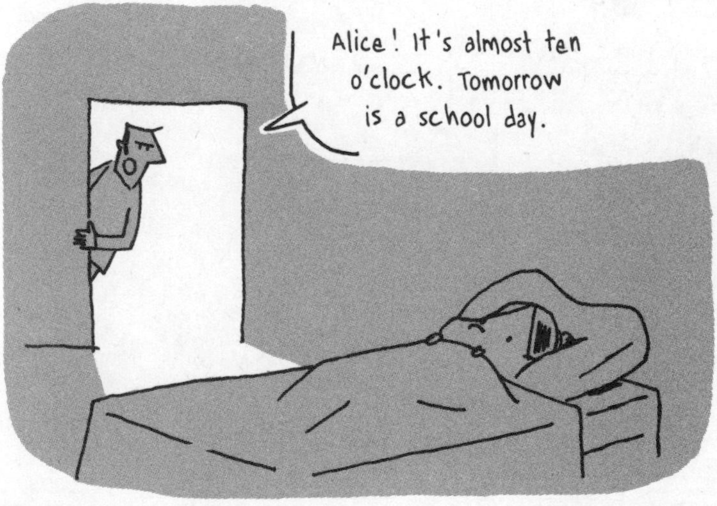
Alice! It's almost ten o'clock. Tomorrow is a school day.

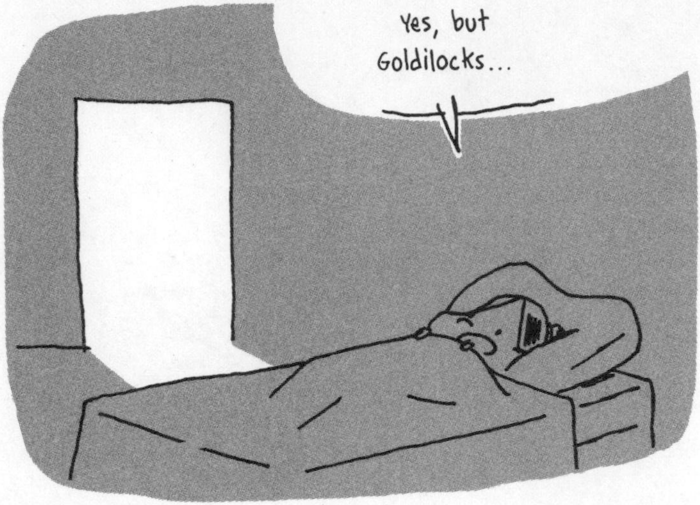
Yes, but
Goldilocks...

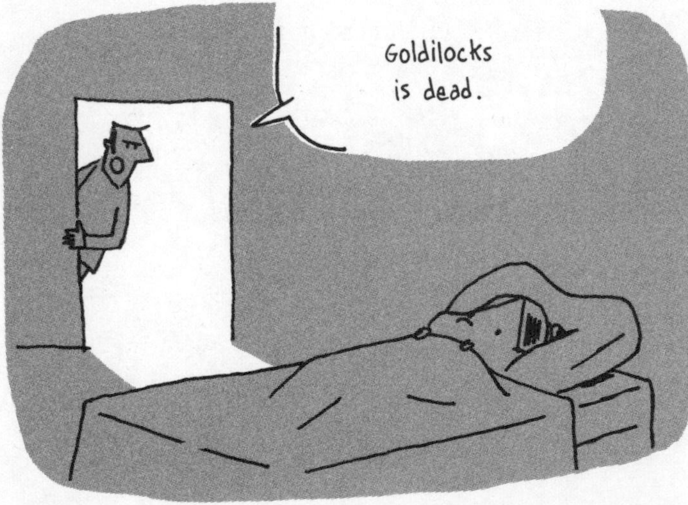
Goldilocks
is dead.

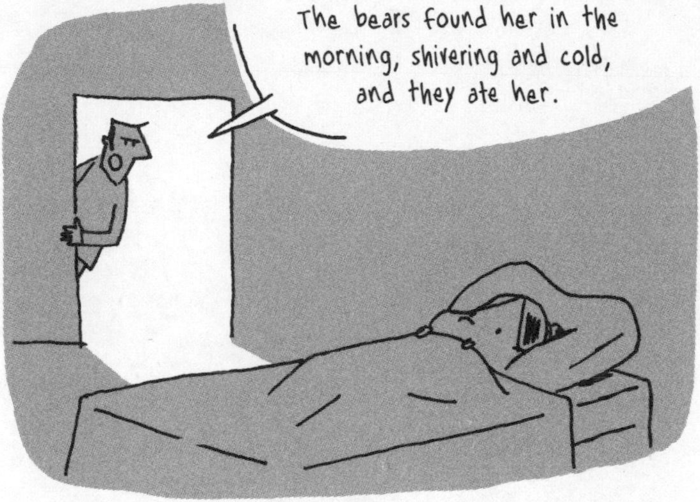
The bears found her in the morning, shivering and cold, and they ate her.

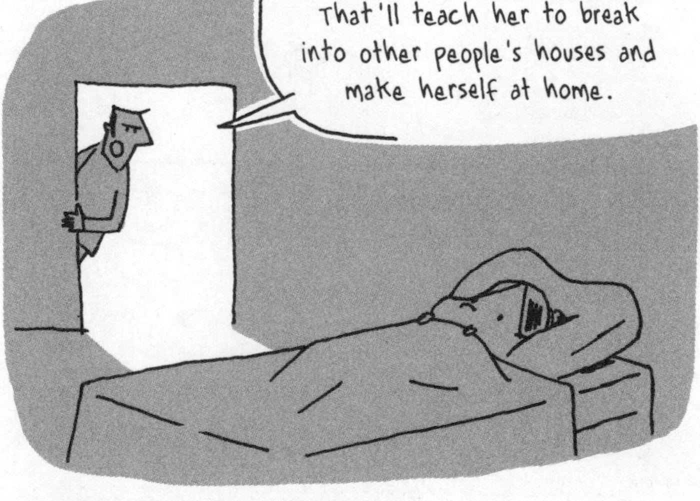
That'll teach her to break into other people's houses and make herself at home.

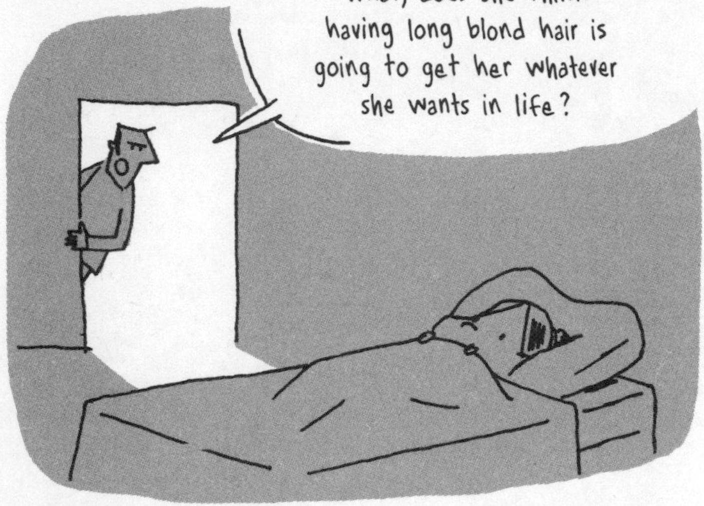
What, does she think having long blond hair is going to get her whatever she wants in life?

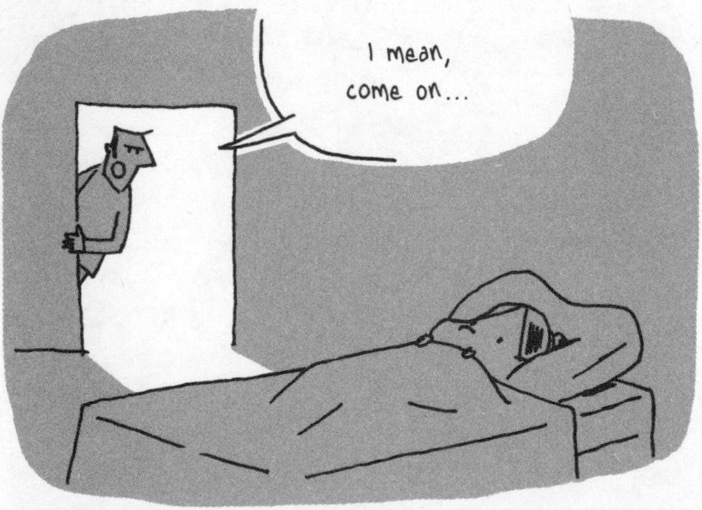
I mean, come on...

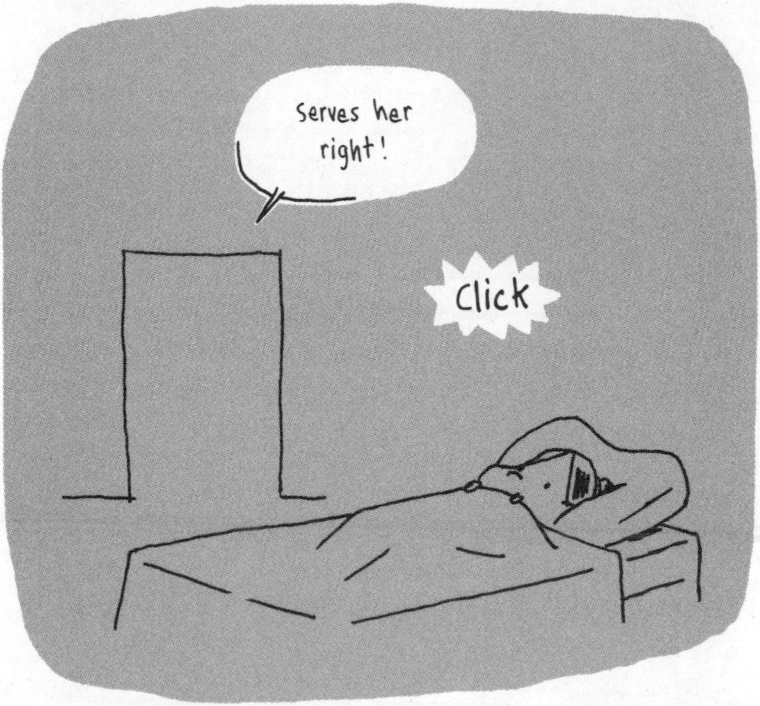
Serves her right!
Click

Delisle

- On the plane

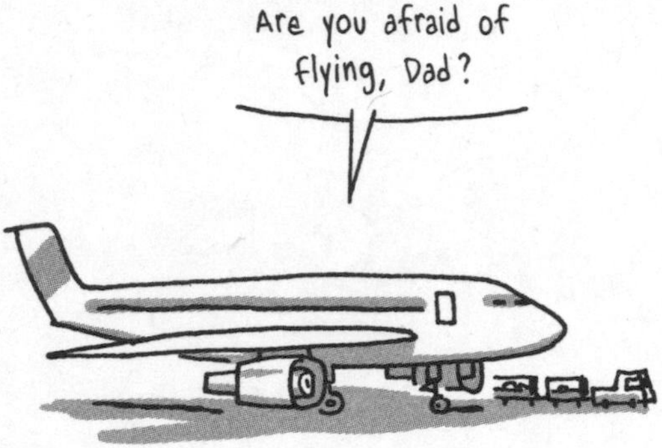
Are you afraid of flying, Dad?

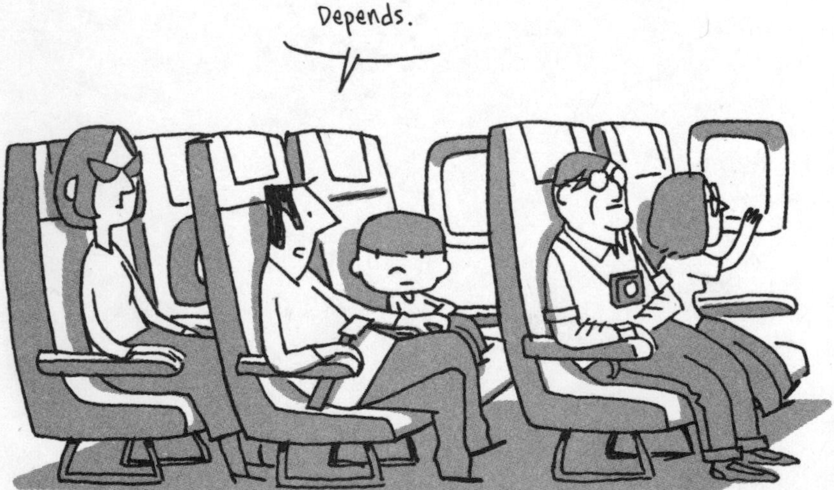
Depends.

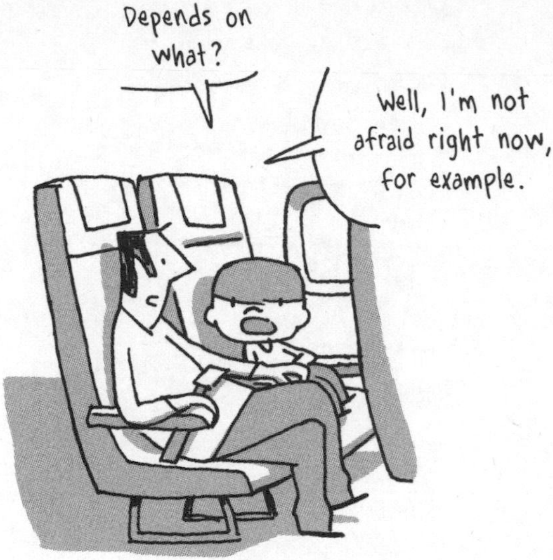
Depends on what?
Well, I'm not afraid right now, for example.

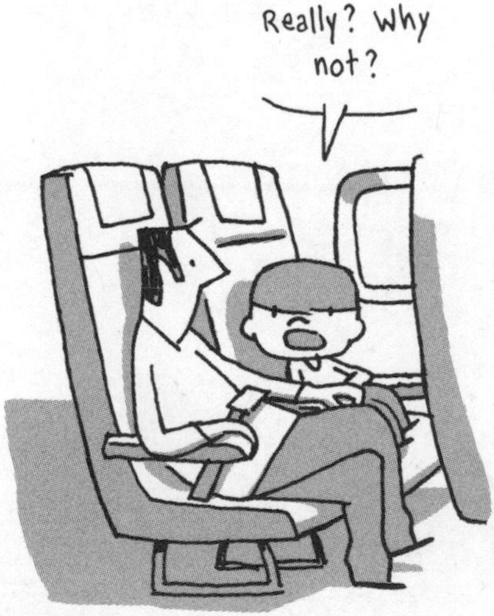
Really? Why not?

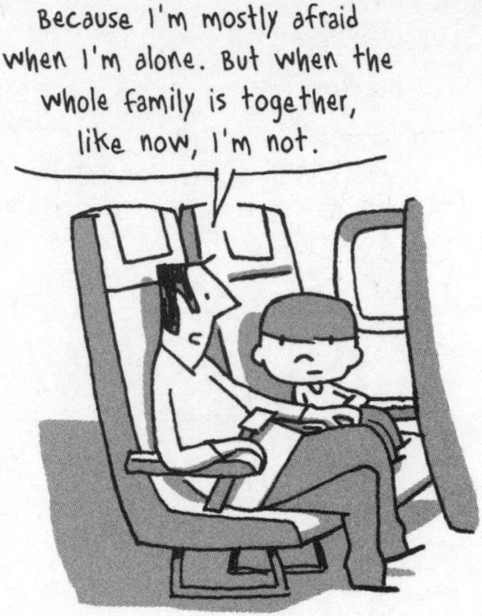
Because I'm mostly afraid when I'm alone. But when the whole family is together, like now, I'm not.

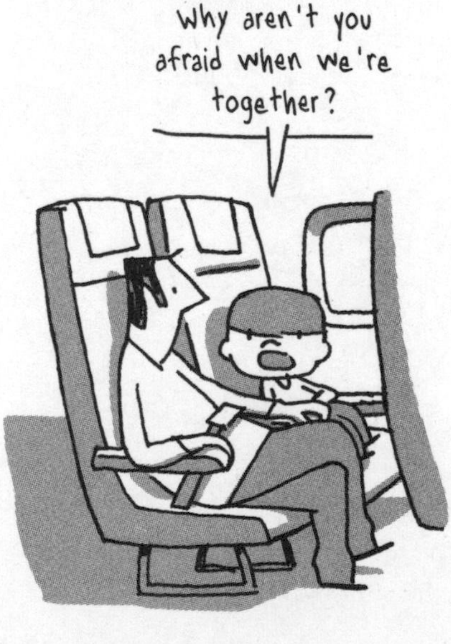
Why aren't you afraid when we're together?

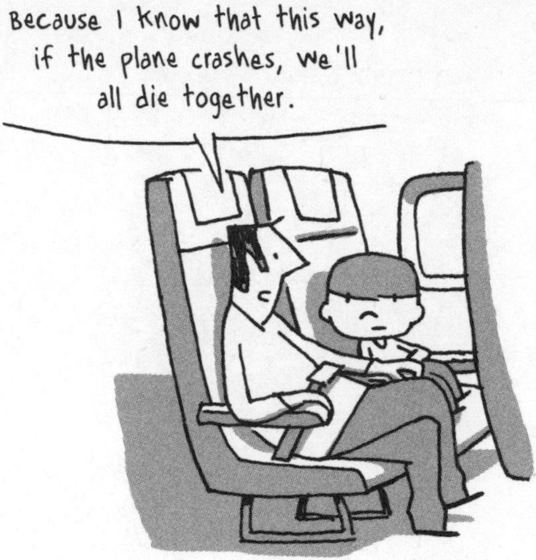
Because I know that this way, if the plane crashes, we'll all die together.

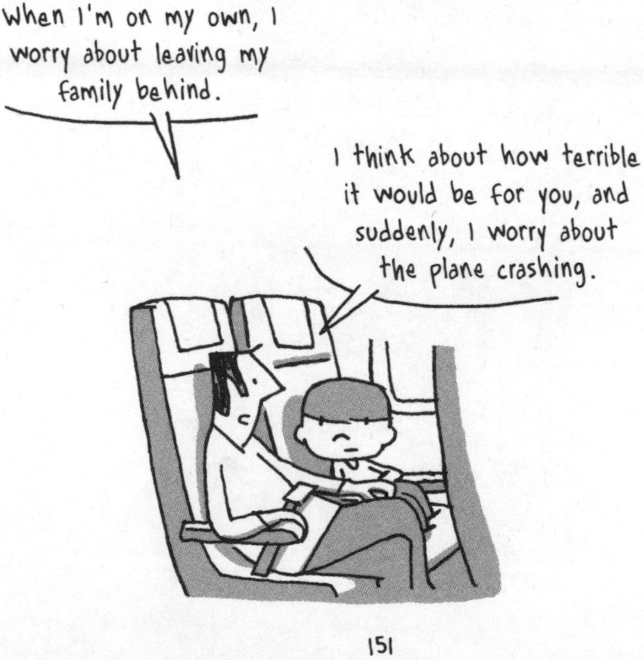
When I'm on my own, I worry about leaving my family behind.
I think about how terrible it would be for you, and suddenly, I worry about the plane crashing.

So, basically, you
want us to die
with you?

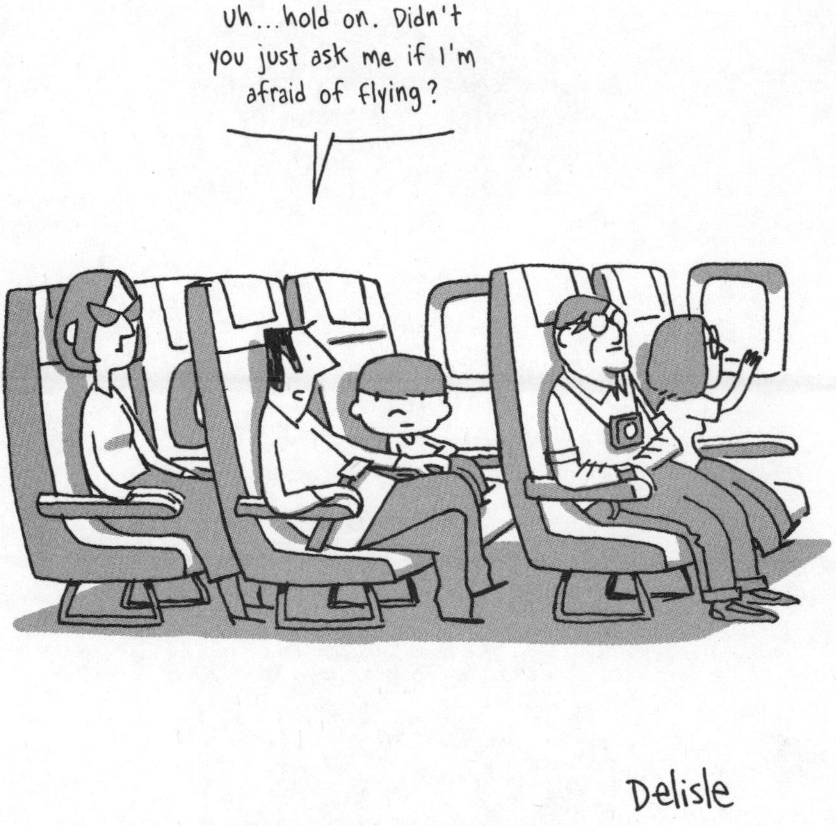
Uh...hold on. Didn't you just ask me if I'm afraid of flying?
Delisle

- Science

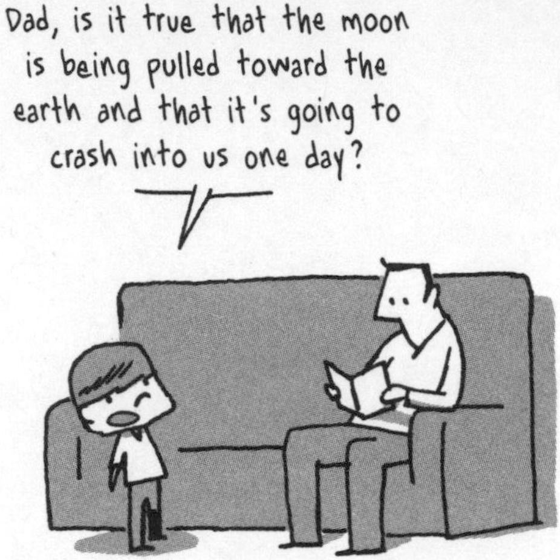
Dad, is it true that the moon is being pulled toward the earth and that it's going to crash into us one day?

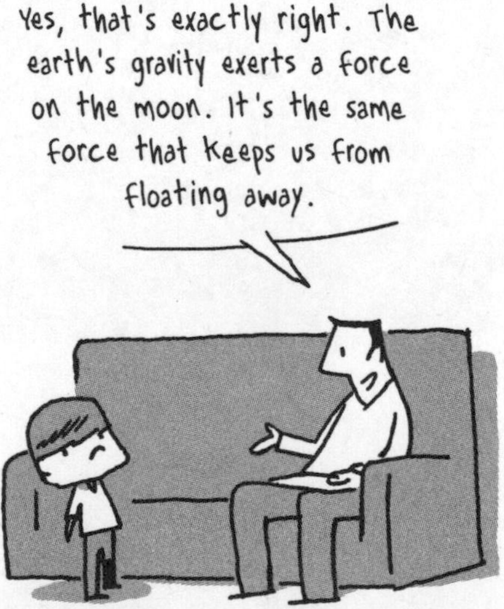
Yes, that's exactly right. The earth's gravity exerts a force on the moon. It's the same force that keeps us from floating away.

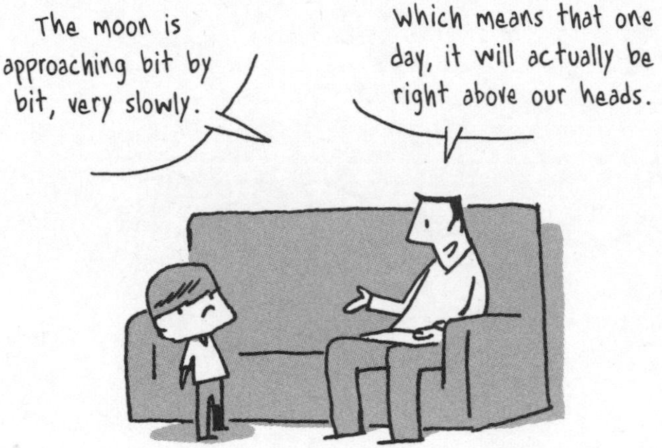
The moon is approaching bit by bit, very slowly.
Which means that one day, it will actually be right above our heads.

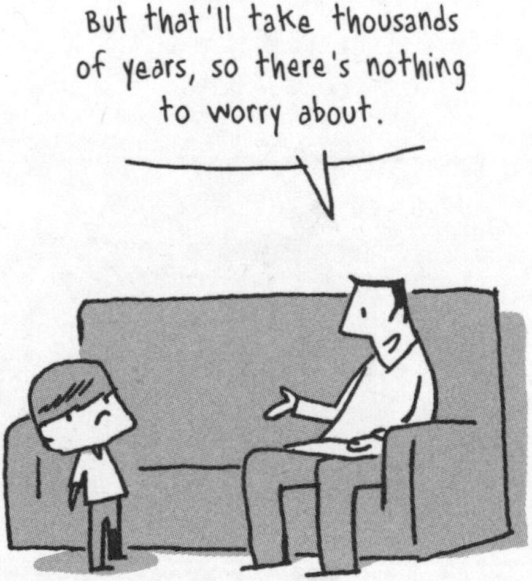
But that'll take thousands of years, so there's nothing to worry about.

Eventually, the moon will come so low, people will have to duck every time it passes by.

Which will be a drag, but thankfully, it only passes by once a month.

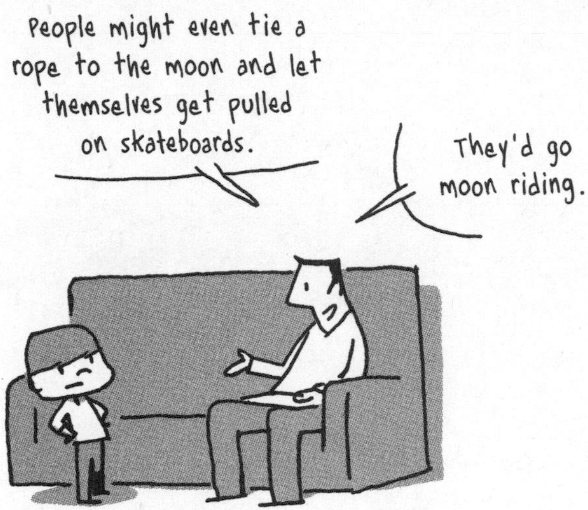
People might even tie a rope to the moon and let themselves get pulled on skateboards.
They'd go moon riding.

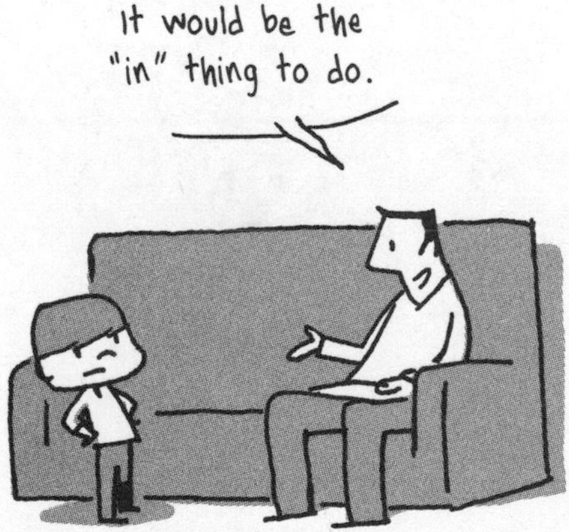
It would be the "in" thing to do.

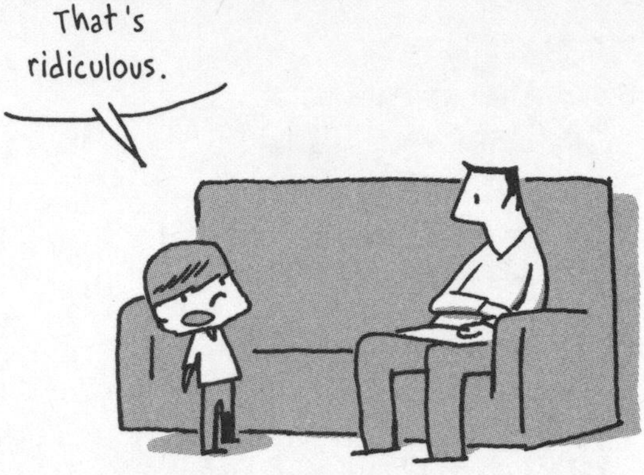
That's ridiculous.

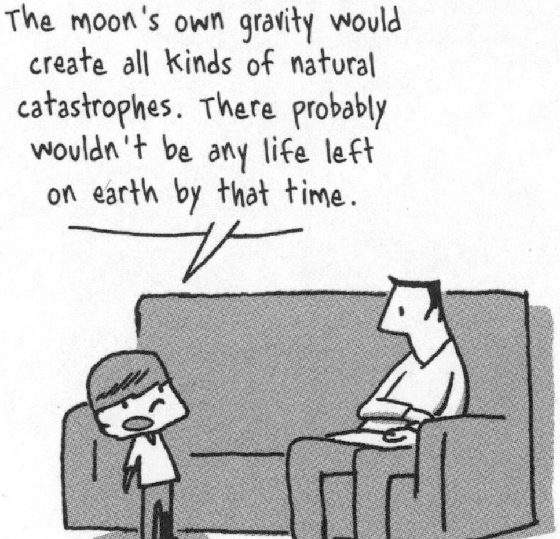
The moon's own gravity would create all kinds of natural catastrophes. There probably wouldn't be any life left on earth by that time.
There'd be nothing but rocks, and they can't moon ride.

But you could put this in your "Bad Dad" books.

You should go write it down so you don't forget.

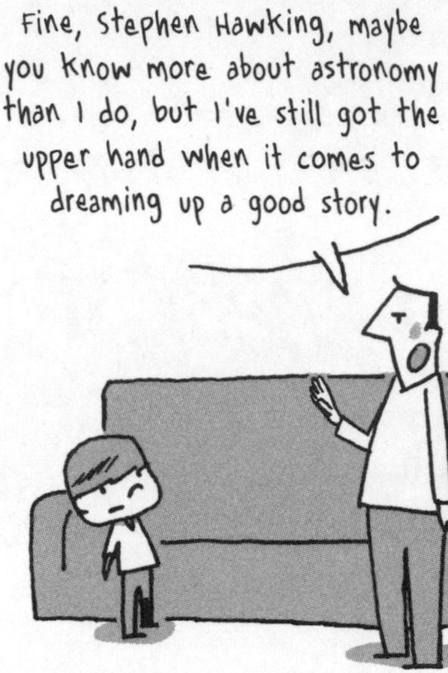
Fine, Stephen Hawking, maybe you know more about astronomy than I do, but I've still got the upper hand when it comes to dreaming up a good story.

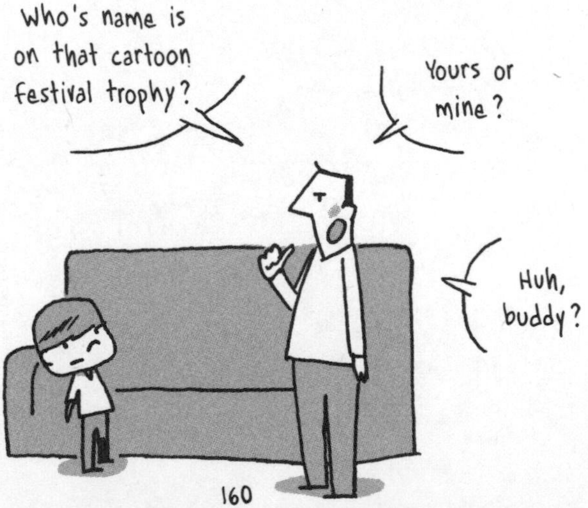
Who's name is on that cartoon festival trophy?
Yours or mine?
Huh, buddy?

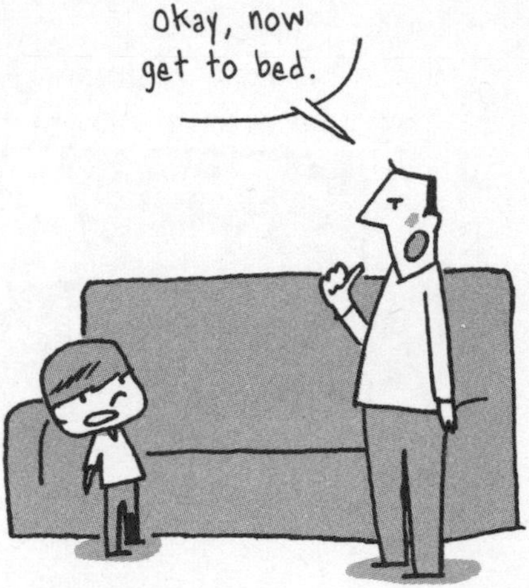
Okay, now get to bed.

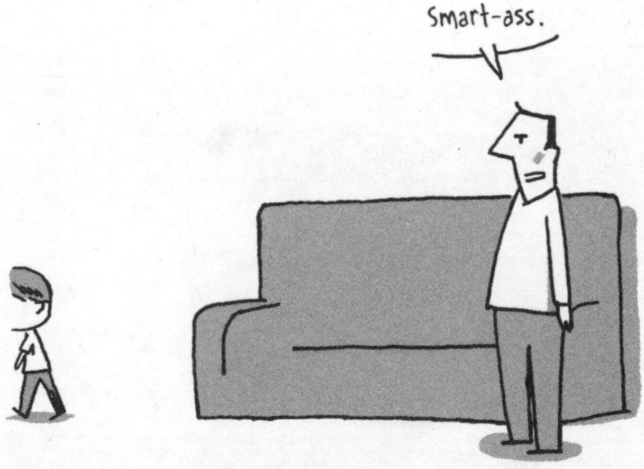
Smart-ass.

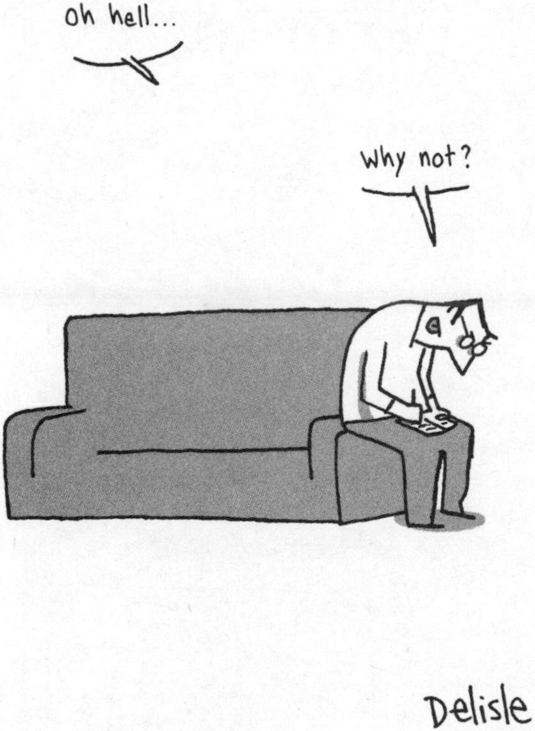
oh hell...
Why not?
Delisle

-At the store

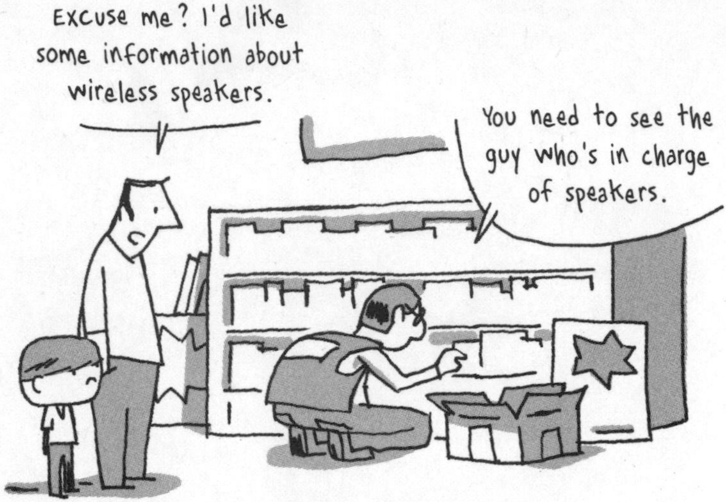
Excuse me? I'd like some information about wireless speakers.
You need to see the guy who's in charge of speakers.

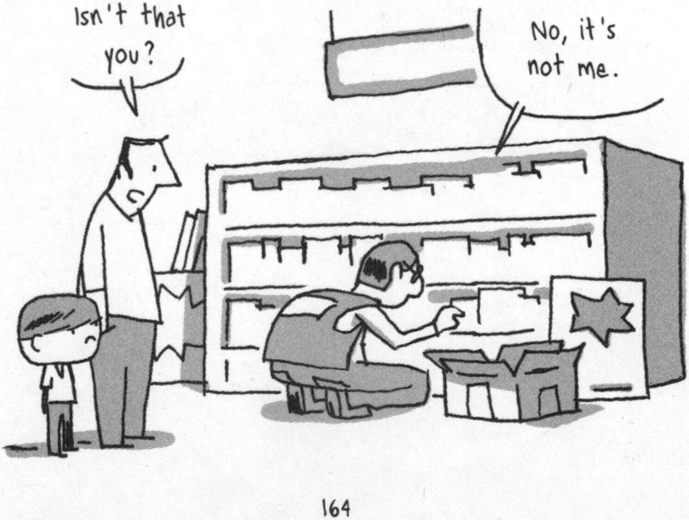
Isn't that you?
No, it's not me.

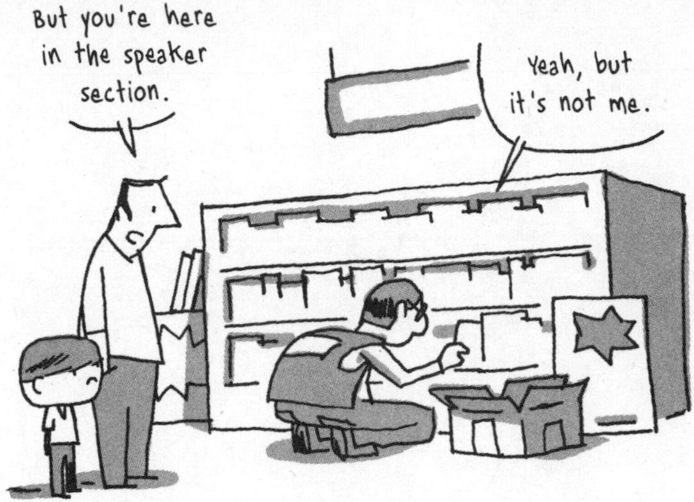
But you're here in the speaker section.
Yeah, but it's not me.

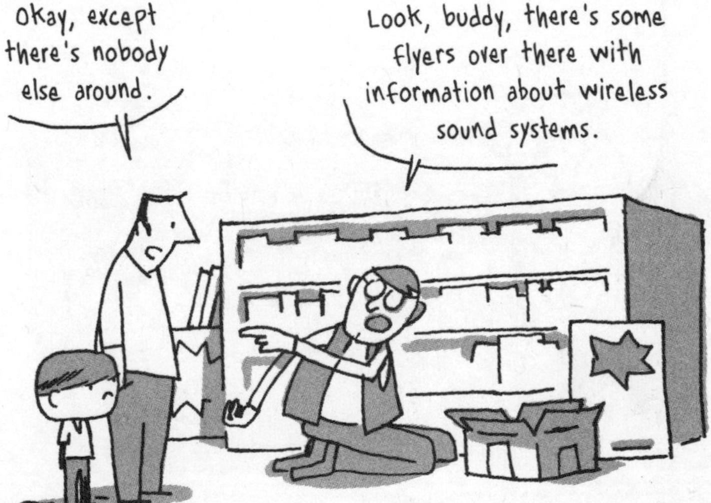
Okay, except there's nobody else around.
Look, buddy, there's some flyers over there with information about wireless sound systems.

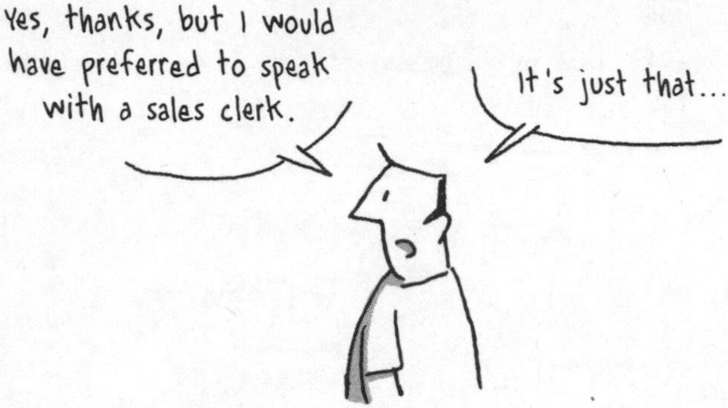
Yes, thanks, but I would have preferred to speak with a sales clerk.
It's just that...

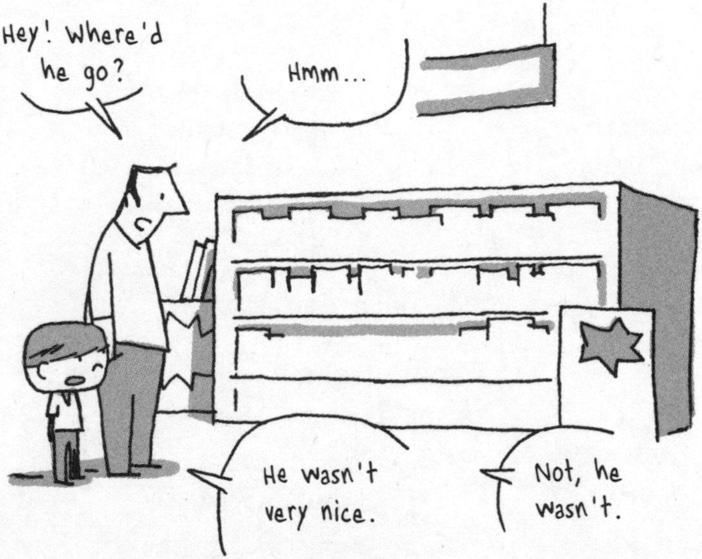
Hey! Where'd he go?
Hmm...
He wasn't very nice.
Not, he wasn't.

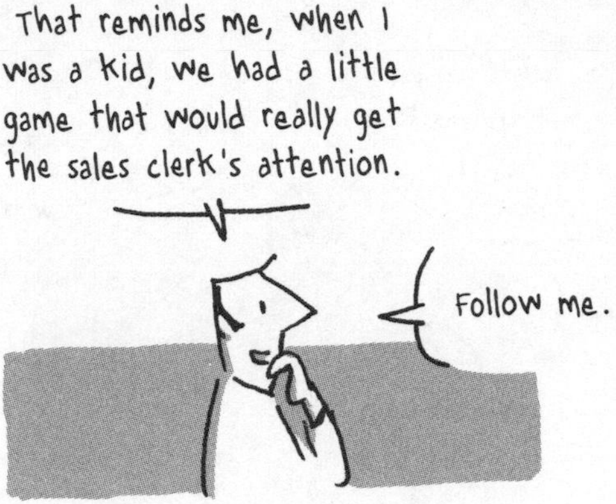
That reminds me, when I was a kid, we had a little game that would really get the sales clerk's attention.
Follow me.

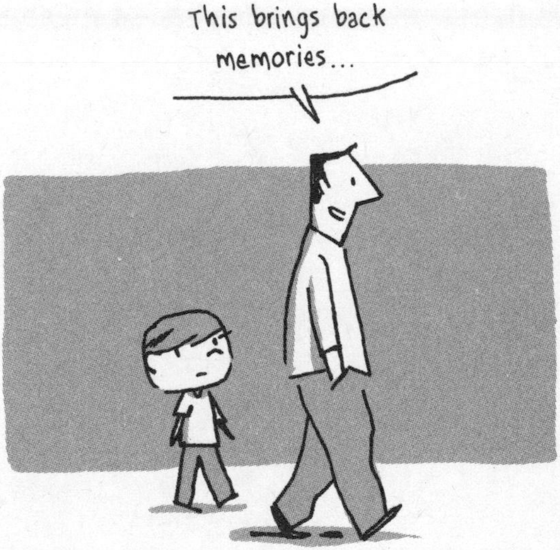
This brings back memories...

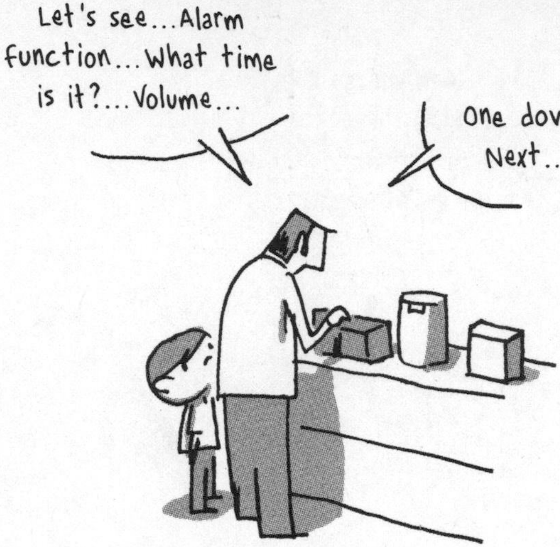
Let's see... Alarm function... What time is it?... Volume...
One down. Next...

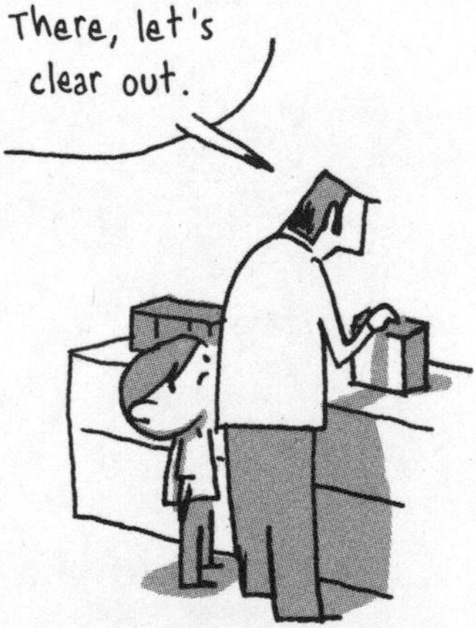
There, let's clear out.

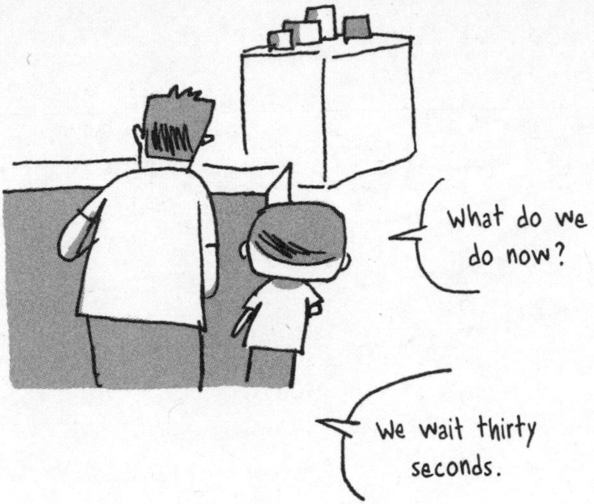
What do we do now?
We wait thirty seconds.

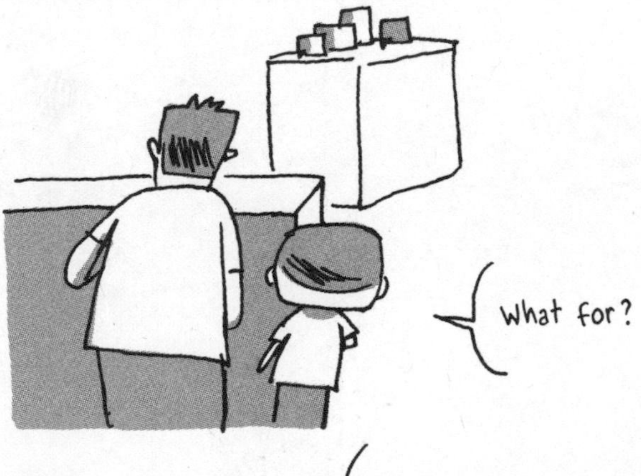
What for?
You'll see.

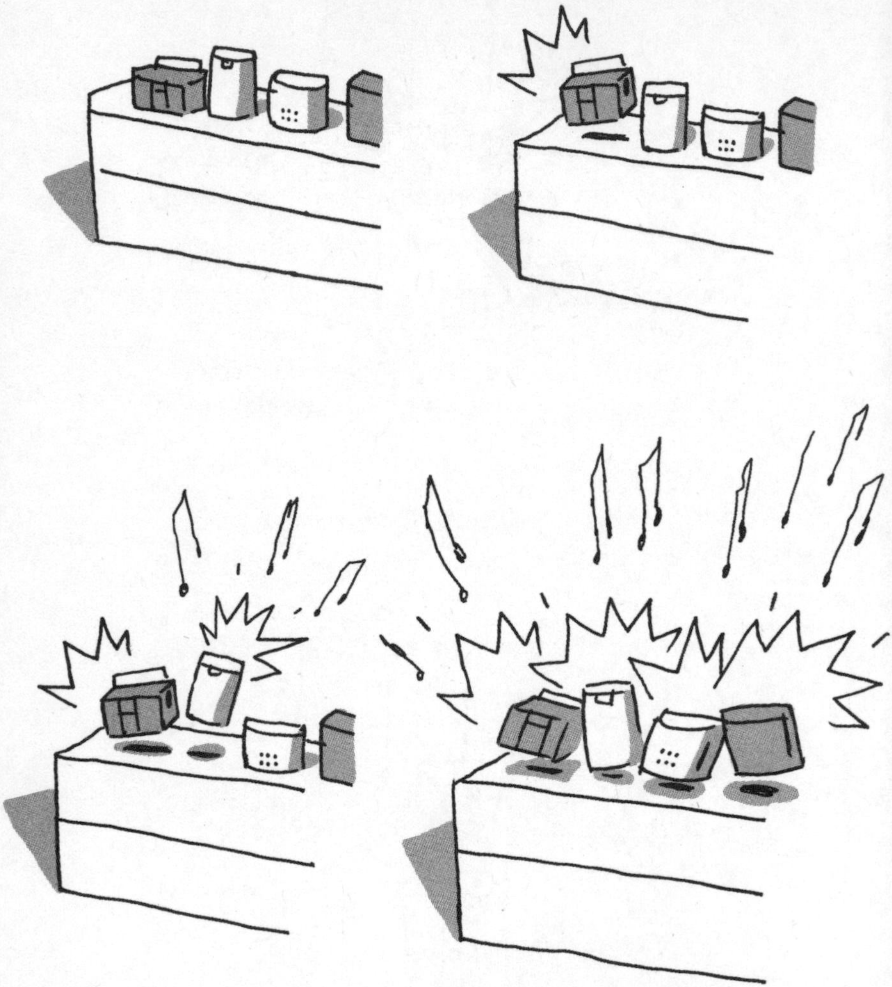

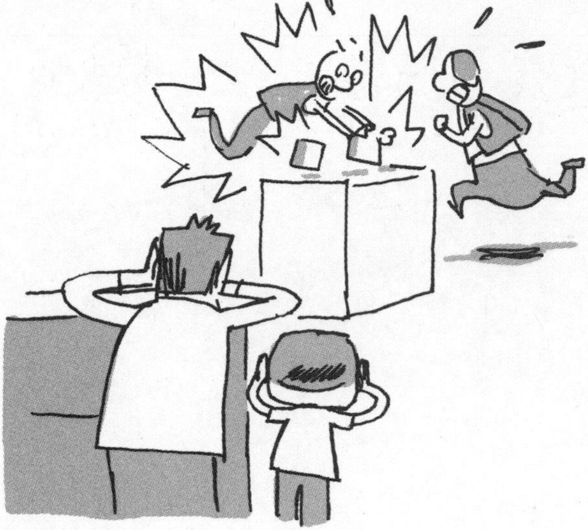

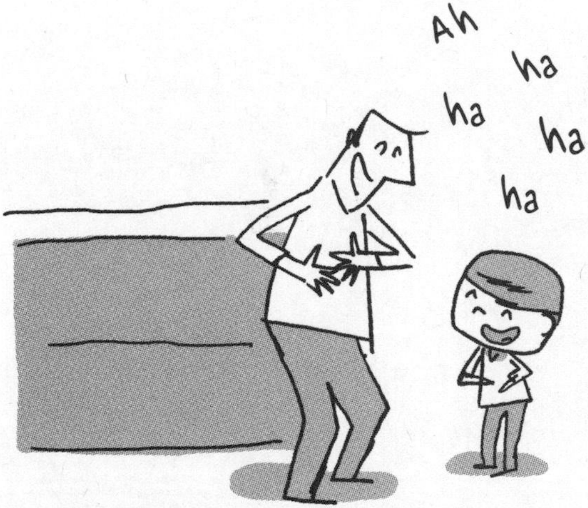
Ah
ha
ha
ha
ha

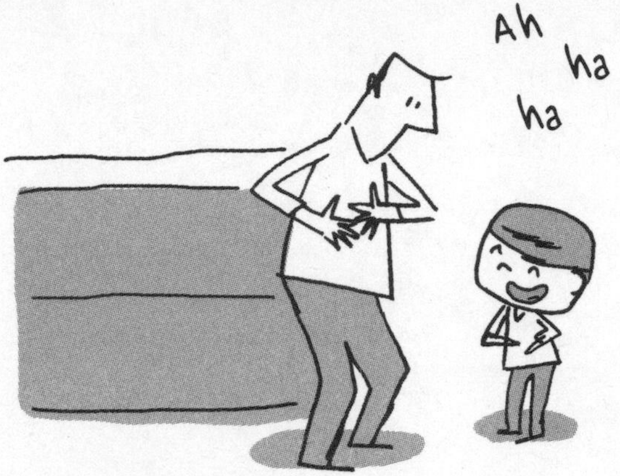
Ah
ha
ha

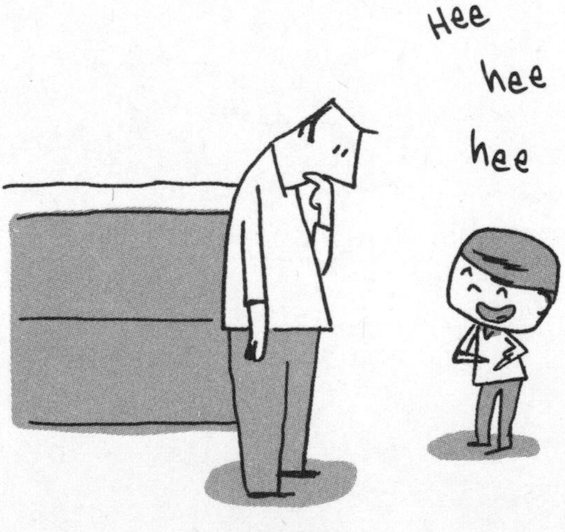
Hee
hee
hee

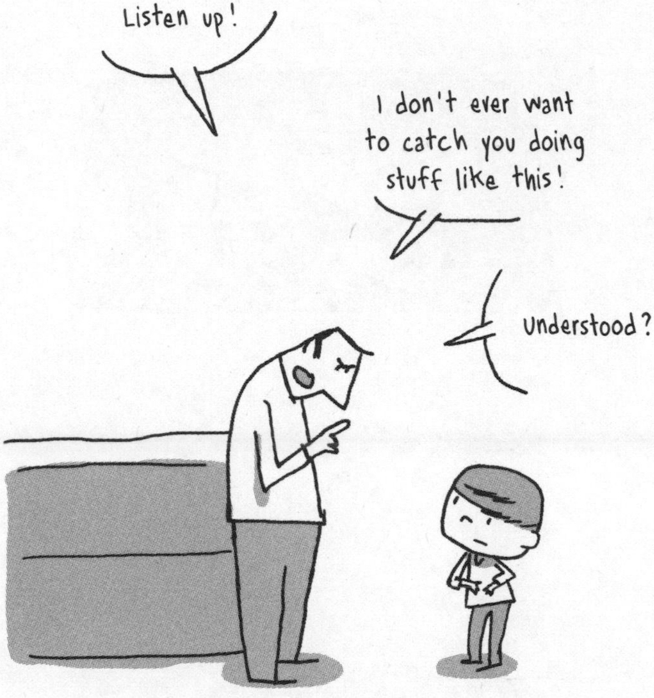

Listen up!
I don't ever want to catch you doing stuff like this!
Understood?
Delisle

- Down the chimney

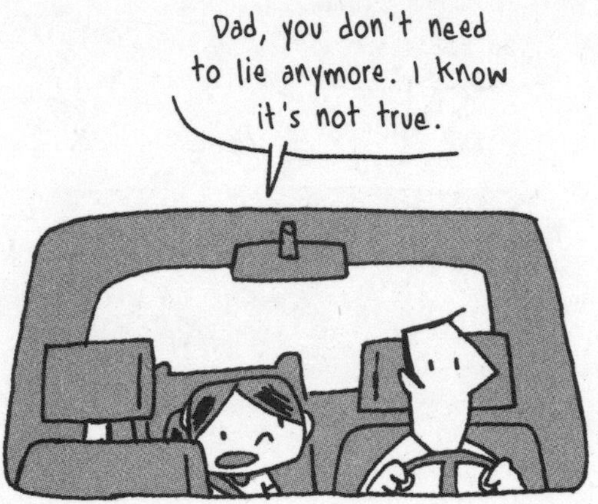
Dad, you don't need to lie anymore. I know it's not true.

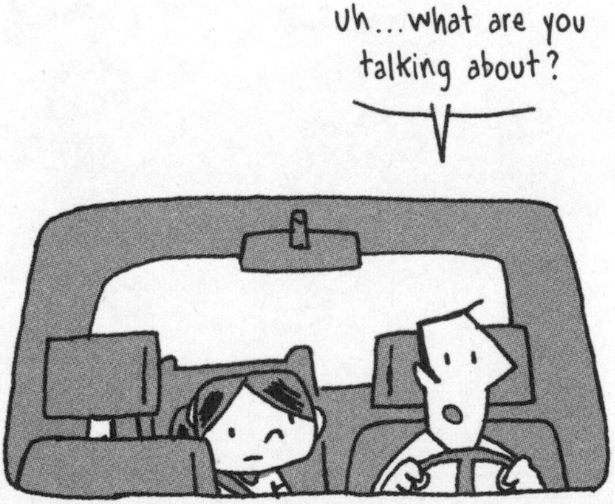
Uh...what are you talking about?

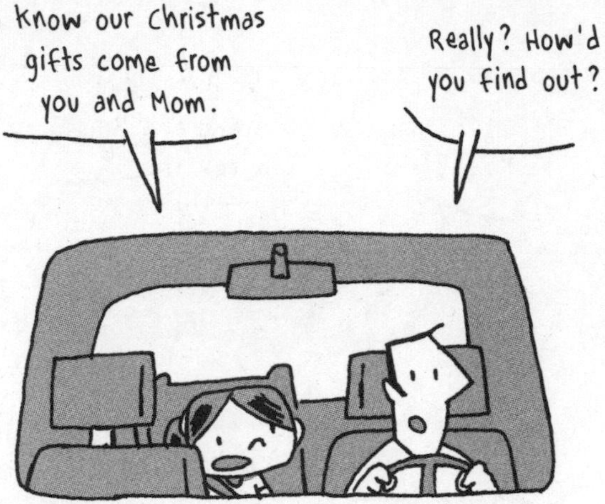
I know our Christmas gifts come from you and Mom.
Really? How'd you find out?

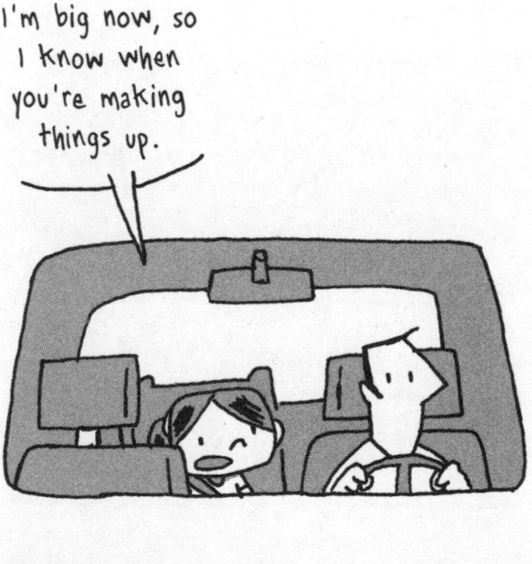
I'm big now, so I know when you're making things up.

I suppose you discuss stuff like this at school?
Yes, at recess. We talk with the bigger kids.
Well, there you go. Now you know.
I won't have to pretend anymore.

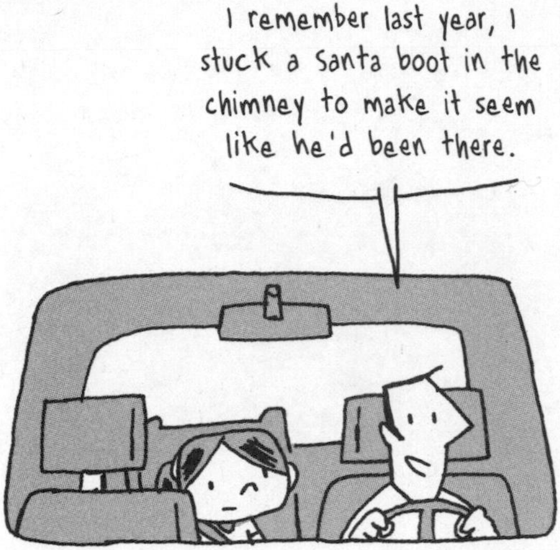
I remember last year, I stuck a Santa boot in the chimney to make it seem like he'd been there.

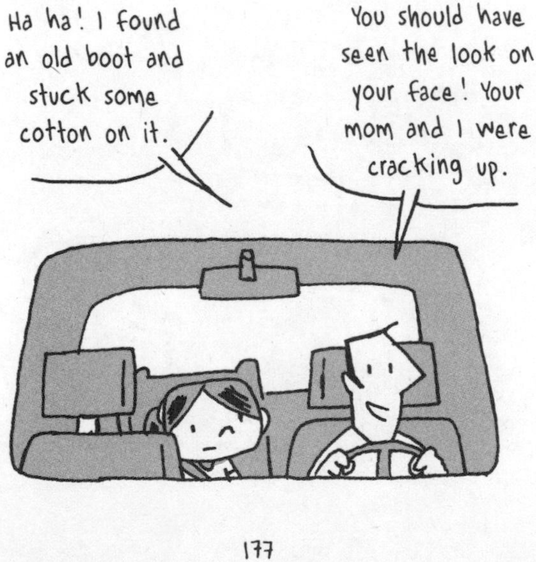
Ha ha! I found an old boot and stuck some cotton on it.
You should have seen the look on your face! Your mom and I were cracking up.

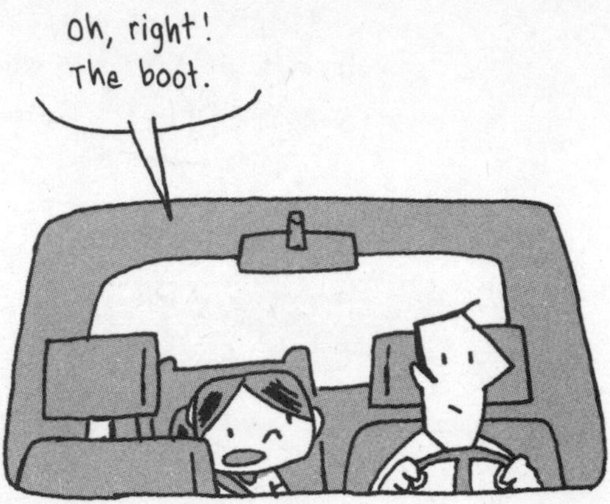
Oh, right! The boot.

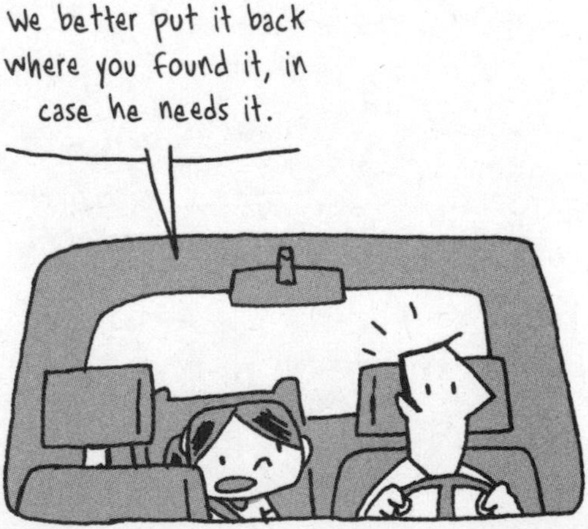
We better put it back where you found it, in case he needs it.

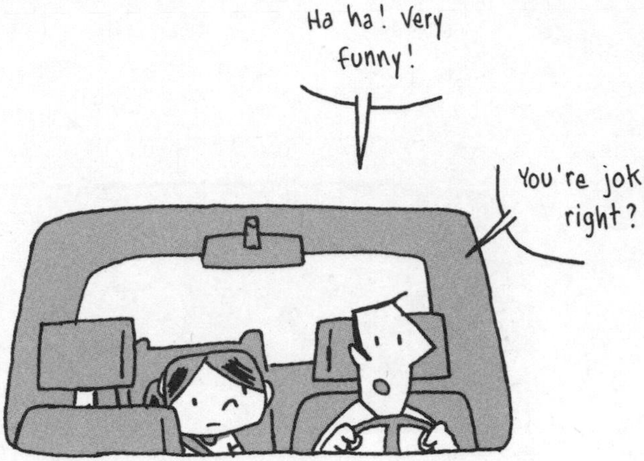
Ha ha! Very funny!
You're joking, right?

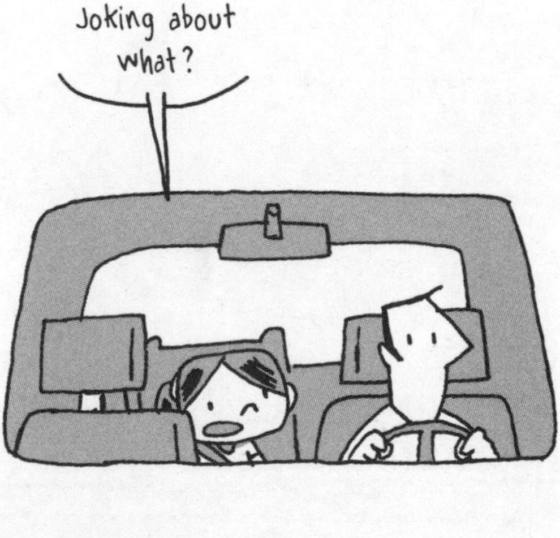
Joking about what?

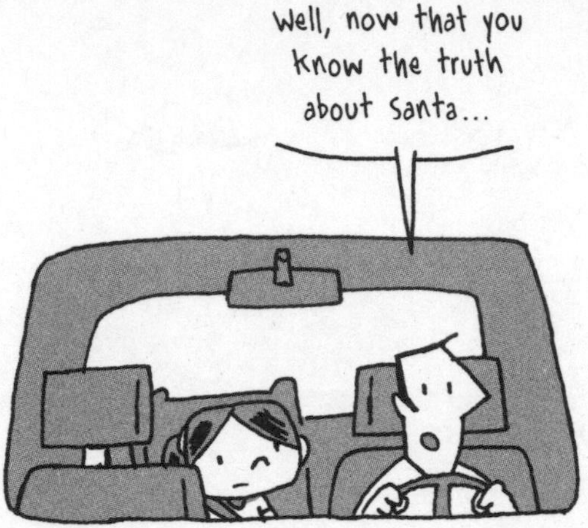
Well, now that you know the truth about Santa...

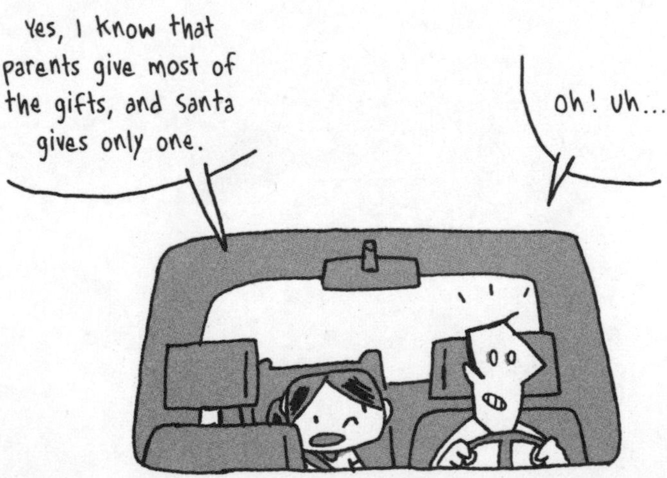
Yes, I know that parents give most of the gifts, and Santa gives only one.
Oh! Uh...

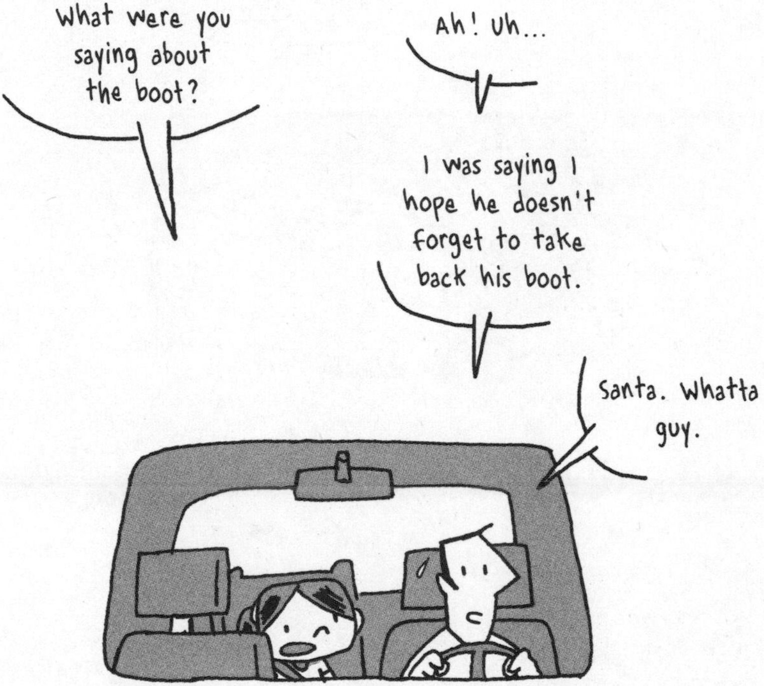

What were you saying about the boot?
Ah! Uh...
I was saying I hope he doesn't forget to take back his boot.
Santa. Whatta guy.

Delisle

– The console

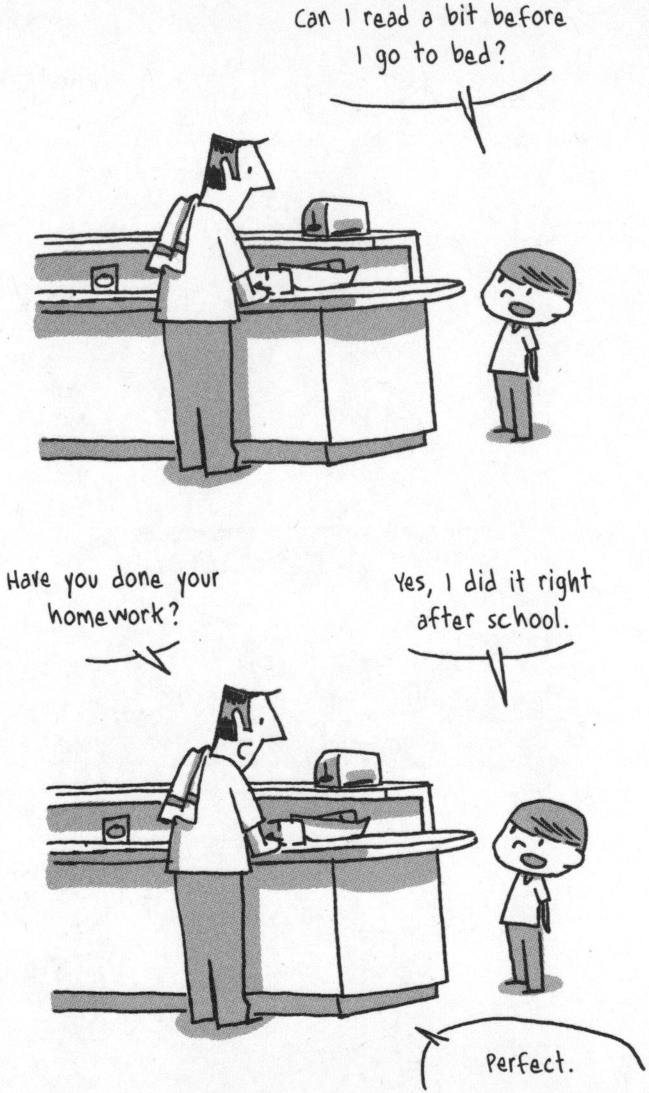
Can I read a bit before I go to bed?
Have you done your homework?
Yes, I did it right after school.
Perfect.

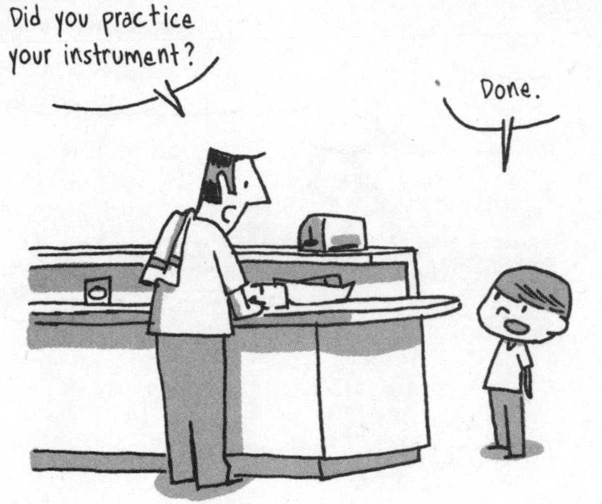
Did you practice your instrument?
Done.

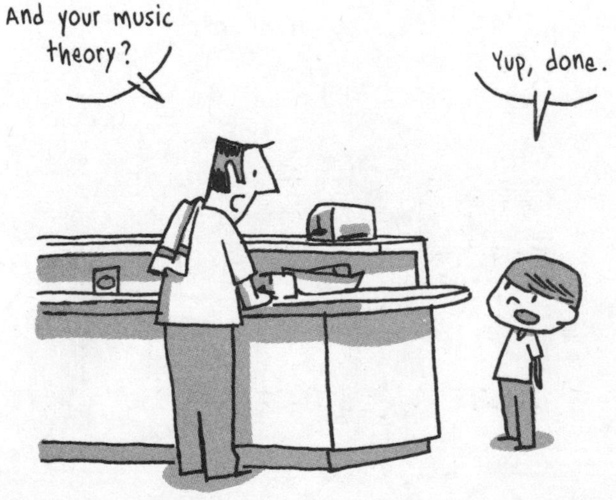
And your music theory?
Yup, done.

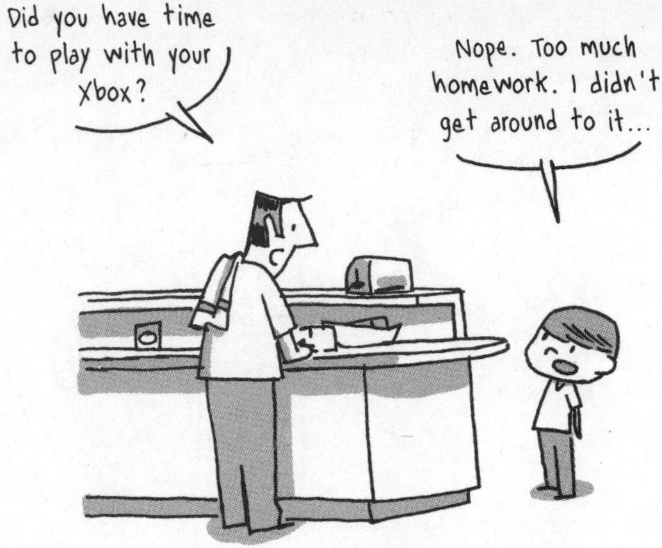
Did you have time to play with your Xbox?
Nope. Too much homework. I didn't get around to it...

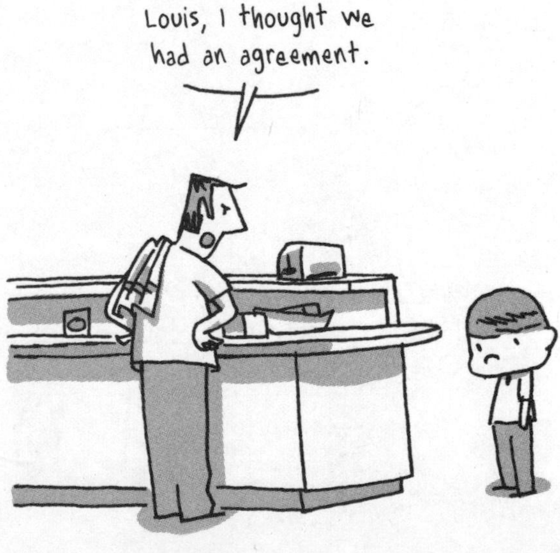
Louis, I thought we had an agreement.

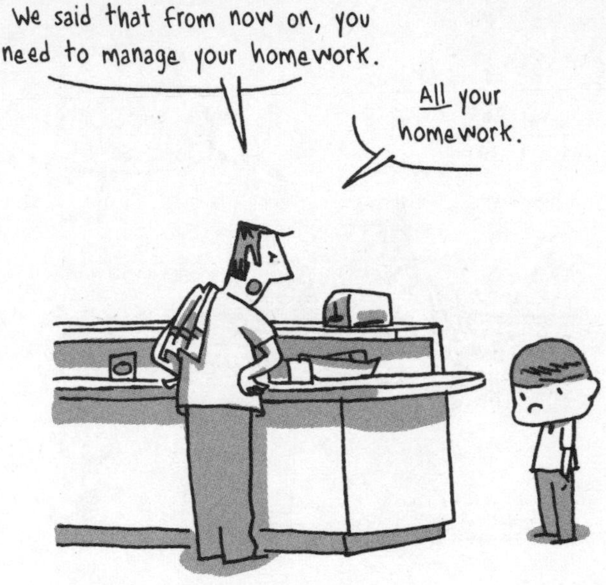
We said that from now on, you need to manage your homework.
All your homework.

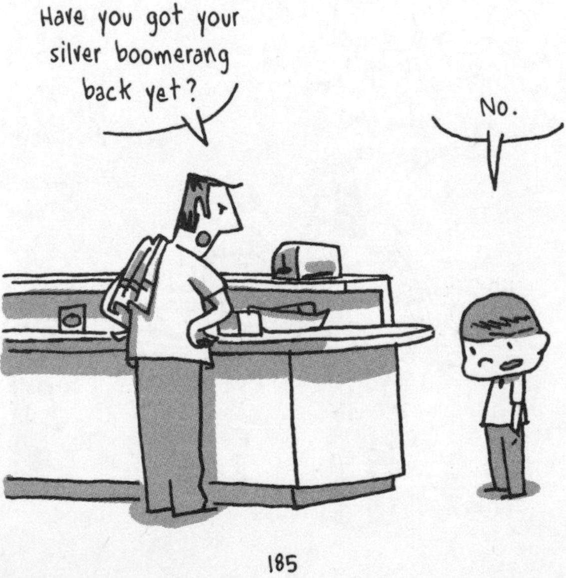
Have you got your silver boomerang back yet?
No.

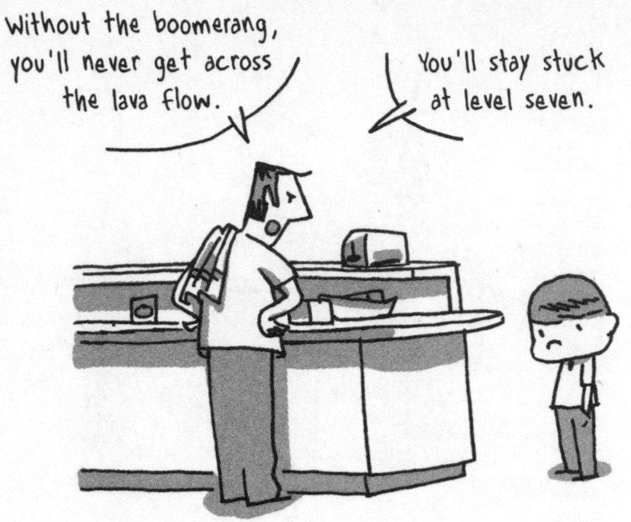
Without the boomerang, you'll never get across the lava flow.
You'll stay stuck at level seven.

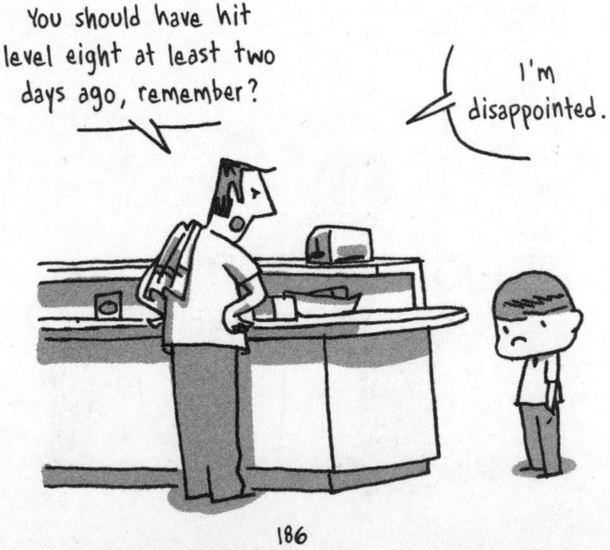
You should have hit level eight at least two days ago, remember?
I'm disappointed.

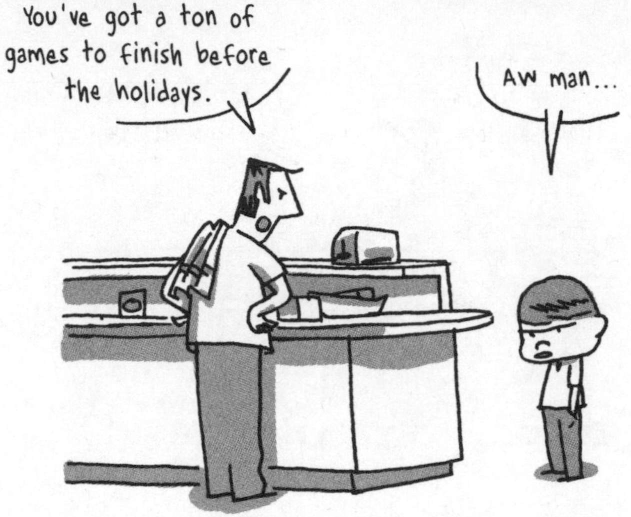
You've got a ton of games to finish before the holidays.
Aw man...

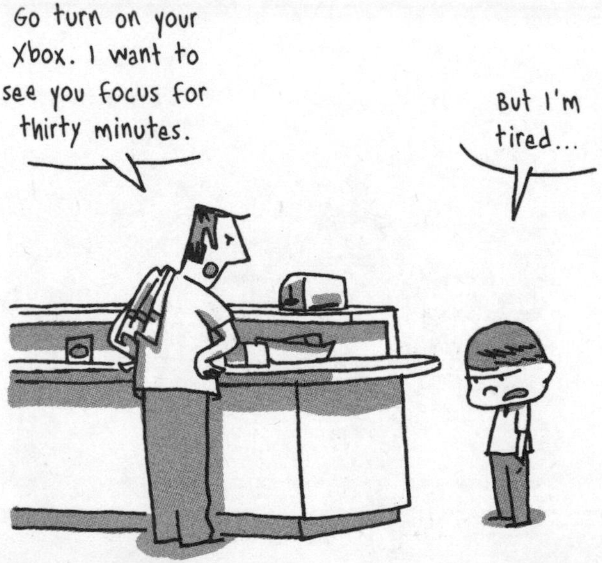
Go turn on your Xbox. I want to see you focus for thirty minutes.
But I'm tired...

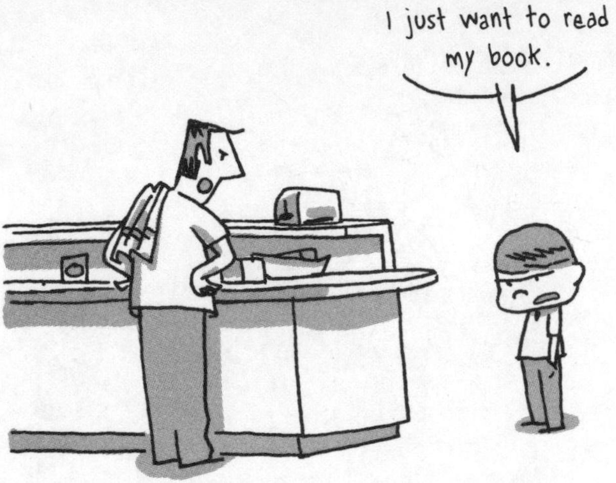
I just want to read my book.

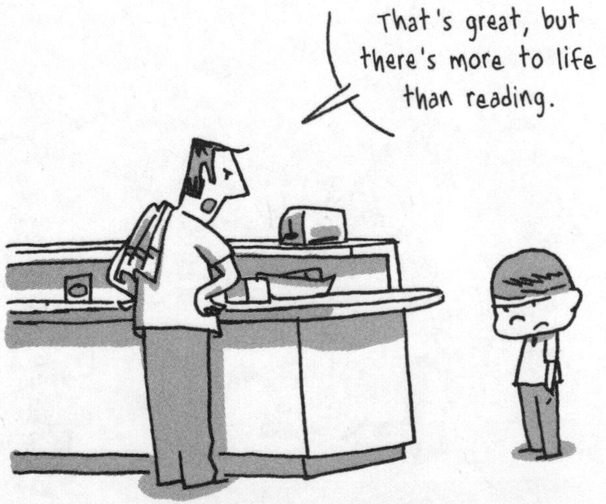
That's great, but there's more to life than reading.

Ugh...I hate video games.

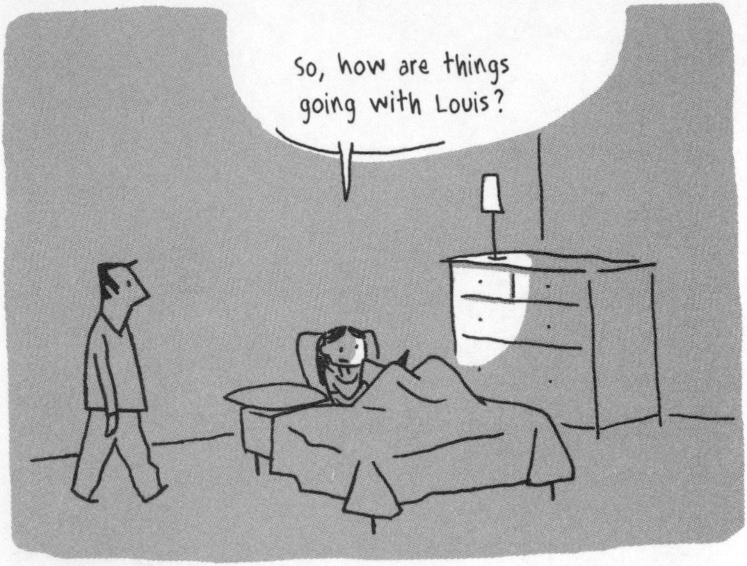
So, how are things going with Louis?

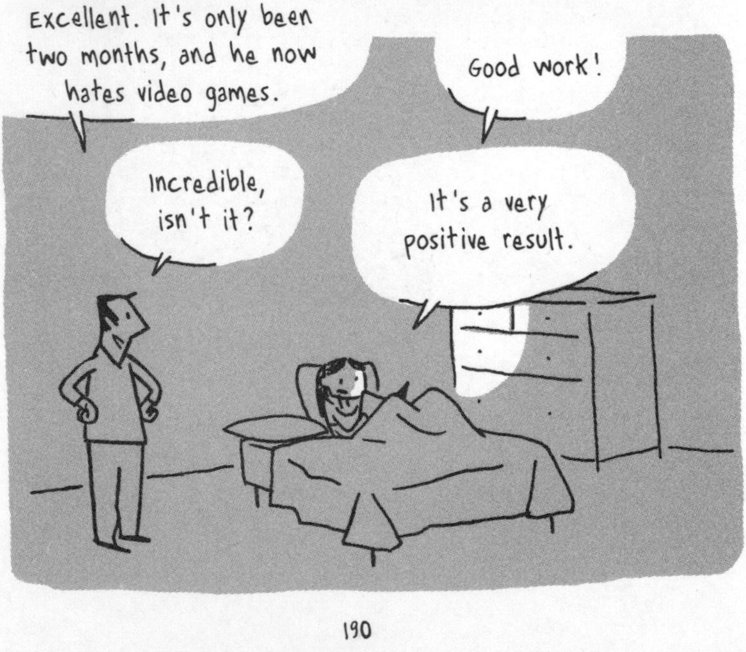
Excellent. It's only been two months, and he now hates video games.
Good work!
Incredible, isn't it?
It's a very positive result.

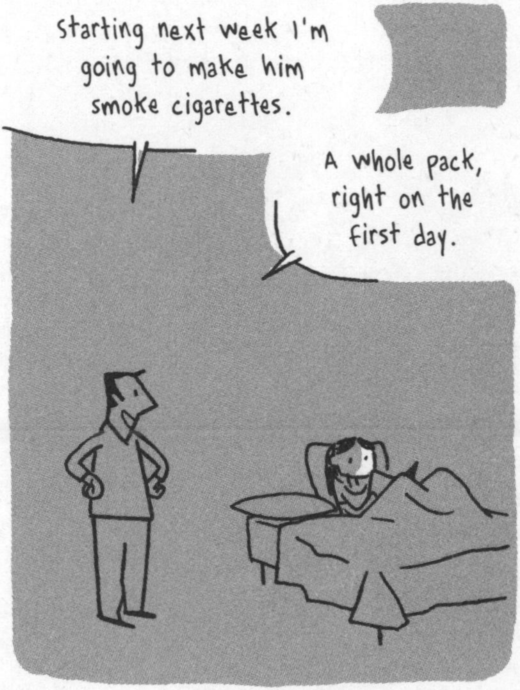
Starting next week I'm going to make him smoke cigarettes.
A whole pack, right on the first day.

Delisle

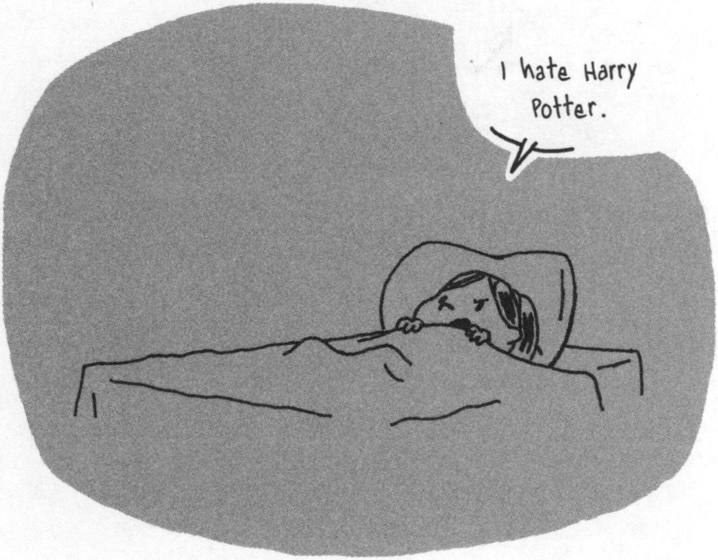
I hate Harry Potter.

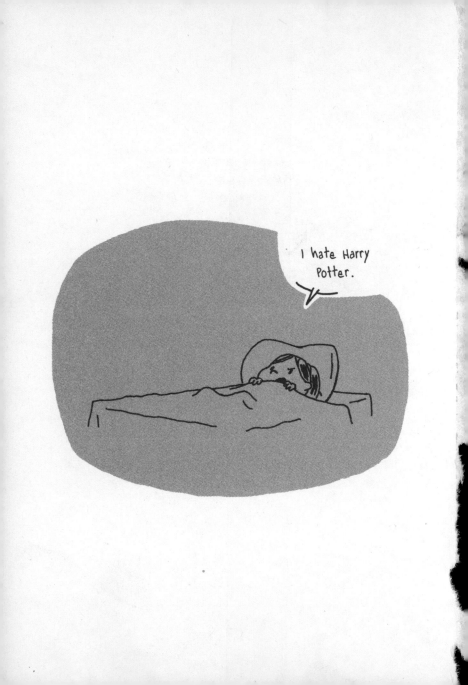